TESTIMONY OF THE HEAVENS

God's Redemptive Plan Preserved in the Stars

Dana Sherstad
and
B. J. Barbich

Illustrations by Dana Sherstad

A Good Name Publishing

Woodinville, WA

Cover graphics by Michael Sherstad, Savanna Sherstad and Dana. Sherstad. Background photo from NASA, ESA, and The Hubble Heritage Team (STScI/AURA).

ISBN-13 :9781494764098

ISBN-10 :1494764091

Library of Congress Control Number: 2011940277

Dedication

This study is dedicated to the Lord, Who has guided us in every step of this study — from conception to completion to publishing. It is also dedicated to the hard, foundational work of two others, Frances Rolleston and E. W. Bullinger.

Table of Contents

iv

Book II - The Redeemed

Book III - The Redeemer, His Glory

Appendix

Preface

Psalm 19:1 says, "The heavens declare the glory of God …" All of mankind is moved by the heavenly display. We may recognize that the heavens display God's power, His majesty, His creativity and His strength. But what if even more about Him can be learned from the heavenly display? The very choice of the word translated "declare" is intriguing. It could be translated, "write, narrate, or tell." We believe there is more told in the stars than a view of the greatness of its Creator. We have found there a story. It is a story that narrates in pictures God's redemptive plan for mankind. And it is written without words in the night sky.

We acknowledge the reservations and misgivings many may have embarking on a study that explores the constellations in the stars, many of them known today as signs of the Zodiac. Generally, unless you are an astronomer,[1] your only knowledge of these signs is that they are joined to the occult. It is an old problem dating all the way back to the tower of Babel. It is also mentioned as an idolatrous religion in 2 Kings 21:1-6 and 23:5. However, we have become convinced that astrology is a perverse corruption of an original revelation from God. Corruption or perversion of original truth is Satan's mode of operation. He distorts and deforms what God has made. He has done this work so cleverly in this instance that we have almost lost something very precious.

As you work through this study, we hope you will conclude with us, that the sky pictures originated out of the inspiration of God to reveal the Redeemer: His character, His righteousness, His glory, and His work. They have nothing to do with predicting our personality or our personal futures. What we have found in these pictures matches perfectly God's written revelation, The Holy Scripture. Had the stories revealed in the stars not been found in or been in contradiction to the revealed Word, we should and would reject them.

We have been amazed to discover how fully God's Gospel, His good news story, is on display every night for all to see. This study has increased our awe and wonder of both the night sky and its Creator. To think that the One who placed these pictures in the sky has time and patience for us, causes our hearts to sing with David, "What is man that You are mindful of Him? Yet you have made him a little lower than the angels and crowned him with glory." We cannot wait for you too, to discover God's oldest revelation of Himself and His plan.

---

[1] Today, astronomers use the constellations to order the sky, to identify numerous stars and objects in the heavens.

Please, Please Read Before Beginning This Study!

It is our desire, as much as is possible, to guide participants of this study in discovery rather than simply relating what we've discovered. Because of our preference for this style, you will find questions embedded throughout a day's lesson, rather than numbered at the end. Also because each day's lesson builds upon discoveries made in that lesson, answers to many questions follow the space provided for your answers. We hope you take the opportunities provided to search Scripture yourself for answers. We believe there are many exciting insights awaiting you in this study; but these are made most exciting through your own personal time in God's Word. Our words are passing, but His Word is eternal, living, and active!

Most importantly, be patient with yourself in the first week of this study! Much of the information in the first week is unfamiliar to most people and technical. We have discovered that some people struggle to understand the explanations and discussions of astronomy in the first week of lessons. And then also feel discouraged. **It is not necessary to understand astronomy to enjoy this study. You do not need to be able to find the constellations in the sky or understand how they move to enjoy this study.** You also do not need to understand the ancient historical references in the first week to enjoy and learn from this study. **The astronomical and ancient history is provided for those that need these contexts to accept our conclusions.** Some of us need that, but if you're not one of them, then you may not need the first week. So if you find it hard to follow the astronomy or any other technical aspect of the first 5 lessons, be encouraged, these are the only lessons with that kind of information in them, and you don't need to understand it. Just get through those first 5 lessons, or skip them (you have the author's permission to do so) and enjoy the rest of the study.

We hope, during the course of this study, you gain an even greater appreciation for God, our Creator, by Whose wisdom all the lights of heaven were placed and named; and for the Son, our Redeemer, by Whose unsearchable love and power purchased our redemption and shared His inheritance.

The heavens declare the glory of God;
And the firmament shows His handiwork.
Day unto day utters speech,
And night unto night reveals knowledge.
Psalm 19:1-2 [NKJV]

Day One – Evidence from the Antiquity and Uniformity of the Constellations

For any study to have any power, any long-term meaning, it must be a study in and about God's Living Word. There will be much time spent in Scripture. But much of this introduction will be technical and historical facts that are extra-Biblical. In this first week, we aim to prove the validity of our conclusion that the 48 original constellations in the sky are a recording of the same prophecies found in Scripture.

Purpose of the Stars

> "And God said, 'Let there be lights in the expanse of the heavens to separate the day from the night. And let them be for signs and for seasons, and for days and years …'" Genesis 1:14 [ESV]

According to Genesis 1:14, why did God create lights in heaven? (List all reasons.)

In the modern era, we have lost, almost completely, our dependency on the heavenly bodies to mark days, months, seasons, and years. But the ancients kept all these measures of time by them. Our clocks and calendars are based upon them and their movements even though modern man has left off looking skyward to keep time.

The Hebrew word translated "signs" here may also be translated "banners, pledges or witnesses." *(Some translations do not say "for signs **and** seasons," and lose the concept that they are used for more than marking seasons.)*

In what way might the lights of heaven be used as signs apart from marking seasons?

Can you name any instance in Scripture where stars served or will serve as a sign? (Hint: See Matthew 2)

Not many events have or will eclipse the importance of the incarnation. If stars are for signs, then we should expect, as the wise men did, a sign in the heavens at His birth. We believe that stars together with the darkening of the sun, served as a sign at His death also – we will explore this later on in the study. The Lord speaks again of the heavenly bodies serving as signs of His return.

> "Immediately after the tribulation of those days the sun will be darkened, and the moon will not give its light; the stars will fall from heaven, and the powers of the heavens will be shaken. Then the sign of the Son of Man will appear in heaven …" Matthew 24:29-30 [NKJ]

Stars Contain a Revelation from God That Preceded the Written Revelation

There is at least a 2,500 year space of time from Adam to the first written Scripture. We believe that God did not leave these generations without a revelation.

God, through His earliest prophets, revealed His redemptive plan. These early prophets, those from Adam forward, recorded and preserved the prophecy, apparently not through words on a scroll, but through emblems in the sky. In the ancient constellations we will see that these pictures, their names and the names of stars within them, reflect the same predictions of the Christ found in the written revelation. Later, the prophets who wrote Scripture again used the same words found as names for stars in the sky. These ancient star names and their meanings can also be found in the mythology of many nations.

How does Romans 1:18-20 describe the order of truth and its suppression?

What does 2 Thessalonians 2:10b-12 give as the reason for obscuring the truth?

How does 2 Timothy 4:3-4 describe the reason for changing the truth and what is the substitute?

It will be clear as you continue in this study, that **mythologies were invented long after these constellations** and not the other way around. The truth came first, fables were invented later. But the fables still bear recognizable shadows of the truth from which they came.

The Antiquity of the Signs

Astronomers have been unable to find the origin of the constellations we will be studying. Rather, they find their presence already existent in all ancient cultures, Chinese, Egyptian, Chaldean, and Hebrew. This has led many to conclude that these constellations are so ancient as to have been in existence since the very beginning of mankind.[1] Among the evidences to their antiquity is the ceiling of a portico in the Egyptian Temple of Denderah. Though we know that the temple was built only 2,000 years ago, internal evidence found in the famous circular Zodiac indicates it is a copy of a Zodiac dating back to at least 4000 BC.[2]

A large astrological work compiled by the Babylonians is displayed at the British Museum. The Fifth Tablet of the "Seven Tablets of Creation," 12th Century BC says,

> "Anu[the Creator] made excellent the mansions of the great gods [twelve] in number. The stars he placed in them. The lumasi [groups of stars or figures] he fixed. He arranged the year according to the bounds [i.e. the twelve signs], which he defined. For each of the twelve months three rows of stars he fixed … [3]

Ok, even the translation doesn't really translate. So we'll summarize what is important to our study from the above quote.

---

[1] Rolleston, Frances. "Mazzaroth by Frances Rolleston." *Philologos*. Web. 30 Aug. 2011. http://philologos.org/__eb-mazzaroth/103.htm

[2] Buchwald, Jed Z "Egyptians Stars under Paris Skies," Caltech 2003 Web, 30 Aug 2011. http://eands.caltech.edu/articles/Buchwald%20Feature.pdf

[3] Bullinger, Ethelburt William, *Witness of the Stars*, (Cosimo, Inc., NY, 2007—originally published 1893) pp 12-13; and also found in The Seven Tablets of Creation, Leonard King, 1902, pp 18

The Creator made 12 boundaries in the heavens each with stars in them which govern the year. (There are 12 months in the year governed by 12 constellations in the sky.) The Babylonians recognized fixed figures or constellations in each of the groups of stars. For each one of the 12 constellations the Babylonians also recognized 3 other constellations connected to it in rows. 12 x 4 equals 48 constellations organized in groups of 4.

The pattern or arrangement we follow in this study is ancient according to this quote from 12th Century BC.[4] It's not important to be able see this in the sky for yourself, though I recommend it.

Also, the early corruption of constellations is reflected in the quote above. It speaks of "mansions of the great gods." This is the occult of astrology, which believes constellations are the homes of gods. Did you know that behind astrology is the belief that it is the nature or personality of a god living in a constellation producing the personality, nature and future of a person born under it? There is no place for a believer in the true God or His word to touch, test or handle anything connected to such a lie, even as a matter of "curiosity".

Ancient Persian, Jewish, and Arabian traditions assign the invention of astronomy (not astrology) to "the family of Seth" or Adam, Seth and Enoch.

> They [family of Seth] also were inventors of that peculiar sort of wisdom which is concerned with the heavenly bodies, and their order.[5]

> The Egyptians credited Thoth with its invention, which is likely a variation of the name Seth.[6]

Numerous artifacts, including coins and boundary stones from various civilizations dating back to at least 700 BC have been found bearing constellation pictures.

There is evidence that the tower of Babel included a temple for the worship of the stars and their constellations. We will explore this more in 4th day of this week's lessons.

The Uniformity and Organization of the Signs Across Cultures

The 12 signs had the same meaning of name and order in the entire ancient world. Chinese, Chaldean and Egyptian records date back to 2000 BC.[7] You can find the signs in Arabian and Persian cultures and on the Indian subcontinent.[8]

---

[4] A History of Ancient Mathematical Astronomy, O. Nuegebauer, 1975, pp 560-561
[5] Josephus Flavius, Antiquities of the Jews, pg 27.
[6] God's of the Egyptians Vol. I, E.A. Wallis Budge, 1904, pp 414.
[7] Rolleston, Frances. "Mazzaroth by Frances Rolleston." *Philologos*. Web. 30 Aug. 2011. http://philologos.org/__eb-mazzaroth/201.htm#authorities
[8] The key word here is ancient, since more current Chinese and Indian star atlases have completely abandoned even the division boundaries of the constellations--having reorganized the sky by the moon's travels. Rolleston sets forth much evidence of the ancient Chinese original agreement with our division and order of the signs under the heading "The Twelve Signs, Sanscrit and Chinese": http://philologos.org/__eb-mazzaroth/203.htm#twelve.

Many of the constellation pictures are hardly, if at all, reflected in the shape made by their stars; in many cases they are arbitrary. Sometimes there is nothing in the stars themselves to suggest the figures, yet all the ancient cultures had nearly identical figures for the 12 constellations of the Zodiac. Consider Virgo here:

This configuration of stars does not necessarily suggest a person. But had you decided it was a person, nothing in the pattern distinguishes between a male and a female figure. And yet figures from across cultures agree on these details and more. How can this be if they were not all descended from a single source?

Here are more star patterns with their corresponding constellation pictures below. Take a stab at matching them with their ancient, universal pictures. We really don't expect you to match them all correctly. (Only prominent stars are pictured.)

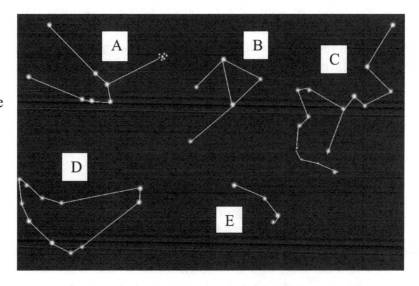

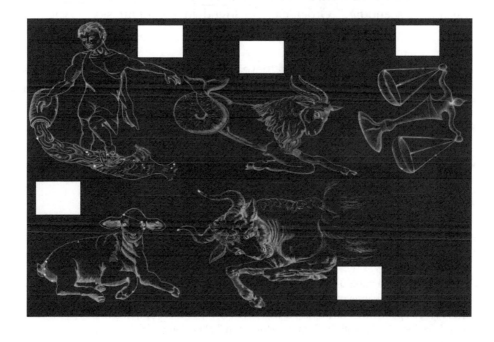

Since the stars do not obviously suggest these shapes, nor necessarily should they be grouped together as they are, why are they viewed with such uniformity across so great a space of time and by so many different cultures? It is the amazing uniformity of the pictures across time and culture that makes the greatest case for a single authorship that is also very ancient. Just matching the star shapes to the figures, in many cases demonstrates how arbitrary the pictures can seem. Besides the basic pictures, many details are consistent. The strange goat-fish creature, though neither the stars suggest it nor has any such creature existed, is found in all ancient zodiacs. The bull is always pictured in the attitude of charging. The scales are always shown with the northern scale higher in balance than the southern scale. The man is always shown pouring out a great stream of water from a small vessel. And the lamb is always seated in repose.

The ancient cultures recognized the same 12 signs along the sun's path with little or no variation. These 12 are called the Zodiac in this study. It is necessary to point out here that the word "zodiac" today is inescapably tied to the occult religion of astrology. And this has been the case a long time. However, this is not our meaning. We wish to emphasize again that we do not believe that these constellations influence us, our personalities or futures, in any way. Zodiac simply means either "circle of animals" or "way in steps or by progression". It is referring to the circle of constellations that are in the same path as the sun as we view them from earth. Many cultures have drawn them with the sun and moon among them on domes and pictures. These pictures we call Zodiacs, only meaning they picture these 12 constellations.

The other 36 constellations in our study (called Decans) had more variation in type but amazing consistency of meaning.[9] And are sometimes found on ancient cultures' zodiacs. Today astronomers identify 88 sky pictures or constellations, but only 48 of them are ancient.

It is important to understand how greatly our daily and especially nightly lives differ from the ancient peoples who preserved and studied these constellations. There was no television, no radio, no internet, no city lights in their day. The night sky was their tv or book. It was the source of much information and it also was the source of entertainment. And in many cultures today without ready accessible light or nightly entertainment it still is. For all who were and are shown these divisions of stars and their corresponding pictures, the night sky is transformed from a chaotic smattering of stars, to recognizable picture book that is ever spinning, rising and descending. Order can be found in the night sky. And that alone makes for interesting sky gazing.

It has been my experience, after drawing each of these lovely figures, that though many say the stars do not trace the constellations, they are easily traceable and recognizable by their star groupings once they are found. I can easily imagine these figures in the stars. I can imagine how much mystery they must have held. And how the ancients must have wondered at and discussed their meanings.

In view of this, we suggest reading Psalm 19. It will prepare you for tomorrow's lesson as well.

Answers in order from left to right beginning at top left box: C, D, B, E, A

---

[9] Information provided in today's lesson should not be considered an exhaustive look at the antiquity and continuity of the constellations. It is a summary of conclusions reached by Frances Rolleston and confirmed by our own investigation. If you want to know more about the evidence upon which these conclusions are based, Frances Rolleston's book *Mazzaroth* is available for reading online.- Rolleston, Frances. "Mazzaroth by Frances Rolleston." *Philologos*. Web. 30 Aug. 2011. http://philologos.org/__eb-mazzaroth.

Day Two - The Testimony of the Scripture Concerning the Stars and Constellations

Job, believed by many to be the oldest book in the world, refers to the stellar revelation and assigns the constellations to the work of God.

Read Job 9:9 and write below the names of the constellations mentioned there. (The Pleiades are not a constellation but a star cluster within the constellation of Taurus. You'll find them in the shoulder of the bull.)

These three (or really two constellations and a star cluster) are mentioned again in Job.

Can you bind the chains of the Pleiades, or loose the cords of Orion? Can you lead forth a constellation in its season, and guide the Bear with her satellites? Job 38:31-32 [NASB]

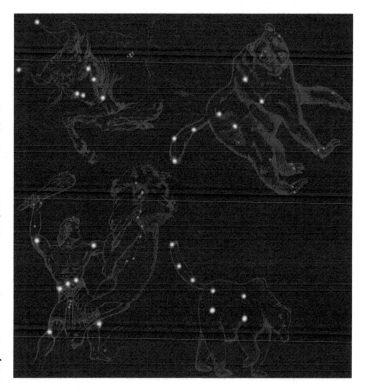

Some versions keep the Hebrew word *Mazzaroth* instead of translating it "constellation." The best theory as to the original meaning of this word is that it refers to the 12 Zodiacal signs.

Another verse which refers to the constellations is Isaiah 13:10 "For the stars of heaven and their constellations will not flash forth their light ..." [NASB]

That the constellations are well known by the Old Testament writers points to their great antiquity.

Amos 5:8 "He made the Pleiades and Orion ..." [NKJV] God is attributed with the creation of constellations. He not only made the stars, but also the constellations.

Now turn to Isaiah 40:26. List the three actions performed by God regarding the stars in this passage.

In Psalm 147:4, Which two of the three actions above are mentioned again?

Here, God is not only credited with creating the stars, but also naming them. We believe the ancient prophets, living before the written revelation; through the inspiration of the Holy Spirit received some of these names for the transmission and preservation of prophecy. We believe the ancient star names known to astronomers today are the same given by the prophets. Over 100 of the principal stars in our sky are still known by their ancient names. And the roots of these names can be traced to Hebrew words used by Isaiah, David, and other prophets.

Frances Rolleston, a 19th century scholar of the ancient classics and the history of language was struck by Psalm 147:4. She spent most of the rest of her life studying the root meanings of the names of the stars in many ancient languages. She published a book entitled, *Mazzaroth*, in 1863, to prove that the ancient names for the constellations and preserved star names were inspired by God and transmitted through the early prophets. We have drawn the translation for the ancient star names from her work. We use these names together with their meanings to understand the meaning of the constellations.

The written revelation is not shy about the constellations. Rather it assigns their creation, their order, their march across the sky and the names of their stars to the work of God. But there is so much more.

What Do These Stars Declare?

Before we turn to our next passage, list what you can know about God from gazing at the heavens.

Read Psalm 50:6. And fill in the blank.

"And the heavens declare _____ _____,
For God Himself is judge."
[NASB]

Did God's righteousness make your list? If not, you will be discovering for the first time in the coming weeks how the heavens really do display the righteousness of God as well as Him as judge.

As we look intently at Psalm 19, we will find a greater purpose for the heavenly revelation.

Read the entire Psalm and record the two things compared in this Psalm. (Hint: The Psalm naturally breaks into two halves between verses 6 and 7.)

From a cursory view, it is surprising that "the heavens" should be compared to "the Law of the Lord." In fact, it is so surprising that scholars have postulated whether or not this Psalm is made from two unconnected fragments and just put together arbitrarily. We are convinced that this is not so. The internal structure joins both halves together in one complete Psalm. The shepherd had studied both the heavens and the Law and found in them the same Truth.

Tomorrow we will analyze this Psalm.

Day Three – Evidence in Psalm 19 and Romans 10

Psalm 19 in Depth

Yesterday we looked at Psalm 19 as a whole. Now let's take it verse by verse. (We have used the NASB version to fill in the blanks.)

Verse 1

Look again at verse 1 and fill in the blanks.

"The heavens are _____ of the glory of God.

And their expanse is _____ the work of His hand."

David says the heavens "tell or narrate" the glory of God and the work of His hand. Doesn't the verb narrate imply that a story is being told?

Verse 2

The thrust of this verse is the unceasing nature of the revelation.

What does this verse say is revealed?

The Hebrew word here *da'ath* is used commonly for "knowing." It is used in Genesis 2:9 "the tree of the *knowledge* of good and evil" [NASB] and Proverbs 9:10b "And the *knowledge* of the Holy One is understanding." [NASB] These are two of many occurrences of this word. Again, David is implying that there is a whole lot more to be gained from the night sky then a general idea of the power of the Creator. The skies reveal knowledge!

Verses 3 and 4

These verses together present a paradox.

> "There is no speech, nor are there words;
> Their voice is not heard.
> Their line [sound] has gone out through all the earth,
> And their utterances to the end of the world …"
> [NASB]

What is the apparent contradiction?

How can this apparent contradiction also be true? Can you think of an example where clear communication is made without sound?

We know communication occurs often without words. The New King James version offers another take on the translation, equally intriguing.

> "There is no speech nor language
> Where their voice is not heard.
> Their line (sound) has gone out through all the earth,
> And their words to the end of the world."
> [NKJV]

Rather than presenting a paradox, how does this translation presents David's message as an expansion on a single theme?

Compare Psalm 19:1-4 to Romans

Now take a look at Romans 10:16-18. What passage does Paul quote to substantiate his claim that all have heard the Gospel?

Wow!! Stop for a moment and take this in. Is Paul saying that all have heard the Gospel through the testimony in the heavens?

Look at Romans 1:18, 19. In your own words summarize these verses.

We believe Paul's discussion, in Romans, chapter 10, explains further the statement he put forward in 1:19. In Romans 1, Paul says God has shown all of mankind what they need to know of Him; in Romans 10:18, he says all have heard the word of God. The passage Paul uses to prove his case is Psalm 19:4a.

Again, just to labor it a bit more to make sure the point is clear, according to the Apostle Paul, whose sound has gone out through all the earth so that all have heard the Gospel?

This is a profound truth is it not?

Psalm 19:4b

The sun now takes the central place in the discussion of the heavens. "In them He has placed a tent for the sun," can be understood as, "In the heavens He has assigned a place for the sun." The sun is the central fixture of the heavens to both the uneducated and to those who are experts in astronomy. The course of the sun determines the principal 12 constellations among the 48. The sun's apparent course through the sky is called the **ecliptic**. The 12 signs of the Mazzaroth or Zodiac lay in a band along this course. So even with just a cursory knowledge of astronomy, we can see that the path, or assigned place, of the sun has significance in relation to the stars and their constellations.

Verses 5 and 6

After reading the above verses in Psalm 19, turn to Luke 1:76-79. This is Zacharias's prophecy after the birth of his son who would be John the Baptist. The NASB version says, "the Sunrise from on high shall visit us," in verse 78. Here Christ is called the "Sunrise," a direct comparison between Him and our sun.

According to verse 79, what does the Sunrise do for us?

This is not the only place in Scripture where the coming Messiah is compared to the sun.

Turn to Malachi 4:2. Here Christ is called the _____ of righteousness.

Now turn to Ezekiel 43:1-2. From which direction will Christ return, shining in glory?

How does this compare to the course of the sun?

In all these verses, the Son is likened to the sun. In Psalm 19, David is talking about more than simply the closest star to our planet. He is using a metaphor here.

List other language in verses 5 and 6 that is also used for Christ.

The rest of Psalm 19

The rest of Psalm 19 explores which revelation of God?

Ethelbert Bullinger in his book, *Witness of the Stars*, does a fantastic job analyzing the structure of Psalm 19.[1] We would love to explore this here, but for the sake of your time, we have included his work in Appendix A. Needless to say, the perfect structure of the two halves as they compare the testimony of the heavens and the testimony of the Word is good proof that its author has written a single psalm and is comparing these two revelations.

The Superior Revelation

According to the Psalmist, circle which revelation is superior.

                    The written revelation   or   The revelation in the heavens

---

What does Isaiah 40:8 say about the written Word?

---

[1] Bullinger, Ethelburt William, *Witness of the Stars*, (Cosimo, Inc., NY, 2007—originally published 1893) page 17

And what does Isaiah 13:10 say about the stars and their constellations?

Though the revelation of the heavens is inferior to the Word, since the stars and their constellations yet remain, it is a blessing to explore this ancient revelation.

Day Four – The History of the Heavenly Revelation in Scripture

The First Recorded False Religion – Worship of the Stars

The Founder

Corruption of the original purpose of the revelation in the heavens happened so early in human history, it staggers the mind. It occurred with the first appearance of the word "kingdom" in Scripture and is found in Genesis 10:10.

What is the infamous name of this kingdom?

Go back to verse 8. Who is its founder?

Take a look back a bit further; how is he related to Noah?

Only [____] generations from Noah and [____] from his sons, who were among the eight eyewitnesses of God's wrath poured out on a rebellious world, was Nimrod, whose name means, "The rebel." The two kingdoms founded by him, Babylon and Assyria were eventual conquerors of the nation Israel.

"He began to be mighty on the earth" is understood to mean he struggled to achieve power. The word translated, "mighty" can also be translated "chief."

How is Nimrod twice described in verse Genesis 10:9?

This is not a complement. It should be read "a mighty hunter **in the face** of the LORD." It is a long standing Jewish tradition and is also found in stories of him from extra-Biblical sources that Nimrod was an evil tyrant who hunted both men and animals and rebelled against the Lord.

Though Nimrod is not mentioned in Genesis 11, we know from chapter 10 that he founded Babel. Read Genesis 11:1-9.

His project – The tower at Babel

Its Purpose Understood from the Biblical Account

Most translators insert words in verse 4 that are not found in the original. This has led to misconceptions about the purpose of the tower. Verse 4 in most translations reads, **"Come, let us build for ourselves a city, and a tower whose top *will reach* into heaven …"**

A good translation will have the words "will reach" in italics. This indicates that these words are inserted by the translators to help the translation make sense, but they are not found in the original. The original only has a preposition that can be translated "<u>in, with, on, into or by</u>."

Rewrite the above phrase leaving out the inserted words – "will reach" – and replace the preposition "into" with another possible preposition. (Use the underlined words in the previous sentence. You can also put the article "the" ahead of heaven – that would be your translator insertion to help the sentence read well in English.)

Your sentence might read, "Come, let us build for ourselves a city and a tower whose top with the heavens …" That the builders desired a very tall tower is certainly implied, but the insertion of words like "will reach" causes readers to believe that the height of the tower was its chief and only aim. This is a misunderstanding. A tower whose top "with the heavens" means a tower whose top contains a representation of the heavens.

Its purpose as evident from archeology

All commentators we have read agree this tower was likely a ziggurat similar to those excavated in Mesopotamia. These structures had several levels with stairs leading to a temple on top. The Incas and Mayas on the American continents also built their temples this way. From the names of ancient ziggurats, even the name Babel, "Gate of Gods," we can safely assume that the chief function of this tower was religious. The reference "top with the heavens" likely means the temple atop this ziggurat was dedicated to the worship of the heavens or contained the representation of the heavens; i.e. zodiacal signs. The "Seven Spheres" ziggurat found in Iraq has seven levels; each level is dedicated to heavenly bodies – five planets, the moon, and the sun – and a temple on top with the signs of the zodiac.

Additional Scriptural Evidence

The name Nimrod means, "the rebel." In 1 Samuel 15:23, the prophet Samuel equates rebellion with witchcraft, "For rebellion *is as* the sin of witchcraft …" [NKJV] The italicized words are not in the Hebrew but added by translators. They reflect interpretation of the meaning of this sentence. It could also be translated, "for rebellion *is* the sin of witchcraft …" Certainly then, with such a man – whose very name means rebel – it is no surprise that he would be a founder of an occultist religion such as astrology.

Revelation 17:5 designates Babylon – the kingdom whose roots are at Babel – as the "mother of harlots." Since idolatry is often called harlotry in Scripture we believe Revelation 17:5 is speaking of Babylon as the birth place of false religion. Genesis 11 likely records the first organized false religion, and this religion likely included worship or some perversion of the constellations. Notice what Isaiah says about Babylon.

> "Stand now with your enchantments
> And the multitude of your sorceries,
> In which you have labored **from your youth** –
> Perhaps you will be able to profit,
> Perhaps you will prevail.
> You are wearied in the multitude of your counsels;
> Let now the astrologers, the stargazers,
> And the monthly prognosticators
> Stand up and save you
> From what shall come upon you."
> Isaiah 47:12-13 [NKJV emphasis added]

This passage referenced not only astrology but "monthly prognosticators." These are still found in every newspaper in the U.S. No wonder so many of us have steered clear of this subject!

The spread of this false religion

Read 2 Kings 23:5. In which kingdom were priests burning incense to the sun, moon, and the constellations?

Dare we wonder at God's wrath against them?

A Short Astronomy Lesson

Today's study will conclude with a technical discussion of astronomy. Since most of us do not spend frequent hours throughout the year gazing at the night sky, and since this is a subject almost completely ignored even at the college level, most of us can benefit from some basic knowledge.

An Important Term

We've referred to this term a few times, but it bears more explanation.

Ecliptic: It is the apparent path of the sun among the stars over the course of a year. The path is "apparent" because the sun does not move, but we orbit the sun. Over the course of a day, we see the sun make an arc in the sky from east to west. From the Northern Hemisphere, the ecliptic arc appears high in the sky in the summer and closer to the horizon in the winter. From our vantage point on earth, the 12 constellations of the Zodiac are in the sun's ecliptic path. When night falls, and you look into the night sky, if you look in the direction that the sun had traveled earlier that day you will find the constellations of the Zodiac or ecliptic. (Not all at once, they rise and set just like the sun.) In other regions of the sky are the rest of the constellations.

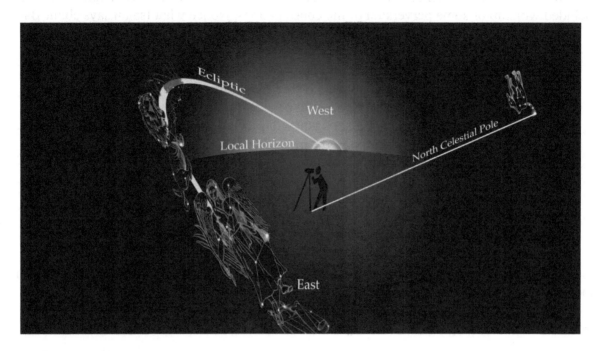

Modern Additions by Astronomers to the Original Constellations

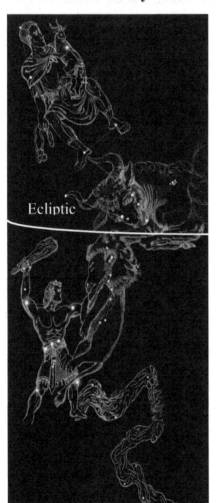

There are 48 ancient constellations. Astronomers Hevelius and Halley, both of the seventeenth century, added 37 constellations to these 48 to include stars that were not embraced by the ancient 48. Since astronomers had found the constellations valuable in organizing and identifying the stars of heaven, they added their own constellations. Actually, the very fact that the original 48 constellations did not include all the stars seen in the night sky is proof that organizing stars was not their purpose. The art that follows in this study does not include these modern inventions since we are concerned with the ancient preserved revelation not star mapping.

The Organization of the Original 48 Constellations

The 48 constellations are organized as follows: The twelve along the ecliptic – these are the ones most familiar to us because their names appear daily in the paper – have three parts or sub-constellations connected to them.

For instance, look at Taurus. The bull, known for its Latin name "Taurus" is the constellation found on the sun's ecliptic path. This makes it a Zodiacal sign and the central sign. Connected with it are three other constellations in this order: Orion, Eridanus (a river), and Auriga (the shepherd). These sub-constellations are located roughly along the same longitudinal plane as Taurus: One is above Taurus – Auriga – and two are located below – Orion and Eridanus. In our picture the river is not proportional. It is a very long constellation ending far into the Southern Hemisphere.

26

This is just one set of the twelve sets we will study. The organization of the 48 ancient constellations we use in this study is consistent with the organization found in ancient zodiacs. You will discover that they all work together to tell God's story.

Our Organization of the Original 48 for the Purpose of Reading God's Revelation

As we look into the heavenly revelation, we will see that the twelve signs with their sub-constellations can be organized into three books – four chapters per book (12 *ecliptic constellations*/3 *books* = 4 *chapters per book*); i.e. Book III contains Taurus, Gemini, Cancer and Leo as its four chapters. Each chapter has four total constellations to express a theme – the Zodiacal constellation plus the three supporting constellations; i.e. Taurus plus Orion, Eridanus and Auriga together make up Chapter One. (If this is still confusing, hang in there, by the time you complete subsequent lessons you will have a firm grasp of this!)

Day Five – How Should We Read the Heavenly Scroll

We are just on the edge of looking into that heavenly revelation. But first, we must decide where to begin reading. This is not obvious because our scroll is circular. So where do we break in and begin?

Traditionally, Aries, the lamb or ram is considered the beginning. But astronomers and astrologers no longer look into the scroll with the purpose of seeing God's revelation or redemptive story.

Take a look yourself at the circle of ecliptic constellations. Circle the one you think may best begin the story. The description of the picture is given in place of their Latin name. In quotes is meaning of their ancient name.

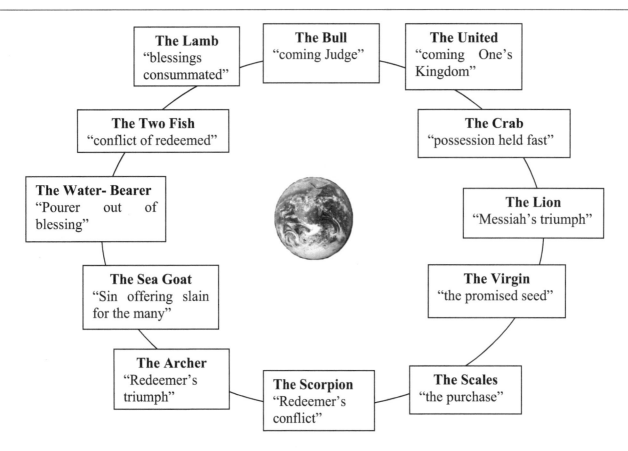

It certainly is hard. We think that the ancients invented a tool to help them remember where the scroll begins. In one of the most ancient zodiacs, the ceiling of the Temple Esneh, a sphinx is placed between Virgo and Leo. The sphinx has the head of a woman and the body of a lion. The word sphinx means "to bind closely together". The head of a woman then would indicate that we should begin with Virgo. While the hind end of a lion indicates we end with Leo. This would solve the riddle of the original purpose of the sphinx. We believe it was designed to show where the two ends of the Zodiac are bound together.

Below is a copy of a tracing from a drawing done by Signor Bossi in 1820.[1] It shows the Sphinx between Leo and Virgo.

The Signs of LEO and VIRGO, from the ceiling of the Portico of the Temple of ESNEH, showing the SPHINX between, uniting the beginning and end of the Zodiac.

The Gospel in the Heavenly Revelation

> Having established a place to begin, what can you expect to find when reading the heavenly scroll? Read Genesis 3:15.

Here is the first Gospel given to man. God, in the midst of pronouncing judgment on Adam and Eve, also pronounces their blessed hope. It is this hope that Adam preserved and shared with the generations after him. Scripture teaches that the Lord has always used prophets, even before Moses. Zacharius and Peter claim that God has spoken through his prophets **since the world began.** (Luke 1:70 and Acts 2:21) We believe the ancients preserved the prophecy in the stars; that night after night it should pour forth speech; that its words may reach the ends of the earth. Before moving forward into the examination of this heavenly revelation, we suggest you memorize Genesis 3:15. It will be narrated by the stars over and over again!

The Contents for the Heavenly Book

Ethelbert Bullinger does a fabulous job organizing the signs into three books with four chapters each.[2] He does such a wonderful and convincing job, we will use his outline for our study. You will find that each book has its own emphasis. And each book speaks in wonderful harmony with the written revelation!

---

[1] Bullinger, Ethelburt William, *Witness of the Stars*, (Cosimo, Inc., NY, 2007—originally published 1893) page 21
[2] Bullinger, Ethelburt William, *Witness of the Stars*, (Cosimo, Inc., NY, 2007—originally published 1893)

Table of Contents

Book One: The Redeemer
(His Person, His Work)

Chapter One: The Redeemer the Seed of a Woman *(Virgo)*
Chapter Two: The Purchase *(Libra)*
Chapter Three: The Redeemer's Conflict *(Scorpio)*
Chapter Four: The Redeemer's Triumph *(Sagittarius)*

Book Two: The Redeemed
(The Results of His Work)

Chapter One: The Blessing Obtained *(Capricorn)*
Chapter Two: The Surety of These Blessings *(Aquarius)*
Chapter Three: The Conflict of the Redeemed *(Pisces)*
Chapter Four: Their Blessings Consummated and Enjoyed *(Aries)*

Book Three: The Redeemer
(His Kingdom, His Glory)

Chapter One: The Coming Judge of the Earth *(Taurus)*
Chapter Two: The Messiah's Kingdom *(Gemini)*
Chapter Three: The Redeemed Possession Held Safe *(Cancer)*
Chapter Four: The Coming One's Absolute Triumph *(Leo)*

We are so excited to get started! Before you break from this study for the week, why not list two or three reasons why you think this ancient revelation has been almost lost.

Book I – The Redeemer – His Person, His Work

Lesson Two – Chapter One – The Coming Seed

Day One – Virgo – The Promised Seed

This book opens with the person of the coming One – the promised seed – then tells of His conflict and victory. It opens with the promise and closes with the dragon cast down. In so doing, it tells and expands upon God's ancient promise, "And I will put enmity between you and the woman, and between your seed and her seed; He shall bruise your head; and you shall bruise His heal." Genesis 3:15 [NKJV]

The Sign Virgo – The Promised Seed

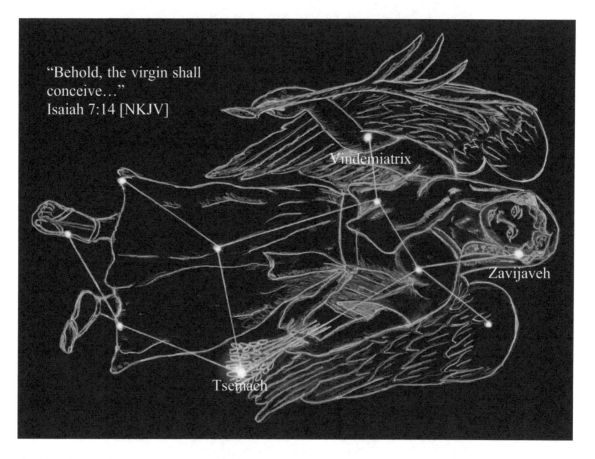

Today we begin the exciting discovery of God's revelation in the heavens! The first part of Genesis 3:15 – the seed of the woman – is our starting point. This picture of the woman lies along the sun's ecliptic path, so it is the first constellation of the set. In the coming days of this week, we will examine the three supporting constellations of Virgo.

Virgo, as she is known today, means virgin in Latin. It is a translation of her ancient Hebrew name, Bethulah, which also means virgin. She is always shown holding a branch, probably a palm branch, in her right hand and a handful of wheat or corn in her left. She is drawn with or without wings. We have opted to include the wings for reasons that will be apparent later in the lesson. The names on the picture are names of stars found on star atlases.

> "Therefore the Lord Himself will give you a sign: Behold, a virgin will be with child and bear a son, and she will call His name Immanuel." Isaiah 7:14 [NASB]

If you have notes in your Bible use these or turn to Isaiah 8:8, 10. What is the meaning of the name Immanuel?

We could almost end today's lesson here, so clear is the message of the sign. We are certain everyone knows who this virgin is who bears a son with the name "God with us." Immanuel is the promised Seed of the woman. But there is a lot more to see in this constellation.

Although the sign appears to focus on the virgin, all the star names contained within the sign speak, not about her, but her Seed! It is the Seed, not the one who bore the Seed, who is really the subject of this constellation.

The alpha star, or brightest star of the constellation is located in the wheat or corn carried in her left hand. The alpha star being located in the seed carried by the woman and not the woman herself, is another reminder that the constellation has more to do with the woman's seed then the woman. Its ancient name is:

- Tsemach [Hebrew] meaning "the branch" or
- Al Zimach [Arabic] also meaning "the branch"
- Some of today's star maps have the name Spica here. This is Latin meaning "ear of corn." It is a modern replacement for the original name.

There are twenty words in Hebrew that can be translated branch. However, this Old Testament Hebrew word, *tsemach*, is translated "branch" only five times. Each time the inspired writer used this word for branch it was a reference to the Messiah. We will look at each for there is something profound in them.

Jeremiah contains two of the five. Find the verse and fill in the missing words.

Jeremiah 23:5, "'Behold, the days are coming,' declares the LORD, 'When I shall raise up for David a _____; and He will reign as _____ and act wisely and do _____ and _____ in the land.'" [NASB]

Jeremiah 33:15 is a repeat of our above verse. "In those days and at that time I will cause a righteous Branch of David to spring forth; and He shall execute justice and righteousness on the earth." [NASB]

●☐In Jeremiah 23:5 and 31:15, in what capacity does the branch serve?

Now turn to the next book, Zechariah. Again fill in the missing words.

Zechariah 3:8 "… for behold, I am going to bring in My _____ the _____."

●☐ What is the Branch called in this passage?

Zechariah 6:12 "… Thus says the LORD of hosts, 'Behold, a _____

whose name is _____, for He will branch out from where He is;

and He will build the temple of the LORD.'" [NASB]

●☐ What is the Branch called in this passage?

Finally turn to Isaiah 4:2:"In that day the _____ of the _____

will be _____ and _____
and the fruit of the earth *will* be the pride and adornment of the survivors of Israel." [NASB]

●☐Here the branch is called the Branch of _____(or Yehovah, Israel's covenant name for God).

Now look again at each of the separate descriptive words used to describe "the branch" [*Tsemach*] in the above verses. (They are marked by a bullet [●] to make them easier to find.) Write your four different answers again on the lines below.

_____   _____

_____   _____

Notice each presentation of the Hebrew word *tsemach* – the alpha (brightest) star in Virgo – uses a separate descriptive word for his office or title. And even more amazing, each of these four titles are a theme for each of the four Gospels.

1. In Matthew, the Messiah's **kingly** role is emphasized
2. In Mark, His role is that of a **servant**
3. In Luke, His role is a **man's**
4. And in John, his place is that of **God**

The star which speaks of a son, or branch, and is found in the bundle of wheat or corn carried by the Virgin, speaks both of the Seed of the Woman and all four of His roles as emphasized in the Gospels.

When Christ came into Jerusalem on the back of a young donkey, the people laid palm branches before Him. This is what is carried in the other hand of Virgo.

This act demonstrated that the people believed Christ was the fulfillment of Jeremiah 23:5, the Branch as king. However, Jesus Christ did not take up that role. Instead, he fulfilled which role above as the coming Branch? (Matthew 20:28)

For those still struggling with "the branch" as synonymous with a son, we will explore this connection a bit further. In Psalm 80:15, 17 we find the Hebrew word, *ben*, translated in verse 15 as branch; but in verse 17 the same word, *ben*, is translated son.

> "Return, we beseech You,
> O God of hosts;
> Look down from heaven and see,
> And visit this vine
> And the vineyard which Your right hand has planted,
> And the branch [*ben*] *that* You made strong for Yourself. …
> Let Your hand be upon the man of Your right hand,
> Upon the son [*ben*] of man *whom* You made strong for Yourself."
> Psalm 80:14, 15, 17 [NKJV]

Besides being a fascinating prophecy of the Messiah, this passage demonstrates that the term branch and son are synonymous in the Hebrew mind. If you are familiar with Hebrew surnames you may recognize the word *ben*. It has been the Jewish practice to follow their first name by *ben* (son) or *bat* (daughter) and then the patriarch's name; i.e. Judah ben Hur (meaning Judah son of Hur).

Virgo is a promise that answers the yearning of this psalmist – He will "visit this vine."

It may seem strange to us, at first glance, to connect the two – branch and son. However, we still use this idea in our own culture as well.

What do we call an ancestral chart?

A family _____ .

Sons and daughters are written upon the _____ .

Let's move on. The second brightest star, or beta star, located in the left wing is Zavijaveh [Hebrew] and means "the gloriously beautiful."

That should sound familiar. Peruse back over the "branch" verses above.

Which verse is the one that also contains this description of the Branch?

The final star name is:
- Al Mureddin [Arabic], "who shall come down, who shall have dominion"

- Vindemiatrix [Chaldean] "the son, or branch cometh"

A parallel to the Arabic name is found in Psalm 72:6-8.

> "May **he come down** like rain upon the mown grass,
> Like showers that water the earth.
> In his days may the righteous flourish,
> And abundance of peace till the moon is no more.
> **May he also rule** from sea to sea,
> And from the River to the ends of the earth."
> [NASB emphasis added]

Finally, we find this constellation described in Revelation 12.

From the first verse, what appeared, and where did it appear?

Again we see an example of the stars fulfilling one of their purposes to act as a _____.

There are three women pictured in the heavens, but only Virgo lies on the ecliptic. Remember, the ecliptic is the apparent path of the sun in the sky. It also happens that the moon and the planets travel along this same path. Of the three depictions of women in the night sky, only the constellation Virgo could have the moon and sun among its stars.

It appears a time frame is marked out by this passage; "… clothed with the sun …" likely means the sun is in this sign. Right now, the sun is in this sign from the third week of September to the end of October. (But because of the procession of the equinoxes, this would be a little earlier in September 2,000 years ago.) The "… moon at her feet …" could mean the new moon. The new moon of the month of September marks the New Year, according to the Jewish calendar, and the Feast of Trumpets or Rosh ha-Shanah. It is a significant day to Jews. Is John giving us the time of Christ's birth? It is a possible conclusion.

The vision continues with the dragon (we'll see him again later) seeking to devour the child who is caught up to God and the woman fleeing to the desert. Then there is a war in heaven in which the dragon is cast down.

Now read Revelation 12:13, 14. What is given to the woman to help her escape the dragon?

With such a visual match to the constellation Virgo, we think the wings belong on this picture.

Day Two –Coma – The Desired

"Your father Abraham rejoiced to see My day, and he saw *it* and was glad."

John 8:56 [NKJV]

Yesterday's constellation, Virgo, is a familiar constellation. Today's constellation may be completely unfamiliar. There is good reason for this. You may remember from our introduction, that each Zodiacal constellation has three supporting constellations. Virgo is the constellation on the Zodiac and Coma, the above picture, is the first supporting constellation and does not appear in any recent star atlas.

The coming Branch will be a son. He is Comah – Hebrew, meaning longing or desire.

Isn't it amazing that this picture follows the virgin. To us who know the written revelation, it couldn't be a more obvious prophecy of our Savior. It should be no surprise to you then, that Satan has all but erased the original and replaced it with a corruption. You will not find this picture on star maps. You will find instead the name "Coma Berenices" and a picture of a wig. Notice the similarity between its ancient Hebrew name, Comah, and the modern Latin name, Coma.

The corruption of this constellation took place during the reign of Ptolemy III, king of Egypt in the third century BC. His wife, Berenice, vowed to consecrate her fine head of hair to Venus for the safe return of her husband from a dangerous expedition. Her hair was hung in the Temple of Venus and subsequently stolen. To comfort Berenice, Conon, an astronomer of Alexandria, told her that Jupiter had taken her hair up and made it a constellation. The Greek word for hair is Co'me; so similar to the original Hebrew, Comah, that the corruption easily caught on.

This is a well known story, but how do we know the above picture was what the wig replaced? There is good evidence that our picture approximates the ancient constellation before Conan corrupted it.

- Ancient zodiacs picture this constellation as a woman with a child in her arms. The Temple of Denderah, which shows a child on a woman's lap, was constructed in the first century BC.
- An Arabian Astronomer of the eighth Century, Albumazar, says:
    "There arises in the first Decan, as the Persians, Chaldeans, and Egyptians, and the two Hermes and Ascalius teach, a young woman, whose Persian name denotes a pure virgin, sitting on a

throne, nourishing an infant boy (the boy, I say), having a Hebrew name, by some nations called IHESU, with signification IEZA, which in Greek is called CHRISTOS."[1]

- Even in the day of Shakespeare, the original picture was known. In Shakespeare's <u>Titus Andronicus</u>, Titus gives arrows with letters on them to his friends to shoot to the gods. All aim at the night sky and shoot. After the shot of one of his friends, Lucius, Titus exclaims, "O, well said, Lucius! – Good boy, in Virgo's lap …" [Act 4, Scene III] In other words, Lucius' shot was aimed squarely at the constellation that contained the boy in the virgin's lap.

- As we become familiar with the mystery and beauty of the other 47 constellations, it will be evident how out of place a wig is among the rest.

If the four evidences above were not enough, the ancient Egyptian name for this constellation is Shes-nu and means "the desired son."

The Hebrew word Comah appears only once in Scripture.

> "O God, You are my God;
> Early will I seek You;
> My soul thirsts for You,
> My flesh longs [*comah*] for You
> In a dry and thristy land
> Where there is no water."
> Psalm 63:1 [NKJV]

Read Haggai 2:6-7.

> "For thus says the LORD of Hosts, 'Once more (it is a little while) I will shake heaven and earth, the sea and dry land; and I will shake all nations, and they will come to the Desire of All Nations, and I will fill this temple with glory,' says the LORD of hosts.'" [NKJV]

We see this prophecy having a partial fulfillment in the visit of the Magi recorded in Matthew 2. These Magi were shaken from their place to seek the desired Son. And they did not come empty handed but brought valuable gifts to this King of the Jews. This is implied here in Haggai – especially if you keep reading to verse 8. It is stated more clearly in a parallel passage, Isaiah 60:5-6.

> What parallels do you see between these verses in Isaiah and the story of the Magi?

It is clear that the Lord has a future fulfillment for these prophecies still in store for Israel; one in which they are completely fulfilled.

Additionally, we would be remiss if we did not take this opportunity to postulate that the star the Magi followed likely appeared in this constellation. These wise men are traditionally believed to be from Persia or the Arabian Peninsula (being from Arabia would make them Midian a fulfillment of

---

[1] Ethelbert Bullinger, *Witness of the Stars*, 1893, pp. 34-35

Isa. 60:6). It makes sense that they traveled to a foreign land for what they saw as an announcement of the birth of the desired Son. He is not only the "King of the Jews", He is the fulfillment of the prophecy spoken to every nation in Genesis 3:15 and testified to in the heavenly display. Secondly, it is interesting that these men knew they were celebrating a king's birth, not his coronation. A star in the constellation picturing a young child on his mother's lap would lend itself to this understanding. Thirdly, a star in this constellation could feasibly shine vertically over Jerusalem or Bethlehem. So this constellation lends itself well to the possibility that the Magi could reach Jerusalem by following a star in it. (How this is possible is explained further in Appendix B.)

How might the Promised Seed be the desire of not only Israel, but the Desire of all Nations?

Read Isaiah 26:7-9. Isaiah expresses his yearning for the Lord. What expectation does he have of the Lord?

Do you think Isaiah's expectation is shared by the nations? Why or why not?

What do you expect He will do when He comes again?

Read Isaiah 9:6-7. How does the Child born to us in these verses fulfill these desires?

Simeon's story in Luke 2:25-32 shows that the expectation of the Jews had not waned even in their long wait for His arrival. He was told he would see the embodiment of his desire before his death.

When he finally saw Him, what hopes did Simeon express Jesus would fulfill?

All men and women have been seeking a savior to right what is wrong in our world since the promise in Genesis 3:15.

List some evidences of this from the secular world.

Though the Promised Savior has already visited us, we now desire His coming again. Read the following passages and describe what the Lord's return will bring or mean for us.

1 Corinthians 1:7

Philippians 3:20-21

Romans 8:22-23

Did you notice the repeated adverb Paul uses to describe how we "await" His return in each of these passages? It is the same in every passage. What is it?

Romans 8, speaks of someone or something else who awaits His coming. Who or what is waiting?

Surely He is desired! Come quickly Lord!

Day Three –Centaurus – The Despised

Alpha Centauri

Hadar

"He came to His own, and His own did not receive Him." John 1:11 [NKJV]

The second constellation under Virgo, pictured as a Centaur, sits so low in the sky most of him is not visible from the Northern Hemisphere. All 48 original constellations were once visible from as far North as North Latitude 40°. *(This latitude is the border latitude between Kansas and Nebraska in the US and runs through the center of Turkey in the Middle East.)* However, because the earth wobbles as it spins upon its axis, stars appear to sink or rise slowly over time and over a period of approximately 26,000 years return to their original positions. This is known as the precession of the equinoxes.

Centaurus is a brilliant constellation, full of bright stars. It is also very large, the 10th largest of the original 48 constellations. He is actually part of a larger picture. The spear he holds is in the act of stabbing an animal. This animal is called "the slain" and is part of the next constellation set. Between his legs sits the famous Southern Cross, also a part of the next constellation set.

Before discussing the meaning of Centaurus, this strange picture deserves our attention: a man's upper half on a horse's body, otherwise known as a centaur. This is a very surprising representation of our Savior.

The centaur pictures a combining of two into one. We believe the purpose is to show this one is the Son of Man and the Son of God.

Read John 1:1-3, 14. Here Scripture teaches that "the Word" existed in eternity as God then took on flesh and became a man. The centaur is a prophetic picture of this same truth.

The use of the upper half of a man in the Centaur to represent Jesus, the Son of Man, is obvious; the hind of a horse is not an obvious representation as Jesus, the Son of God. However, in ancient times, horses were solely the property of kings. There were not middle-class hobbyists or ranchers owning their own horses then, as there are today. So the hind of a horse would speak of His kingship to the entire ancient world. In fact, the Romans called this constellation, Rex Centaurus, "king centaur."

The one preserved ancient star name, Hadar, is a Hebrew word translated, "glory, honor, majesty, beauty, comeliness." It is a word closely connected to kingship. It is commonly used in connection with the Lord. The Lord uses it to describe Himself in Job 40:9-10.

<blockquote>
"Have you an arm like God?
Or can you thunder with a voice like His?
Then adorn yourself with majesty and splendor,
and array yourself with glory and beauty [*hadar*]."
[NKJV]
</blockquote>

This star name is found in the horse part of this constellation, and we believe, is meant to point out that the coming Seed is King and, more exactly, the King of kings, the Son of God.

The brightest star in his forward hoof does not have a preserved ancient name but its modern astronomical name may be familiar. It is known as alpha Centauri and is the third brightest in all the night sky. You may recognize its name. It has long been a subject of interest to astronomers since it is the closest star system to our own.

The ancient names for the sign also help us interpret the meaning of this unusual picture. They are:
- Bazah [Hebrew] meaning "the despised" and another Hebrew name –
    - Asmeath [Hebrew] meaning "sin offering"
- Al Beze [Arabic] derived from Hebrew meaning, "despised"
- Chiron [Greek] meaning "the pierced or who pierces"
    - Frances Rolleston, the 19th century scholar of the history of ancient languages, believes the Greek name Chiron was derived from the Hebrew word karah which means "pierced."[1]

We find the Hebrew word, *bazah* in Psalm 22:6. Psalm 22 is a psalm of David and likely expresses an experience of David, but it is also prophetic and most appropriately applied to the Lord Jesus. Remember the words spoken by Him on the cross, "Eli, Eli, lama sabachthani?" [Matthew 27:46] They were Aramaic for, "My God, My God, why have You forsaken Me?" and are the opening words to Psalm 22. He quoted the opening to Psalm 22, to let us know that this psalm was about Him and His crucifixion.

---

[1] Rolleston, Frances. "Mazzaroth by Frances Rolleston." *Philologos*. Web. 30 Aug. 2011. http://philologos.org/__eb-mazzaroth/202.htm

---

What does He say in verse 6?

The Greek name, Chiron as derived from the Hebrew *karah* is also found in Psalm 22. This ancient Hebrew root is used in Psalm 22:16.

What is pierced?

This detailed prophetic reference to the crucifixion contains two names for this constellation. Look again at the picture on the first page of this lesson. There between the hind feet of the Centaur is the famous Southern Cross! The evidence for the meaning of this picture is already overwhelming – two words for this centaur in a single psalm – a psalm which speaks of the crucifixion in amazing prophetic detail – and between the feet of the Despised is the constellation of the cross.

There is still so much more. The cross' alpha star (brightest star), is known as Acrux, near the right hind ankle. The ancients saw this star as piercing the right ankle of Centaurus. This probably led the Greeks to adopt their own derivation of *karah* as a name for this constellation. How magnificent a match to Psalm 22:16.

We are not nearly done yet. Isaiah 53 is also a very famous prophecy of the Messiah's death. The Hebrew name for this sign, Bazah, is used twice in one verse in this passage.

Since you know *bazah* means "despised," which verse contains this Hebrew word?

We find the star name, Hadar, also here in Isaiah 53. "… He has no form or comeliness [*hadar*]; and when we see Him, *there* is no beauty that we should desire Him." Isaiah 53:2 [NKJV].

This section of Scripture also answers a nagging question for any reader of this heavenly scroll.

Why was the desired [Coma] despised [Bazah]?

In case this was not completely clear, look back at the quote from Isaiah 53:2. Remember that *hadar* is a word very closely connected with kingship. Keeping that in mind, what is implied in saying, "He has no form or comeliness [kingly beauty] when we see Him" and how does that relate to the above question?

Even when He entered Jerusalem triumphantly and received praise as the "son of David," He did not ride in as a king, but He rode a lowly donkey. He did not ride a glorious beast of war, but a humble beast of burden.

He came into Jerusalem, as a servant, with no form or kingly beauty, just as Isaiah 53 prophesied. The Jews saw Pilates' placing the plaque above the cross of Christ, "King of the Jews," as the height of insult. Nothing about His entrance into Jerusalem or His passion week was kingly in their eyes.

The Greeks have corrupted the truth through the invention of myths which now stand in the place of the truth. (As you continue through this study you will see this again and again.) Having somewhere along the way forgotten that the constellation teaches a mysterious truth about the Desired Son, they invented a mythological creature, a centaur. And they gave him the name Chiron or Kheiron. It is such an inferior substitute for the truth.

It is worth telling the Greek fable surrounding Chiron, because in it, traces of the truth are easy to recognize. As you read, make a mental note of the parallels to the true Person represented by Centaurus. You will be asked to list them.

Chiron was a famous centaur who was known for his skill in hunting, medicine, music, athletics and prophecy. He was unique among centaurs, having a unique lineage and character. Centaurs were regarded as wild, overly indulgent drinkers and uncultured. However, Chiron, owing to his godly lineage, was intelligent, civilized, and kind. He was regarded as a great healer and teacher. All the most distinguished heroes of Greece were his pupils/disciples. Because he was the offspring of a god, he was immortal. When accidently pierced in the foot by a poison arrow, the pain of it was so excruciating, he voluntarily gave up his immortality and died. In most versions, it was one of Chiron's own disciples who wounded him with the poison arrow. In some versions, Chiron gave his immortality to Prometheus who had been consigned to eternal torment. Chiron was placed amongst the stars as a tribute to his gracious act.

List as many parallels as you can find between this mythical Chiron and the true person, Jesus Christ.

It is exceedingly evident from this myth that, at one time, there were those among the Greeks who knew the truth. How could they have so many details so similar to the truth? No wonder Paul writes to the Romans, who inherited these myths.

> For the wrath of God is revealed from heaven against all ungodliness and unrighteousness of men, who suppress the truth in unrighteousness, because what may be known of God is manifest in them, for God has shown *it* to them. For since the creation of the world His invisible *attributes* are clearly seen, being understood by the things that are made, *even* His eternal power and Godhead, so that they are without excuse, because although they knew God, they did not glorify *Him* as God … but became futile in their thoughts … Professing to be wise, they became fools, and changed the glory of the incorruptible God into an image made like corruptible man … Romans 1:18-23 [NKJV]

Though this coming Seed will suffer humiliation and be despised as prophesied in the constellation, Centaurus, He is given this promise.

44

"Thus says the LORD, the Redeemer of Israel, their Holy One, To Him whom man despises [*bazoh* from *bazah*], To Him whom the nation abhors, to the Servant of rulers, 'Kings shall see and arise, princes also shall worship, because of the LORD who is faithful, the Holy One of Israel; and He has chosen You.'"
Isaiah 49:7 [NKJV]

Day Four –Boötes – He Comes for His Reward

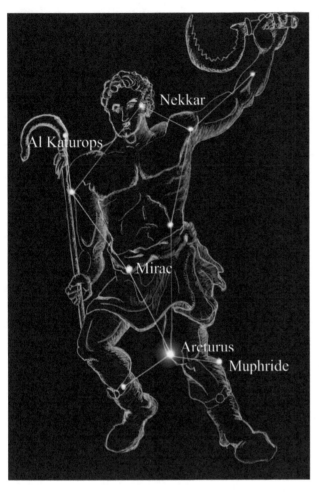

"… Be strong, do not fear!
Behold, your God will come *with* vengeance,
With the recompense of God;
He will come and save you."

Isaiah 35:4 [NKJV]

The third supporting constellation of Virgo was called Smat, "one who rules," by the Egyptians.

The Greeks called him, Boötes, {pronounced bah-OO-tays} which is likely taken from the Hebrew word bo, a common word with various nuances of meaning. But primarily meaning, "to come." Boötes is always pictured as a man walking rapidly, holding a spear or shepherd's staff in his right hand and a raised sickle in his left.

Read the following passages (the brackets tell how the Hebrew word "*bo*" is translated in each) and describe what He is coming to do.

Psalm 98:9 [bo is "come"]

Isaiah 35:3-4 [bo is "come"]

Ezekiel 34:12-16 [bo is "bring"]

Micah 1:3 [bo is "coming"]

All these ideas are represented in this picture.

The passage in Ezekiel speaks of bringing His flock to their own land.

What in the picture might symbolize this?

The star, Arcturus – which happens to be the fourth brightest star in the sky – foretells that He will bring a band of followers at His coming. Its name is Greek, meaning, "the guardian or keeper."

The Greeks, along with all antiquity, saw Boötes as the guardian of the bears, Ursa Major and Ursa Minor. The constellation, Ursa Major is located near the arm with the raised sickle. Boötes is not seen as traveling alone, but leading the bears as their shepherd. We will explore this more when we discuss the bears in lesson 12.

Frances Rolleston believed the name Arcturus came from a Hebrew root 'arach, "to travel or go with a band of travelers." This seems very likely given the ancient world's understanding. Likely the meaning of the name evolved over time to mean guardian.[1]

The passage from Micah said He comes to tread on all the **high places** of the earth. This idea matches the star in the staff, Al Katurops, "the branch, treading under foot"

In ancient times, high places were used for a special purpose. Read the references below and provide the common purpose of "high places."
1 Kings 11:4-8
1 Kings 14:22-24
Ezekiel 16:15-16, 23-25
In Micah 1:3, the treading down on the high places of the earth, is a reference to doing what?

The verses above spoke of the worship of false gods on high places by God's own people. It is a heartbreaking truth when He comes down from heaven, part of His work will be to tread down these false gods and idols, that He may be solely exalted, among His own people.

From Isaiah 2:12, 17 what other "high" things will the Lord tread down when He comes?
In Psalm 108:13, the idea of treading under foot is mentioned again, but what is tread upon here?

---

[1] Rolleston, Frances. "Mazzaroth by Frances Rolleston." *Philologos*. Web. 30 Aug. 2011. http://philologos.org/__eb-mazzaroth/202.htm

The first passage we looked at, Psalm 98:9 said the Lord comes to judge in righteousness and with equity. This idea is spoken by the star, Muphride, "who separates."

Read Matthew 25:31-34, 41. What is separated and for what purpose?

We have already examined how this constellation expresses the idea of the Lord coming to lead His flock. The same Ezekiel passage from the first page of this lesson, also spoke of Him gathering His flock wherever they had been scattered. This is also in this constellation. The idea is captured in the raised sickle in Boötes left hand. The sickle is a reaping tool.

Read Revelation 14:14-16. Who is the one who reaps with the sickle?

This reaping is the gathering or reaping of those who are His sheep.

Continue reading in Revelation 14:17-20. This is another reaping. Who is reaping and what happens to those reaped here?

Amazing isn't it, how well Boötes matches the first reaper in Revelation. The sickle in His hand should be to us a comfort, for we know when He comes He will first gather us together before pouring out wrath on those who remain in unbelief.

Let's summarize what we have already learned from this sign. There is One who is coming; He is the Branch promised in the constellation Virgo. He comes to judge between the sheep and the goats, to gather and lead His flock to safety. He also comes down from heaven to tread on everything high and lofty and to tread down all false gods, so that He alone will be exalted among His people. Wow, the heavens do declare God as Judge! But there is still more to this sign.

The star in Boötes' waist is Mirac, "the coming forth as an arrow."

What is implied by this name?

Finally, the beta star in his head is Nekkar, from the Hebrew word, *daqar*, "the pierced."
This word is found in Zechariah 12:10. From the context, and the expression, "then they will look on Me," we know that this takes place when He returns and all flesh shall see Him.

What will they know about Him at that time, and what will their reaction be?

The "they" in this verse is the Lord's people Israel. It was to them that He came, but they did not receive Him. (John 1:11) The Promised Seed, the Desired Son became the Despised and was pierced – this is the message of the first three constellations of chapter one. Now in the final section of this chapter we have the Branch returning, and He will be recognized as the One who was pierced. This is the Gospel.

You have now heard the declaration of the stars in the first chapter of the first book of the heavenly revelation. This first chapter is Genesis 3:15 told and expanded upon in pictures – the Seed of the Woman(Virgo) will be pierced in the foot (Centaurus) and will crush His enemy's seed (Boötes). This first chapter contains the outline for the rest of Book I and the broad summary of the Lord's redemptive work. Every chapter to come will be an enlargement of many wonderful details within this framework.

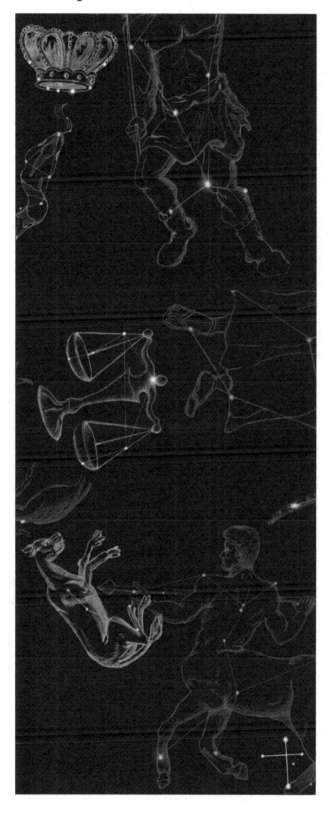

Day One – Libra – The Purchase

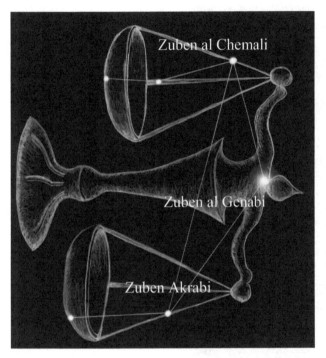

"The LORD redeems the soul of His servants,
And none of those who take refuge in Him will be
condemned."

Psalm 34:22 [NASB]

As with last week's first lesson, this week begins with the constellation along the ecliptic. This will be the pattern for every week to the end. Libra is a picture of scales and has many preserved ancient names.

- Mozanaim meaning "the scales weighing" in Hebrew
- Al Zubena "purchase or redemption" in Arabic
- Lambadia "station of propitiation" in Coptic (Coptic is the Egyptian language written with Greek letters)
- Libra "weighing" in Latin

The Hebrew and Latin merely describe the picture while the ancient Arabic and Coptic tell us much more about the meaning of the picture. It is worth spending some time defining two words above.

- Redemption means, "to buy back," being a bit more specific than just purchase. Redemption includes the idea that what is purchased had once belonged to the purchaser.
- Propitiation, involves an act to appease or satisfy an offended person and hence be reconciled to that person. Since this word is most frequently used in reference to God or a god, the act of propitiation most often involves a sacrifice.

We find both of these words, redemption and propitiation, in Romans 3:23-26. Read this passage and note these words. (The NIV uses sacrifice of atonement instead of propitiation but the meaning is essentially the same.)

We will further discuss how these scales represent the ideas of redemption and propitiation when we move on to the star names in this picture. But first, the verse above brings out something from our first lesson.

What does this passage say is demonstrated by the Lord's act of redemption and propitiation?

But how? This is worth examining. Romans 3:23 states an important truth about all of us.

What is this truth?

This problem presents, as we see it, two obvious options for God.

1. He could leave us in our sin to suffer the consequences of our sins – this would be just and consistent with His righteousness or
2. He could ignore our sin and release us from its consequences – this would be gracious but would be in conflict with His righteousness and His very character. It would make Him unrighteous and is really not an option for Him.

So God took action creating another option. "Because of His forbearance," He supplied the propitiation that justifies us as a gift, purchasing our redemption. This option then demonstrates God's righteousness because He did not overlook our sin. Rather He provided the only way for His justice and righteousness to be satisfied and also reconcile us to Him.

We love how the passage above concludes. It says that God is both "just and the justifier of the one who has faith in Jesus." He has kept His justice intact, while justifying the ungodly. This is an amazing truth.

Scales, in ancient times were the means by which a purchaser made his purchase. They measured the weight of his silver or gold against a standard so that the seller was certain he was receiving the agreed upon sum. Consequently, the Arabic name which means, "purchase" is self-evident – scales were used in sales transactions. The idea of propitiation is also present in scales, though a bit more of a stretch. In the balanced scale, the seller is satisfied or appeased that the purchase price is actually paid and he has not been shorted. There is a spiritual parallel here. We begin in Romans 3:23 with the problem – all fall short – the scales are tipped against us. God, being just does not ignore this truth, but as both the just and the justifier, He pays the high price Himself and purchases us for Himself. As Roman 3 says, God, through the provision of propitiation, demonstrated His righteousness. Since Libra speaks of propitiation (the ancient name Lambadia means "station of propitiation") we can now see how the heavens declare His righteousness as the Psalmist states in Psalm 50:6, "Let the heavens declare His righteousness, for God Himself is Judge." [NKJV]

Now let's look at the individual star names; the above idea is clarified in them. The alpha star, Zuben al Genabi, means "the price which is deficient." The story this sign tells begins just as Romans 3:23-26 does – the problem is that there is a price and a deficiency.

Read Psalm 49:7-8. Why can't we redeem our brother?

Read Psalm 62:9. Here we have a picture of purchasing by weighing on a scale. What is true of men of any rank according to this verse?

Remember when purchasing anything, what is desired is for the scales to be brought into balance, then the seller is appeased that the purchase price is met.

If all men, when weighed on the scales go up and are lighter than air – what is the problem?

The beta star in the higher scale is Zuben al Chemali, "the price which covers."

> "Thou didst forgive the iniquity of Thy people;
> Thou didst cover all their sin."
> Psalm 85:2 [NASB]

> "Blessed is *he whose* transgression is forgiven,
> *Whose* sin is covered."
> Psalm 32:1 [NKJV]

There is a solution to the problem!

Read Revelation 5:9.In these verses we have the purchaser, who is He? (You may need to look back to verse 5.)

Who or what is purchased?

For whom are they purchased?

With what were they purchased?

This leads to the final preserved star name, Zuben Akrabi or Zuben al Akrab, "the price of the conflict."

In the first set of verses, we learned that the price of our redemption was too costly for any man.

The purchase of our sin was the blood of Christ as we saw in Revelation 5:9. It was indeed costly!

In Libra, we have the Gospel simply presented. Every man owes a debt too costly for himself or any other to pay. But, through the precious blood of the Lamb, the debt has been covered; redemption has been purchased. This begs the question, have you received for yourself the propitiation for your sins? Romans 3:26 says, "… that He might be just and the justifier of the **one who has faith in Jesus**." [NKJV emphasis added] The price for your sins is paid, but it is up to each one to receive it.

The final star name includes the idea of conflict. A battle is continually waged by the adversary to corrupt the truth of the Gospel. Look back at the introductory picture to this lesson which includes all the constellations we will be studying as well as the constellations near them. You will notice that the claws of the Scorpion just to the left of Libra are reaching out to hold it. As you would imagine, the scorpion represents a malignant character.

> What do you think the signs of heaven might be telling us in the attempt of Scorpio to hold the scales in its claws?

We see evidence of the enemy's attempt to seize the truth and corrupt it in the Egyptian myth surrounding this constellation. We also see evidence that the original message of the scales was once understood. In the myth, the goddess Ma'at weighs the feather of truth against the heart of one who recently died. If the heart does not succeed in bringing the scale into balance, the heart fails the test, is devoured and the owner of the heart is doomed to suffer for all eternity.

This myth denies several truths taught in the names of the stars, and even in the Coptic itself. The Coptic speaks of propitiation – sacrifice. The stars say there is a price that is deficient, but there is also a price that covers and it is costly. In contrast, the myth tells us that the heart of the individual can pass the test based on its merit. The heart may not be found deficient. The heart of some individuals may actually bring the scales into balance and have no need of a price to cover. The lie in this myth is still believed today but expressed a little differently.

> How is this same lie expressed today?

The scorpion has desired to seize the truth in this constellation and corrupt its message.

"… knowing that you were not redeemed with corruptible things, *like* silver or gold, from your aimless conduct … but with the precious blood of Christ, as of a lamb without blemish and without spot."
1 Peter 1:18-19 [NKJV]

Day Two – Crux – The Place of the Purchase

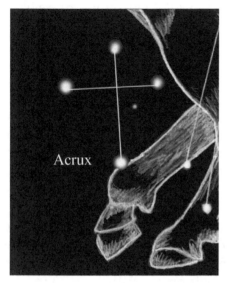

Acrux

"For while we were still helpless at the right time, Christ died for the ungodly."
Romans 5:6 [NASB]

The famous Southern Cross is the first supporting constellation of Libra. Though today it is only visible from the Northern Hemisphere's tropical latitudes during winter and spring, it was once visible in Europe. We discussed the phenomenon that causes stars to sink or rise above the horizon last week. The phenomenon is known as the precession of the equinoxes. By 400AD, all stars in this cross were no longer visible in European countries.[1]

Crux was plainly visible everywhere in the United States some 5,000 years ago, as well as in ancient Greece and Babylonia. According to Richard Hinckley Allen (1838-1908), an expert in stellar nomenclature, the Southern Cross was last seen on the horizon of Jerusalem about the time that Christ was crucified. But thanks to precession — an oscillating motion of the Earth's axis — over the centuries, the Cross ended up getting shifted out of view well to the south.[2]

We do not have ancient names for this tiny constellation, nor for any of its stars. However, it speaks volumes astronomically--no words are necessary:

- First, its shape is an unmistakable representation of a cross. It has been observed and admired by many cultures and has been included on five different country's flags.[3]

- Next, it sits under the belly of "the despised," piercing his right hoof, as we have seen in earlier pictures. The climax of the Redeemer's rejection led Him to a cross and on that cross, He was pierced as Isaiah 53 foretold.

- The cross culminates (reaches its highest point from the viewpoint of the observer) around the end of March or early April, the time of Passover and Christ's crucifixion. It's hard to imagine mere coincidence is behind the placement of these five stars!

- But there is still more. Only four stars are necessary to make the pattern of the cross, but there is a fifth star on the lower right side of the cross. For those not understanding the pivotal event to which this constellation speaks, this fifth star is an annoyance; it breaks the perfect pattern made by the other four. The Portuguese were so bothered by this fifth star, they named it "Intrometida," meaning "intruder."

---

[1]Plotner, Tammy. "Crux." *Universe Today — Space and Astronomy News*. 3 Nov 2008 Web. 30 Aug. 2011.
    http://www.universetoday.com/20563/crux

[2] Rao, Joe. "Doorstep Astronomy: See the Big Dipper | Space.com." *Space, NASA Information & News | Outer Space Flight Videos & Pictures | Astronomy, Solar System Images | Space.com*. 9 May 2008. Web. 30 Aug. 2011.
    http://www.space.com/5323-doorstep-astronomy-big-dipper.html

[3] The five countries with the Sothern Cross on their flag are Australia, New Zealand, Papua New Guinea, Samoa, and Brazil.

Read John 19:33-34. What is marked by this fifth star?

For those who have missed the message of this constellation, this fifth star is foolishness, but for those who recognize its message, it is the glory and wisdom of God! This is one of two stars that shine red. The other red star marks the top of the cross.

What do you think this might signify?

- Sailors have long treasured this tiny constellation because the stars making the long axis of the cross point directly toward the Southern Celestial Pole. Since there is not a star marking the South Pole as there is for the North Pole, this is of tremendous value. However, there are two other asterisms (cluster of stars smaller than a constellation) very near the Southern Cross that also appear as crosses though not nearly as perfect in the placement of their stars. These are called false crosses which have mislead many a careless sailor since their long axis' lead them just off course.

Another interesting astronomical reality for this constellation is it is apparently a counterpart to the "Big Dipper" in the North. As you will see in the final days of this study, the Big Dipper is actually the Greater Flock led by Boötes. The Greater Flock represents those He purchased at the cross. Below are three ways in which these two appear as counterparts though separated by such a great distance in space they cannot both be observed from a single location.

- Both point toward the poles – Acrux (in the cross) is the same distance from the S. Pole as Dubhe (in the Big Dipper) from the N. Pole.
- Both circle their respective poles in 24 hours – The Cross circles clockwise and the Greater Flock/Big Dipper counter-clockwise.
- When the cross is high in the sky at its pole, the Dipper is also high in the sky; when the cross is low in the sky so is the Dipper; when the cross is midway in the sky toward one side, the Dipper is midway on the opposite side.

The stars of the Southern Cross expound upon the price of the conflict.

> "Christ redeemed us from the curse of the Law, having become a curse for us – for it is written, 'CURSED IS EVERYONE WHO HANGS ON A TREE ...'" Galatians 3:13 [NASB]

> "... fixing our eyes on Jesus, the author and perfecter of faith, who for the joy set before Him endured the cross, despising the shame, and has sat down at the right hand of the throne God. For consider Him who has endured such hostility by sinners against Himself ..." Heb 12:2-3 [NASB]

The starry cross is not the only ancient cross. We find a picture of the cross in at least two more places, the arrangement of Israel's encampment and the articles of the Tabernacle.

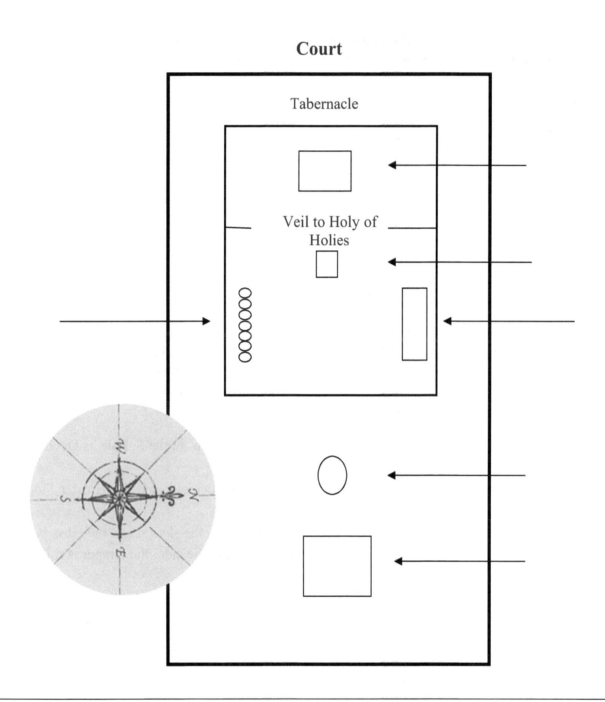

Court

Tabernacle

Veil to Holy of Holies

Using Exodus 40:21-33, name the articles referenced by the arrows. Notice that from a bird's eye view, these objects line up in the shape of a cross. This is repeated in the encampment of Israel around this tabernacle.

Using Numbers, chapter 2, fill in the head tribes and the total number of men.

The boxes are sized relative to the size of these groups. They likely avoided spreading out; but kept their camps due North, South, East, or West of the tabernacle as commanded by God. Notice the tribes North and South are very similar in size. The tribes to the West, the smallest, and the tribes to the East, the largest.

The Tribe of
_____

Numbered men

_____

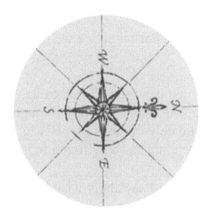

The Tribe of
_____

numbered men

_____

The Tribe of
_____

numbered men

_____

The Tribe of
_____

Numbered men

_____

The timing of Jesus' advent seems, in part, to assure that His death would be by Roman crucifixion.

Galatians 4:4 "But when the fulness of the time came, God sent forth His Son, born of a woman, born under the Law." [NASB]

Romans 5:6 "For while we were still helpless, at the right time Christ died for the ungodly." [NASB]

The violence of that death is difficult to imagine. For Christ, it included beatings, the deprivation of sleep, a Roman flogging, a grueling journey through the streets of Jerusalem to the place where He'd be crucified carrying approximately 100lbs upon His torn back, enormous blood loss, and excruciating pain. In fact the very word, excruciating has crucifixion in its root!

What does Isaiah 52:14 say about what He suffered?

The crucifixion was designed to not only be excruciating but it was intended to humiliate. A Roman citizen was exempt from this type of death; it was reserved for the lower classes: slaves, pirates, and enemies of the state. To be crucified was to be identified with the very lowest social strata. The crucified were not allowed any covering, they hung there naked. Adding to the shame and disgrace of this death, the Romans usually forbade burial of the crucified. They were usually left on the cross to be consumed by birds and vultures. "[Christ] … endured the cross, despising its shame …" Heb 12:2 [NASB] but God did not allow the final humiliation intended for Him, instead He received a proper burial.

We may wonder why God chose such a cruel death, for God is not unnecessarily violent. As we read in Romans, it was the propitiation (this sacrifice) that demonstrates His righteousness.

How can this be so?

This horror, that Christ had to suffer, says much about the wide gap between our sins and God's holiness. He had to pay a sufficient price to cover that gap. His righteousness is so far beyond our reach, the price was very great. It meant this cross and all the cruelty and shame that went with it.

Day Three – Lupus – The Price of the Purchase

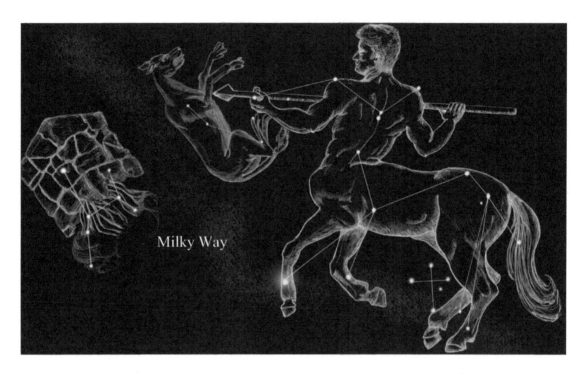

Milky Way

"… but now once at the consummation of the ages He has been manifested to put away sin with the sacrifice of Himself."
Hebrews 9:26 [NASB]

This second supporting constellation of Libra is known today as Lupus, the Latin for wolf. However, it was not recognized as a wolf until the 16th Century. The Greeks called it Thera, meaning "a beast." Before the 16th Century it had always been a generic animal. A picture of this scene drawn by Hyginius in 1 AD has the centaur holding a dying goat. A wineskin also appears in the picture and has been described as a replacement for this animal. Both symbols in Hyginius' scene work well to express the meaning of the constellation – even the wineskin, since Christ compared His crucifixion to a cup from which He must drink.

Its ancient names are:
- **Asedah**, Hebrew, "to be slain"
- **Asedaton**, Arabic, "to be slain"

The Greeks recognized in the stars a story. In it, Centaurus has pierced the animal and is placing it on the altar near it as a sacrifice. This well reflects what we believe is its meaning. Certainly, this matches the ancient Hebrew and Arabic names.

We established in the last lesson, that Centaurus, "the despised," who is in the act of slaying and carrying the beast to be sacrificed, is a picture of our Savior. So also is this beast, whose name means "to be slain." What appears, at first glance, to be a problem is really a perfect picture.

What do you think this picture is saying since the one being slain, and the one doing the slaying are the same person?

Happily, we have the Written Revelation to help us.

"… because He poured out _____ to death,
And was numbered with the transgressors;
Yet He Himself bore the sin of many,
And interceded for the transgressors."
Isaiah 53:12 [NASB]

Do you see that the one pouring out, and the one being poured out are the same person? We can think of no better way to demonstrate this truth in pictures than two separate beings both reflections of the same person. If the picture were of one being, spearing itself, it would look more like a suicide than a willing sacrifice.

Here is the same idea. Hebrews 9:26 "… but now once at the consummation of the ages He has been manifested to put away sin by **the sacrifice of Himself**." [NASB emphasis added]

This is an important theological point; and Jesus wanted to be sure we understood it. He was not a victim. No one had overpowered Him and taken His life! He laid it down Himself.

Read John 10:15, 17-18. How many times does Jesus use the phrase, "I lay down?"

How else does He emphatically express that His sacrifice was a result of His own initiative?

Isaiah 50:5-7 speaks in prophetic detail of the willing sacrifice of our Redeemer. Read this passage.

He knew ahead of time what he would face and He faced its horror. In most versions, He says "I have set My face like flint [or hard stone] …"

What does this mean?

What phrase can you find in Luke 9:51 that correspond to this phrase?

Dare any of us assume this sacrifice was not a difficult labor for the Lord? So far from easy, He had to set His face like stone; He had to resolve unflinchingly to do it.

In all the passion accounts, Scripture clarifies that Jesus went willingly to the cross. The star picture above illustrates the profound truth that He placed Himself there.

"Jesus therefore said to Peter, 'Put the sword into the sheath; the cup which the Father has given Me, shall I not drink it?'" John 18:11 [NASB]

Let's think more about what Jesus meant when He said that no one has taken his life from Him, but He laid it down on His own initiative. Jesus' authority to lay down His life goes further than most of us have thought to take it. Christ held life in a different manner from us. John 1:4 says, **"In Him was life**, and the life was the light of men." [NKJV emphasis added]

What does that mean, "in Him was life?" Certainly, He possessed life in a way unfamiliar to the rest of us. We are given life as a gift – we do not possess it in ourselves. We have no power over our beginning or our life's end; it can be taken from us either accidentally, by disease, or the act of men. But Jesus possessed life. He did not receive it as a gift. He could not then have it arrested from Him. All the suffering and agony of the flogging and crucifixion, the unimaginable loss of blood, none of these things took His life from Him. Rather as the possessor of life, He kept His life until He had borne the sins of the world. Then, by His authority, He gave it up. He did not bleed to death or die because His heart failed; He died only because, as the possessor of life, He laid it down.

"… He said, 'It is finished!' And He bowed His head, and **gave up** His spirit." John 19:30 [NASB]

The Victim as pictured by the Egyptians

The ancient Egyptians in the temple of Denderah had another name and picture for this sign. He is called, Sura, meaning "a lamb." He is pictured as a young boy with a finger over his mouth.

This speaks to the truth that before His accusers, Jesus was silent. Matthew 26:63; Isaiah 53:7

It is a sad commentary that in spite of all that the Egyptians had understood from the testimony of the heavens, they lost themselves in idolatries. As Psalm 19:4 states, "Their [the heavens] line [words] has gone out through all the earth, and their utterances to the end of the world …" [NASB]

Day Four – Corona – The Crown Gained

Al Phecca

"There I will cause the horn of David to spring forth; I have prepared a lamp for Mine anointed.
"His enemies I will clothe with shame; But upon himself his crown shall shine."

Psalm 132:17-18 [NASB]

The ancient names of this third supporting constellation of Libra are:
- Atarah, Hebrew, "a royal crown"
- Al Ielil, Arabic, "an ornament or jewel"

The alpha star is Al Phecca, Arabic, "the shining."

Our time, so far this chapter, has been spent discussing the Coming One's atoning work. The scales are the debt owed, the small bright cross the payment exacted, and then the slain, who laid down His own life that He might taste death for every man.

> "But we see Jesus, who was made a little lower than the angels, for the suffering of death crowned with glory and honor, that He, by the grace of God, might taste death for everyone." Hebrews 2:9 [NKJV]

His suffering is always quickly followed by references to His glory. In the verse above, we see that the suffering to death is quickly followed by a reference to His crowning. In Scripture, His Second Coming may be discussed without reference to His first, but never vice versa.

We will further discuss this crown, but first, we want to confirm the truth above.

Let's look at the passages we used earlier. Psalm 22, which began with, "My God, my God why have You forsaken Me?"

Summarize how it ends in verses 27 through 31.

Isaiah 53, another passage which discusses His suffering at length, says in verse 12, its final verse, "Therefore, I will allot Him a portion with the great, and He will divide the booty with the strong; ..." [NASB]

In the previous lesson, we quoted Hebrews 9:26 "... He has been manifested to put away sin by the sacrifice of Himself." [NASB] Continue reading to the end of this chapter.

What event is discussed?

Let's now look at this crown.

Read Revelation 4:9-11. The Apostle John sees the throne room. Why is the Lord receiving worship?

This song is going to have a *new* song added to it as we will see when we read further.

Read Revelation 5:1-4. These verses present a problem in heaven, what is it?

Since the Bible does not tell us exactly what this scroll is, we will have to make an educated guess. We know that the scroll has seven seals upon it. According to Ethelbert Stauffer, Roman law required a will to be sealed with seven seals. Each seal was of a witness to the validity of that will.[1] This then may indicate that the scroll in Revelation 5 was a type of will. If so, such a will might contain God's final settlement of the affairs of the universe as well as dominion over it. The dilemma contained in chapter 5 of Revelation might be that this inheritance had been intended for Adam's race, but neither Adam nor any of his offspring were found worthy to open this will and receive this inheritance.

As we read further in Revelation, One is found worthy to take the scroll and open its seals. Write below the description of this worthy One as He appears in the midst of the throne in verse 6.

Notice, He appears as a Lamb that is slain! Why do you think He appears this way at this moment?

Now continue reading to verse 12 of Revelation 5. Notice, first of all, that the song in vs. 9 and 10 is a **new** song.

---

[1] Stauffer, Ethelbert, *Christ and the Caesars,* (London, SCM Press, 1955) pp 182-83.

According to the words of this song, why is the Lamb worthy to take the scroll and open its seals?

Libra – the scales, the cross, the slain, and the crown – are all summed up for us in Revelation 5:12.

> "… Worthy is the Lamb who was slain
> To receive power and riches and wisdom,
> And strength and honor and glory and blessing!" [NKJV]

This crown, at the end of the second chapter of Libra, is not the crown He already had as creator of the universe. It is the Victor's crown; the crown He earned by His sinless life and His atoning death. Imagine – the God of the universe earned a crown! It is a profound idea.

There is something else very exciting in this passage we want you to see before we leave it. Look at the new song again, paying special attention to its final lines in verse 10.

What will we be doing after Jesus comes back?

The slain Lamb has earned the right to take the will of God, likely containing the deed to the earth and the heavens. He inherits rulership over it. Even more amazing, He shares this inheritance with us! We will share in this kingdom that **He has earned** and reign together with Him. It is grace and gifts beyond comprehending.

> "Thus says the LORD:
> 'In an acceptable time I have heard You,
> And in the day of salvation I have helped You;
> I will preserve You and give You as a covenant to the people,
> To restore the earth,
> To cause them to inherit the desolate heritages;'"
> Isaiah 49:8 [NKJV]

Christ's life and death was not only necessary for our personal salvation, but also, in God's mysterious plan, for the righting of all creation. Not only this, but His act **earned** for Him something new.

The Written Revelation is not quiet about this. It is amazing how often I have missed what is plainly there.

Read Philippians 2:8-9. Notice in this familiar passage, the word "therefore" which could also be translated consequently.

How does this word affect the meaning of this passage?

We will conclude today's study with another proof text and one with which we began our day. Return to Hebrews 2:5-8.

67

What has God put under whom?

He also states, in verse 8 that we still don't see everything subjected to him. We daily witness this truth. For all our gains technologically, the earth is still for us a wild and often times destructive beast. Somewhere on the globe, at almost any time of the year, people die and/or property is destroyed by a 'natural' disaster.

In verse 9, we see that Jesus also took a place with us; a place lower than the angels so that He could gain a crown.

Just to labor the point a bit, how is this crown earned?

Finally, verse 10 continues this profound truth. What is true about Christ according to the opening of this verse?

In bringing many sons to glory, what happened to Jesus and how was it accomplished?

The first Adam lost dominion over the earth given to him in the Garden of Eden.

> "Then God said, 'Let Us make man in Our image, according to Our likeness; and let them rule over the fish of the sea and over the birds of the sky and over the cattle and over all the earth …' And God blessed them; and God said to them, 'Be fruitful and multiply, and fill the earth, and subdue it; and rule over the fish of the sea and over the birds of the sky and over every living thing that moves on the earth.'" Genesis 1:26, 28 [NKJV]

In the Garden of Eden, through the disobedience of man, dominion was lost, [Heb 2:5-8]. In the Garden of Gethsemane, through the obedience of the Lamb, who is the Son of God and the Son of man, it was regained.

Isn't it amazing! What a mysterious and awesome message.

Day One – Scorpio – The War

"Blessed be the LORD, my rock, who trains my hands for war, and my fingers for battle"

Psalm 144:1 [NKJV]

This sign is one of our favorites because it truly speaks without words.

Here is your opportunity to interpret the art of the heavens. Take some time to study this starry scene and write in the space provided the story as you see it.

This sign is unique in its interconnectedness. The first three constellations are all touching and telling a story together. We will begin with what is recognized as the first constellation of this sign, Scorpio. As with all the signs, it is the sign along the ecliptic that is the first and main sign of the group.

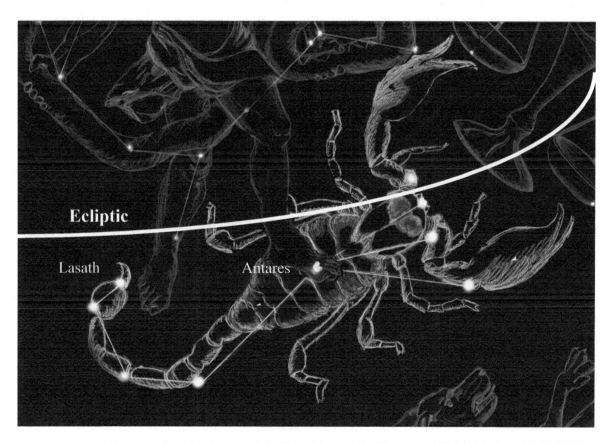

Scorpio is the only malignant character among the twelve ecliptic constellations (or the Zodiac). So it seems out of place. An additional complication of this sign is that it spends so little time in the sun. We have drawn an arc across our picture to show the ecliptic line. Notice that Scorpio is almost entirely beneath that line. Only a bit of his "nose" is on it, meanwhile the line of the sun also spends time in Ophiucus, the man standing on Scorpio – the third constellation of the sign. Because the sun also passes through Ophiucus, astronomers can count thirteen constellations of the Zodiac, not twelve. But because the circle of the sun, or 360 degrees, divides evenly by twelve, many continue to count only twelve ecliptic or Zodiac signs. The constellation Scorpio, is disruptive to order. We believe that even this, the disruptive nature of the constellation Scorpio and the placement of these starry pictures along the sun's path, conveys meaning. Remember our chief proof text for the starry revelation, Psalm 19? It discusses the significance and prominence of the sun and its circuit across the sky. Here is an example of the importance of the stars and their placement against the path of the sun. We will look at a spiritual parallel later, but first, we'll look at Scorpio itself.

Its ancient Hebrew name is Akrab, "scorpion or the conflict/war." David uses the word in the verse quoted with the opening picture, but worth repeating.

"Blessed be the LORD, my rock,
Who trains my hands for war [*akrab*] ..."
Psalm 144:1 [NKJV]

71

How well this verse applies to the scene. Certainly the Savior has been prepared for the "Great War," pictured above. And truly, it is the war to end all wars, in the seen and unseen world!

In previous chapters of this heavenly book, the stars told us that our coming Savior would be wounded and would suffer, not as a victim, but by a sacrifice of Himself. Here, we are introduced to His enemies. In these pictures, we see Jesus in the arena. He has emptied Himself and become one of us to step inside the ring. In the ring, He must contend against two foes at once. The serpent in his arms is a familiar picture of the old enemy, Satan. The scorpion, beneath His feet, is a less familiar representation but, knowing its nature, it is not hard to imagine it as a picture of evil. We see it as a picture of Satan but more exactly his co-conspirators: darkness and death.

The traits of a scorpion provide a good representation of this malignant foe. In front, are claws that seize; at his rear is a tail with poison to paralyze and kill. Its traits gave birth to the ancient Akkadian name for this constellation, Gir-tab, "the seizer and the stinger."

In the starry revelation, what is the scorpion seizing and what is he stinging?

Take some time to write any of your own ideas on what this could mean. (If this is a struggle now, hopefully it will be easy by the end of this lesson.)

Scripture connects scorpions with the enemy. Read Luke 10:19. What two beasts are named here?

According to this verse, what do these represent?

Read Revelation 9:1-6. The creatures that rise from the abyss, though they are called locusts, are given power like scorpions.

Immediately preceding the rise of these creatures from the abyss, what happens to the sun and air?

How perfect! The darkened sky creates circumstances on earth favorable for another trait of the scorpion; it is a nocturnal creature. Not only so, but it is photophobic (has an aversion to light).

How does this match those who do evil in John 3:20?

In light of the verse above, it will not surprise you that the ancient star in the scorpion's tail, named, Lesath, means "perverse."

Read Colossians 1:13. This verse speaks of two kingdoms. What are the two kingdoms compared here?

Again, we see a literary comparison between the Son of God and our sun; for His kingdom is the opposite of the dominion of darkness. Ephesians 5:8 also makes this comparison. It is the heavens, not only its stars, which declare the glory of God.

When Christ is arrested at Gethsemane He says, "While I was with you daily in the temple, you did not try to **seize** Me. But this is your hour and the **power of darkness**." Luke 22:53 [NKJV emphasis added]

The Lord's statement was true in both the literal and spiritual sense. It was perverse desires that sought out our Savior under the cover of darkness. Like the scorpion, this perverse evil sought to seize Him. In this hour, the foe stung Him in the heel. It had pursued him since the promise in Genesis 3:15.

In fact, we need to only turn to the next chapter from the promise in Genesis 3:15 to witness the first skirmish. Read Genesis 4:6-8. This is not an obvious attempt by the enemy to destroy the seed of the woman.

According to 1 John 3:12, why did Cain kill his brother?

Considering Abel's works, and because Christ was despised by many for the very same reason, he is a type of Christ. Death, or the seed of the serpent, was at war with the seed of the woman. We see this in her naming of Seth, "For God has **appointed another seed** for me instead of Abel, whom Cain killed." (Genesis 4:25) [NKJV emphasis added]

Follow the story further. God told Jacob, who came out of Seth, that the promised seed would be through him. And so the focus of death's pursuit narrows and Pharaoh issues an edict to destroy all the male children of Israel. (Exodus 1)

Athaliah sought to kill all the seed of David. The focus of death's pursuit narrowed further since the promised seed had been promised to David's house, the house of Judah.

Read 2 Kings 11:1-3. How was death's pursuit avoided?

Haman sought to destroy all the Jews living under the rule of Persia. At his time, this was all of the promised line known to be left. Esther 3:13

Through Herod, death found a narrower focus for pursuit since the seed had come. Herod issued an edict that killed all the male children under the age of two in the vicinity of Bethlehem. Matthew 2:16

Finally, death, through the perverse desires of the Pharisees, pursued the promised seed Himself. It was not until its hour had come that it prevailed. John 8:59 and John 10:31 are examples of attempts to stone Him before the crucifixion.

In the scorpion, we find a good representation of two formidable foes, death and darkness.

What does Ecclesiastes 8:8 say about our chances in the battle against death?

This is a bleak picture were it not for the Promised Seed's foot upon the very heart of Scorpio. Ultimately, the Seed prevails! To ensure this message is not lost, a star named Antares, lies directly under the foot of the man. Its name means "wounding" and shines with a deep red glow.

With the meaning of this picture now clear, let's look at the placement of Scorpio on the ecliptic. We see a spiritual reality reflected in it. This formidable foe represented in Scorpio disrupted the creation as God had intended it. God did not design man to live under the domination of death, evil, and darkness. The scorpion has stuck its nose where it did not belong and disrupted the perfect order. By all rights, Ophiucus, the serpent holder, should be the main sign of this group. The sun shines among his stars for 19 days. The sun shines in Scorpio just short of a week. Why, we ask, has Scorpio ever been considered the Zodiacal sign? In the heavens, as well as here on earth, things are not what they should be. The foe of the coming victor has been given its time of power and influence.

The parallel goes even further in the number of days it has been allowed to shine in the sun's path; a week cut short. Is that a familiar span of time to you? There is not space to fully explain the 70 weeks of Daniel, but the one whose works are in accordance with Satan is given one week (which represents seven years) to have his way until the consummation or end of the allotted time. (Daniel 9:27) It is known as the 70th Week of Daniel or as the Great Tribulation. But Jesus Christ later reveals that that week is cut short for the sake of the elect in Matthew 24:22. Undeniably, the stars speak without words and serve as signs; we just need to look for them.

Day Two – Serpens – The Serpent's Ambition

"For you have said in your heart,
'I will ascend into heaven,
I will exalt my throne above the
stars of God ...'"

Isaiah 14:13 [NKJV]

Though the serpent's stars are divided with some on each side of Ophiucus, it is still seen as a single constellation and the second constellation of this sign. It is the other enemy and a familiar foe. It is found on the earliest pages of Scripture.

> "Now the serpent was more cunning than any beast of the field which the LORD God had made ..." Genesis 3:1 [NKJV]

By his cunning, he deceived the woman and robbed the first man of dominion.

How does this starry revelation demonstrate that the serpent sought dominion for himself?

Scripture describes the serpent's attempt to gain dominion in Isaiah 14:12-15.

"How you are fallen from heaven, O Lucifer, son of the morning!
How you are cut down to the ground, you who weakened the nations!
For you have said in your heart:
'I will ascend into heaven,
I will exalt my throne above the stars of God;
I will also sit on the mount of the congregation on the farthest sides of the north;
I will ascend above the heights of the clouds,
I will be like the Most High.'
Yet you shall be brought down to Sheol, to the lowest depths of the Pit."
[NKJV]

More than dominion over the earth is an expressed desire here. What did he want?

Did you notice a familiar phrase in this passage; One found in the temptation in the garden of Eden. To refresh your memory you will find it in Genesis 3:5.

What did the serpent say would be the result of a taste of forbidden fruit?

Lucifer used his own sinful desire as a source of temptation for the man. And it was effective. The fall of man, as a result of this deception, has given the serpent rule.

> "We know we are of God, and the whole world lies *under the sway of* the wicked one."
> 1 John 5:19 [NKJV]

What is he called in Eph. 2:1-2?

Three temptations of the second Adam are recorded in Matthew 4; though we are sure Jesus also was tempted daily during His life. These three are recounted because they probably represent a different area of fleshly desire: lust of the flesh, lust of the eyes, and pride of life. (1 John 2:16) It is the final temptation in Matthew 4:8-9, which relates to the picture we are studying.

What does Satan offer?

Satan claims the power to give the kingdoms and their glory to Christ. In order for this to be a temptation, there must be some truth in it. More pertinent to our discussion, it underscores the conflict pictured above. It is a struggle to restrain the serpent who seeks dominion. How surprising and mysterious, possibly even to the serpent, that this struggle was won in apparent defeat, the death of God's anointed.

There is one preserved star name in the serpent. The alpha star is:
- Unuk, "encompassing" or
- Alyah, "the accursed"

Look again at Isaiah 14:15. At Satan's end, he is finally exposed as accursed. Where does he end up?

This verse dispels a modern myth about Satan. He is commonly viewed as having charge over hell. Instead, he is assigned the deepest recesses of the pit. This is not a location of dominion over anyone or anything. This is a location of darkest, deepest punishment and humiliation.

Day Three – Ophiuchus – The Serpent Held

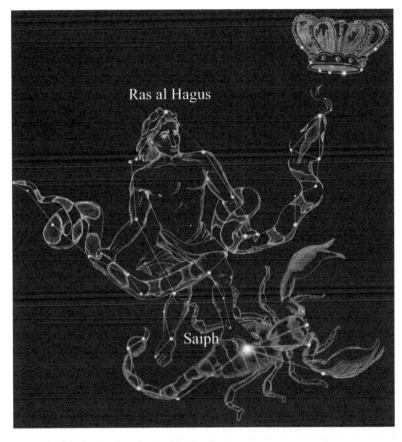

"Inasmuch then as the children have partaken
of flesh and blood,
He Himself likewise shared in the same,
that through death He might destroy him
who had the power of death,
that is, the devil."

Hebrews 2:14 [NKJV]

Here is the Contender; known today by his Greek name, Ophiucus. This name is from the Hebrew, Afiechus; "the serpent held." In our starry scene, He is outnumbered. He contends by himself against two foes, and both his hands and both his feet are occupied in the battle. Could this be a prophetic picture that both His hands and feet would be pierced? Praise be to God that despite this, He overcomes! Without His victory we are hopeless, there is no victory for us in death, nor can we release ourselves from the sway of the evil one.

This picture, however, does not show the serpent defeated but the serpent restrained. This idea is reiterated in the alpha star in His head, Ras al Hagus, "the head of him who holds."

Fill in the blank from 2 Thessalonians 2:7. "For the mystery of lawlessness is already at work; only He who now _____ *will do so* until He is taken out of the way." [NKJV]

The book of Job also illustrates how Satan is restrained. In Job 1:12, Satan is allowed power over all Job's possessions

What is Satan not allowed to do?

Later in Job 2:6, Satan brings further accusation against Job, so he is allowed to touch Job's flesh.

How is Satan still restrained?

In the garden of Gethsemane, the Savior said to Peter, "Simon, Simon! Indeed, Satan has asked for you, that he may sift *you* as wheat. But I have prayed for you, that your faith should not fail; and when you have returned to *Me*, strengthen your brethren." (Luke 22:31-32) [NKJV]

In all these instances, what must Satan do?

How did Christ restrain Satan on Peter's behalf?

This is often the great overlooked weapon of warfare available also to us.

> "For the weapons of our warfare are not of the flesh but have divine power to destroy strongholds. We destroy arguments and every lofty opinion raised against the knowledge of God, and take every thought captive to obey Christ," 2 Corinthians 10:4, 5 [ESV]

Ephesians chapter 6:13-18 lists the weapons of our warfare.

What is the final weapon listed and how often should it be engaged?

While the serpent is restrained, the scorpion receives a mortal wound from Ophiucus. His foot is directly over its heart.

Read Hosea 13:14. What has Jesus done to defeat death?

Death's defeat required a ransom. That is mysterious and remarkable. In Hebrews 2:9, we see the amazing way in which Jesus paid the ransom and offered redemption.

According to these verses, how did Jesus defeat death?

This is pictured in the heavens which show the heel of Ophiucus stung by Scorpio. A star in that leg, Saiph, means "bruised".

Let's unwrap this mystery; how His taste of death brought defeat to death. Let's continue in Hebrews. Read verses 14 and 15 of chapter 2.

Who in these verses had the power of death?

To what did this power subject us?

By what means did the devil subject us to bondage?

Summarize then, the message of these verses. Why or how did Satan have the power of death?

The things we fear also enslave us. And, if there is one who is both wicked and cunning enough to know what we fear, then he can gain power over us by using against us what we fear. Satan is both cunning and wicked. But this verse says, No longer! No longer are we to be imprisoned by the fear of death. No longer can Satan hang this over our heads to coerce us into doing what he desires.

Paul is a powerful example of freedom from the fear of death. Read Acts 20:22-24. Wow! In the face of tribulations and chains, Paul says that none of those things moved him.

> "For to me, to live *is* Christ, and to die *is* gain. But if *I* live on in the flesh, this *will mean* fruit from my labor; yet what I shall choose I cannot tell. For I am hard pressed between the two, having a desire to depart and be with Christ, *which is* far better." Philippians 1:21-23 [NKJV]

How does Paul take this even further than simply lacking the fear of death in Philippians 1:21-23?

This verse in Philippians should change our views about our own deaths. But now, let's consider how we view the death of others.

> "But I do not want you to be ignorant, brethren, concerning those who have fallen asleep, lest you sorrow as others who have no hope." 1 Thessalonians 4:13

How does it change the way we mourn?

Death yet remains awaiting its ultimate defeat.

Again describe what has changed for us through Christ regarding both our own death and the death of those we love who are in Christ.

Death, darkness and evil still are active in our world today. They are active but have lost their strangle hold on us.

According to 1 John 2:8, what else is passing away?

Again, we see another enemy connected with the scorpion defeated by the work of Jesus Christ.

"For He must reign till He has put all enemies under His feet." 1 Corinthians 15:25 [NKJV]

In the starry revelation, the enemy is under his feet. You will see this theme again tomorrow. Certainly, such pictures could not be the result of some accident, nor could so many coincidental portrayals of truth have their origins in myths. If myths exist around these pictures, and they do, they are the corruption of original Truth.

Before we leave Ophiucus, it is also interesting to note that the Egyptians called him Api-bau, "the chief who cometh." They pictured him with the head of a hawk or eagle to signify he is the natural enemy of the snake and the scorpion. At some point, they had the truth.

"Blessed *be* the Lord,
Who daily loads us *with benefits*,
The God of our salvation!
Our God *is* the God of salvation;
And to GOD the Lord *belong* escapes from death."
Psalm 68:19-20 [NKJV]

Thank you, Savior, Redeemer and Lord!

Day Four – Hercules – The Labor of the Mighty One

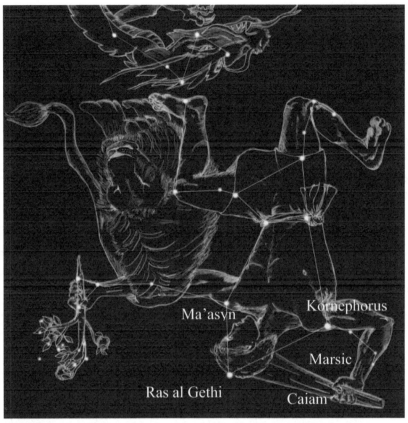

"He shall see the labor of His soul, *and* be satisfied.
By His knowledge My righteous Servant shall justify many,
For He shall bear their iniquities.
Therefore I will divide Him a portion with the great,
And He shall divide the spoil with the strong …"

Isaiah 53:11-12

In Arabic his name is Al Giscale, "the strong one" and in Egyptian, Bau, "who cometh."
He appears on our page as he appears in the sky. He is giant, the sixth largest constellation in the heavens. He is also upside down in the sky so that his left foot can be shown over the head of the dragon. He kneels, while his right foot is lifted up as if wounded. Amazing, is it not? Again, the enemy is shown under his feet and another repeat of Genesis 3:15! With his right arm he wields a club; in his left hand, he is shown holding a branch from the tree of life. Traditionally, he is shown wearing the skin of the lion. We believe this is myth added later by the Greeks. Some pictures also show the dead lion draped over his outstretched arm. Since the lion skin on Hercules is so consistent, we believe the dead lion belongs in the picture.

The stars in this sign are:
- The alpha star in the head, Ras al Gethi, "the head of him who bruises"
- In his raised arm, Kornephorus, "the branch, kneeling"
- Marsic, "the wounding"
- In the hand or club, Caiam or Guiam, "treading underfoot."

All these stars help preserve the picture and its message. The star Kornephorus, "the branch, kneeling," preserves an important truth that must not be missed. We believe this act is important to our understanding this picture.

What do you think is meant in the purposeful portrayal of Him kneeling?

The ancient Greeks thought that the kneeling represented him toiling or laboring at something. The star in his head, is placed forward giving the idea of one wearied under a hard labor. Aratus speaks of this in his poem, "Phaenomena."

> "Near this, and like a toiling man, revolves
> A form. Of it can no one clearly speak,
> Nor what he labors at. They call him simply
> 'The man upon his knees'; In desperate struggle
> Like one who sinks, he seems. From both his shoulders
> His arms are high-uplifted and out-stretched
> As far as he can reach; and his right foot
> Is planted on the coiled Dragon's head"[1]

by Aratus in Phaenomena (a poem about the constellations written around 277 BC) – Apparently during the time of Aratus, the name Hercules, simply meant, "the man upon his knees."

If you did not conclude that the kneeling represented toil, don't assume you were wrong. That is the wonderful thing about art, it can mean many things at once. An additional idea could be that he kneels because He must stoop in order to do His mighty work.

How might Philippians 2:6-7 teach this same idea?

We are convinced that toil is an important message of this constellation.

The final ancient star name is Ma'asyn, "the sin offering." This mighty one is also the One who was Himself slain.

Isaiah 53:10-11 brings this constellation's message into focus. We have bolded the parallel concepts.

> "Yet it pleased the LORD to **bruise** Him;
> He has put *Him* to grief.
> When You make **His soul an offering for sin**,
> He shall see *His* seed, He shall prolong *His* days,
> And the pleasure of the LORD shall **prosper in His hand**.
> He shall see the **labor of His soul**, *and* be satisfied ..."
> [NKJV]

For each of the following words or phrases, explain how this sign, either in its picture or the names of the stars, matches these concepts.

- Bruise

---

[1] Bullinger, Ethelburt William, *Witness of the Stars*, (Cosimo, Inc., NY, 2007—originally published 1893) page 60.

- His soul an offering for sin

- Prosper in His hand (especially Hercules' left hand)

- Labor of His soul

We believe the phrase in Isaiah, "the labor of His soul," focuses our attention on the particular story in this sign. The work He did while in the flesh that procured Satan's defeat is the mighty act represented here. So we are not tempted to diminish the might and strength He demonstrated in the flesh, the picture is called, "the mighty one." And even better, unlike Aratus in his poem above, we **can** speak of this toil, for the written revelation has revealed it to us.

First is the mighty act in willingly leaving His place in eternity, taking on flesh, and walking in this fallen place. Is it easy for any of us to give up a place with comfort and safety to go to a place where these do not exist at the level we are accustomed? And of course, our experience is only in a matter of degrees – His was the true sacrifice of these things.

Describe what mighty acts are performed in the verses below.

- Luke 2:49-51

It is so difficult to be subject to someone who either is, or we deem is more ignorant than we are. In the Lord's case, His parents truly were more ignorant of the Father's will.

- Hebrews 4:15

There is great force of strength involved in remaining sinless under temptation. A person under a temptation can be compared to a power lifter attempting to lift a great amount of weight against all the natural forces. Everything is against him in the attempt, gravity, his own natural instincts, and the immense weight of the bar and plates. To drop that weight before having stood under it and holding it there is to yield to temptation. If we yield, the full weight of the temptation is never fully realized. But Christ was the ultimate power lifter who truly felt the full weight of every temptation. He lifted each and every one above His head and stood under them. The strength He demonstrated here is beyond the strength of any other man, for all of us have sinned. It is a Herculean feat!

- Luke 22:42 and Heb 10:7

- Philippians 2:8

- Hebrews 7:25-26

These are some of the labors by which Jesus has secured victory over formidable foes. We will see that the Greeks had warped this truth in foolish imaginings.

Before we examine the parallels between the toils of Hercules in Greek myths and the toils of the true Mighty One, we do not want to miss other similarities between this starry revelation and the written one. For each verse, note how they parallel the starry picture.

- Psalm 91:13 (Remember that this sign usually has the skin of a lion as a part of the sign.)

- Psalm 136:10-12 (Remember to look for the physical resemblance of the constellation and the verses paying close attention to verse 12.)

- Isaiah 51:9 (Rahab is a name for Egypt, a symbol of the world system.)

With the many parallels to Scripture and the testimony in the very names of the stars in this sign, it is sickening that its true meaning has been so thoroughly perverted. Still, even in the perversion of this sign, we can see the seeds of truth.

Hercules is best known for his ten or twelve labors (there is disagreement as to the number). Mixed among these labors are found the truths in the picture. He defeated an "invulnerable" lion and retrieved golden apples from the tree of immortality. These two labors are found in the above picture.

What do you think the dead lion draped over the arm of the mighty one represents? (See 1 Peter 5:8)

In the hand of Hercules' outstretched arm is a branch. Look at the picture again, paying attention to this part of it. Doesn't Hercules appear to be proposing? He is down on one knee and he offers this branch. The Greek myth says these are the golden apples from the tree of immortality obtained by Hercules in his eleventh labor. There is a great deal of foolishness in the myth, but perhaps truth lies hidden behind it. This branch could be a symbol of the tree of life, access to which has been taken from mankind. But Christ has opened the way through the labor of His soul, and He offers eternal life to mankind again. He, through His might of sacrifice has defeated the enemy, conquered sin, and opened the way. "… as You have given Him authority over all flesh, that He should give eternal life to as many as You have given Him." John 17:2 [NKJV]

Revelation 22:12-14 speaks to this same truth.

The myth of Hercules teaches that he had to complete twelve labors as payment for his own sin. It appears that the Greeks, in times past, were aware of the meaning of the star Ma'sayn, "sin offering." Obviously, their understanding of how this star fits the original meaning of this picture has been thoroughly corrupted. How their hearts became darkened in the perversion of Truth. This Mighty One did not labor as an offering for His own sin, but He labored for the sins of the whole world. He bore our iniquities, thereby conquering the foe, and now offers us eternal life.

In the time of the Greeks, heroes went to war many times, not for preservation of country or for the exacting of justice, but merely to be immortalized by the performance of mighty deeds. None of their acts shall compare to the deeds of the true Mighty One.

> "Great *is* the LORD, and greatly to be praised;
> And His greatness is unsearchable.
> One generation shall praise Your works to another,
> And shall declare Your mighty acts.
> I will meditate on the glorious splendor of Your majesty,
> And on Your wondrous works.
> *Men* shall speak of the might of Your awesome acts,
> And I will declare Your greatness."
> Psalm 145:3-6 [NKJV]

Lesson Five – Chapter Four - The Redeemer's Triumph

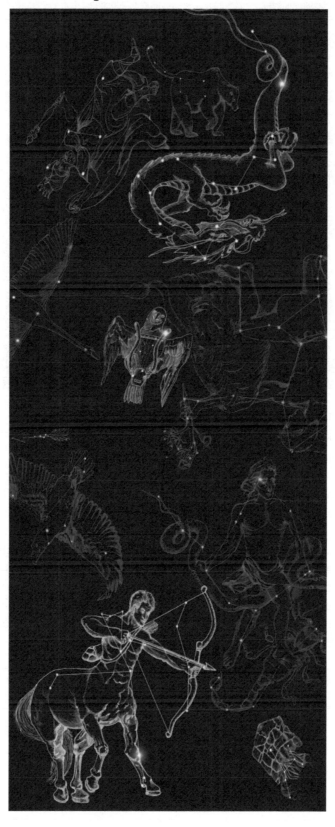

Day One –Sagittarius – The Redeemer's Return

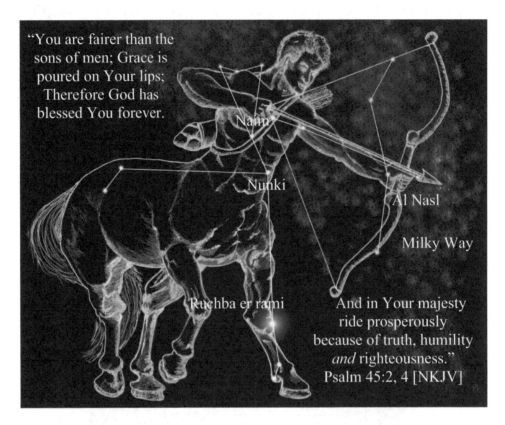

"You are fairer than the sons of men; Grace is poured on Your lips; Therefore God has blessed You forever.

Naim

Nunki

Al Nasl

Milky Way

Ruchba er rami

And in Your majesty ride prosperously because of truth, humility *and* righteousness." Psalm 45:2, 4 [NKJV]

- The Latin name for this constellation, Sagittarius, means "the archer."
- The Hebrew name, Kesith, carries the same meaning.
- The Coptic name, Pimacre, means "beauty of the coming forth"

What a lovely name the Coptic represents, "the beauty of the coming forth." This is the occupation of this final chapter in Book 1, His coming forth victorious.

The stars in this sign create the shape of a bow preserving this picture. Again, we find a centaur and are reminded that He is the God/man. Remember back in the first chapter of this book, the centaur there was located far south of the ecliptic. So far south that nothing of him or only a portion of him can be seen in most of the Northern Hemisphere. In contrast, this centaur rides the ecliptic and is visible from both hemispheres. Though He gave up His life going down to death, as represented by the lower centaur, He is not defeated, but has returned from death glorious and triumphant.

The star Al Nasl means, "the arrow." At what is the point of His arrow aimed? (See the whole picture of Sagittarius for help.)

What enemies were represented in Scorpio?

What does 1 Corinthians 15:26 say will be the final enemy to be defeated?

This is the final triumph yet future. The arrow aimed at the heart of Scorpio speaks to this future, but the beauty of communicating in art is that it can picture more than one aspect of the truth at a time. There is a present truth also portrayed, in which the arrow from this archer's bow has already been released. Our Savior's work did not end with His resurrection and ascension into heaven.

Read Matthew 28:18-20. He spoke with His disciples after His resurrection, what did He command them to do?

What did He promise?

His final words before His ascension are recorded in Acts 1. Read verse 8. What does He promise the disciples they will be?

This becomes the preoccupation of the book of Acts – the march of the Gospel. Indeed it is like an arrow sent forth from the Lord's bow to pierce the heart of death – for by God's power through the Gospel many multitudes will be delivered from it.

> "For I am not ashamed of the Gospel of Christ, for it is the power of God to salvation for everyone who believes, for the Jew first and also for the Greek." Romans 1:16 [NKJV]

Read Acts 2:41. How many believed after Peter's first sermon?

What does Verse 47 of the same chapter tell us?

This great conversion of many Jews occurred in Jerusalem. Acts records the spread of the Gospel from there outward and its spread continues today. (Read Colossians 1:5, 6.)

That is why though Ophiucus has crushed the heart of the Scorpion, the arrow of Sagittarius is aimed at its heart also. Death suffers a dual defeat. By losing its battle with the Seed of the woman, it not only suffered the loss of Him, but through the spread of the Gospel, it suffers daily the loss of a multitude of souls. We believe this multiplication of the work He began is part of what He meant in saying, "Truly, truly, I say to you, he who believes in Me, the works that I do shall He do also; and greater *works* than these shall he do; because I go to My Father." John 14:12 [NASB]

In agreement with the name for this sign, Pimacre, "the beauty of the coming forth" are the words of Isaiah 52:7.

According to this verse what is beautiful?

In fact, what must happen before the end according to the Lord Jesus (Matthew 24:14)?

Let's move on to the stars. The brightest star is Ruchba er rami, Arabic, "the riding of the bowman."

Other stars are:

- Nun-ki, Akkadian, "prince of the earth"
- Naim, Hebrew, "gracious one"
- Al Nasl, "the arrow" (as we saw earlier).

The star names match well Psalm 45:2-6. Fill in the lines with the names of the stars that match the concepts in the verse.

You are fairer than the sons of men;

Grace is poured upon Your lips;

Therefore God has blessed You forever.
Gird Your sword upon *Your* thigh, O Mighty One,
With Your glory and Your majesty.

And in Your majesty ride prosperously [   ] because of truth,

humility, and righteousness;
And Your right hand shall teach You awesome things.

Your arrows *are* sharp in the heart of the King's enemies;

The peoples fall under You.
Your throne, O God, *is* forever and ever,

A scepter of righteousness *is* the scepter of Your kingdom.
[NKJV]

It is amazing that each star name in Sagittarius finds a matching concept in this passage. Again how wonderfully these two Revelations agree.

The dual meaning of Sagittarius is also in the above verses. This is an obvious reference to the Lord's return when He shall ride forth and the peoples of the earth fall beneath Him. Preceding the description of this war, the psalmist says, "Grace is poured upon Your lips."

How does this make any sense in the context of destroying His enemies?

He is wholly gracious to provide a chance, for those even in the farthest corners of the earth, to receive salvation before He comes to judge.

There is a very interesting astronomical fact connected with Sagittarius worth noting before we leave it. If you are lucky enough to observe Sagittarius outside the light pollution of a city, you will notice that the Milky Way glows distinctly bright in the region of Sagittarius' bow and arrow. When you look toward that region, you are actually looking into the center of our galaxy and the center is exceedingly dense with stars and gas. It is probably not some lucky coincidence that Sagittarius stands with his bow and arrow directing our attention to our galaxy's center.

> What do you think this could mean?

Our guess is that it may be to confirm that this rider is at the center of everything. Notice that the descriptions of Him enthroned, describe Him in the center.

> Revelation 4:6 "… and before the throne *there was*, as it were, a sea of glass like crystal; and in the center and around the throne …" [NASB]

> Revelation 5:6 "And I looked, and behold, in the midst of the throne and of the four living creatures, and in the midst of the elders, stood a Lamb as though it had been slain …" [NKJV]

> Revelation 7:17 "For the Lamb at the center of the throne shall be their shepherd …" [NASB]

> In Ezekiel 48:21, talking about the new temple and the division of the land it says, "… the sanctuary of the LORD *shall be* in the center." [NKJV]

It could also mean that this victory and the news of it (the Gospel) is a triumph at the very center of all things. This triumph is not like any other, it changes everything right to the very heart of all things.

> "And He who sits on the throne said, 'Behold, I am making all things new.' …" Revelation 21:5 [NASB]

> "Therefore, if anyone *is* in Christ, *he is* a new creation; old things have passed away; behold, all things have become new." 2 Corinthians 5:17 [NKJV]

> "For behold, I create new heavens and a new earth;
> And the former shall not be remembered or come to mind."
> Isaiah 65:17 [NKJV]

Finally, we cannot leave this picture without noting its match in Revelation 19:11.

> "And I saw heaven opened; and behold, a white horse, and He who sat upon it *is* called Faithful and True; and in righteousness He judges and wages war." [NASB]

Day Two –Lyra – Praise for the Conqueror

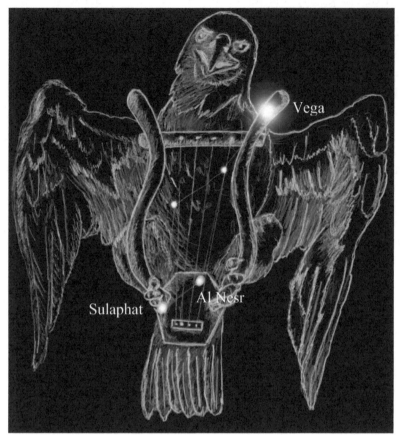

"Praise is awaiting You,
O God, in Zion;
And to You the vow shall be performed."

Psalm 65:1 [NKJV]

The picture is that of an eagle ascending and carrying a harp. Two of the ancient star names have preserved this picture: Sulaphat, "springing up or ascending" and Al Nesr, "an eagle."

The Egyptian name for this sign is Fent-kar, "the serpent ruled" and is pictured only as an eagle. In some modern representations, only the harp is shown. The Latin name Lyra, has not carried forward the image of an eagle. However, the star Al Nesr requires the eagle.

As an aside, notice how similar the official seal of the United States is to Lyra.

Vega is the alpha star of this constellation and the fifth brightest in the heavens. Vega is easy to find and beautiful in brilliance. Its name is from the primitive Hebrew root, ga'ah, "to rise up or triumph," and translates, "He shall be exalted." We find this root used only once in Scripture in the Song of Moses found in Exodus 15:1 "… I will sing to the LORD, for He has triumphed (ga'ah) gloriously …"

Moses' song is sung again according to Revelation 15:3. What event follows this song?

This judgment by the LORD is preceded by praise; praise that calls, in parallel with the name Vega, for Him alone to be exalted.

Turn to Philippians 2:9-11. This is a familiar passage to most of us. What two things will we all be doing at the mention of His name?

Looking back to the previous verse, 2:8, why is Jesus given a name above every name?

How well this fits with the flow of this book in the sky. In the previous chapter, Scorpio, we saw Him humbled and toiling. In the first picture of this final chapter of Book I He is seen victorious. He sends forth the good news for the salvation of many from every nation and tribe. This is praise ascending; for many voices are added to praise the One who has saved them.

Psalm 65:1 is beside the picture of Lyra. The second half reads, "… to You the vows shall be performed." This could be translated; to You the voluntary offering shall be completed. During David's time, voluntary gifts and offerings were offered at Zion, but in the fullness of time the Perfect One voluntarily offered Himself, finishing and completing all need for sacrifice. Now, praise awaits Him for what He has done. Read Psalm 65:1-5. Don't these verses describe the results of the salvation He is gained for us?

We have looked at this before, but it is worth repeating here. Turn to Revelation 5:8-10. For what work do the creatures around the throne sing a new praise song to Him?

Read Revelation 14:6-7. In verse 6 the everlasting Gospel is preached. What is going to follow?

Since the constellation before this, Sagittarius, also speaks to His return, Lyra, speaks not only of the praise given Him for His salvation, but the praise He receives on the day He returns.

> "Enter into the rock, and hide in the dust,
> From the terror of the LORD
> And the glory of His majesty.
> The lofty looks of man shall be humbled,
> The haughtiness of men shall be bowed down,
> And the LORD alone shall be exalted in that day.
> For the day of the LORD of hosts
> *Shall come* upon everything proud and lofty,
> Upon everything lifted up –
> And it shall be brought low – "
> Isaiah 2:10-12 [NKJV]

We see Him exalted above _____. He shall occupy sole exaltation.

Read Isaiah 2:18, which is still in the context of the above verses. What else will He end?

Isaiah 42 also fits well with the flow of all the signs in Sagittarius.

> "'I *am* the LORD, that *is* my name;
> And My glory I will not give to another,
> Nor My praise to carved images.
> Behold, the former things have come to pass,
> And new things I declare;
> Before they spring forth I tell you of them.'
> Sing to the LORD a new song,
> *And* His praise from the ends of the earth …
> … The LORD shall go forth like a mighty man;
> He shall stir up *His* zeal like a man of war.
> He shall cry out, yes, shout aloud;
> He shall prevail against His enemies.
> I have held My peace a long time,
> I have been still and restrained Myself.
> *Now* I will cry like a woman in labor …
> … They shall be turned back,
> They shall be greatly ashamed,
> Who trust in carved images,
> Who say to the molded images,
> 'You *are* our gods.'"
> Isaiah 42:8-10, 13-14, 17 [NKJV]

In this passage we see several of the concepts we have been discussing. Notice that the Lord has said in the opening verse quoted here, that He means to put an end to idols.

Then what immediately follows?

We left off quoting the second half of verse 10 through 13. These verses discuss all the places on the earth that will praise the Lord; then follows a description of His coming like Sagittarius. Following all this He says, "I have held My peace a long time." Isn't this interesting? When does the Lord ever say anything is "a long time?" But His wait for vengeance and the abolition of false gods is a demonstration of His longsuffering. When He returns, He alone will be exalted.

Day Three –Ara – The Finishing

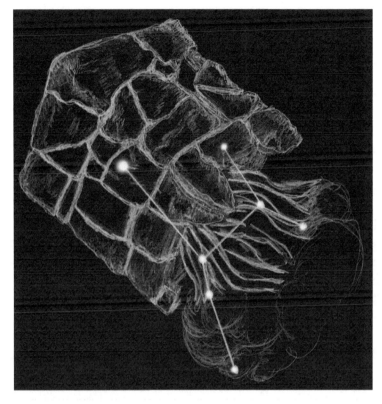

"For behold, the day is coming, Burning like oven,
And all the proud, yes, all who do wickedly will be stubble."

Malachi 4:1 [NKJV]

The constellation name, Ara, is Greek and means "altar." This constellation has an ancient Arabic name, Al Mugamra, "the completing, finishing."

The altar is pictured upside down in the sky with the fire pouring forth toward the earth.

Read Hebrews 10:11-14, 18, 26-27. What are two likely meanings of this overturned altar whose name means, "completing?"

In the Zodiac of Denderah, it is a different picture. It is a man enthroned whose name is Bau – same as Hercules and Boötes – "he cometh." In his hand he holds a flail. This was an instrument used to thresh grains. This Egyptian picture brings to light another layer of meaning for this constellation. Read Matthew 3:11-12. These verses have parallels to this constellation, both to the altar or the Egyptian picture of the man who cometh holding a flail.

flail

What are these parallels?

It is also important to note something else. In the verses above, what is burned up with fire?

What happens to the other part that is not burned?

Take comfort, if you belong to Him you are the wheat and are not destined to endure His burning anger.

> "For God did not appoint us to wrath, but to obtain salvation through our Lord Jesus Christ."
> 1 Thessalonians 5:9 [NKJV]

Instead, we shall be gathered into His barn, 1 Thessalonians 4:15-18.

We can see this truth in Malachi as well.

> "For behold, the day is coming, burning like an oven, and all the proud, yes, all who do wickedly will be stubble. And the day which is coming shall burn them up," says the LORD of hosts, "That will leave them neither root nor branch. But to you who fear My name the Sun of Righteousness shall arise with healing in His wings; and you shall go out and grow fat like stall-fed calves." Malachi 4:1-2 [NKJV]

There is something else worth noting in the quote from Matthew 3 above. It says "He will thoroughly clean out His threshing floor." Did you know that John the Baptist, who is speaking here, was referring to a literal, specific place?

Read 1 Chronicles 21:18-22.

Then Read 2 Chronicles 3:1. What is "His threshing floor?"

We think this offers a wonderful parallel with this sign. We see in it the truth that Christ's work and coming will cleanse His earthly temple and all false religion. For even His temple had become the seat of false religion in Israel's past. In the last days, the man of lawlessness will set up an image to himself there. Since the altar was the heart of religion in the ancient world, we believe the overturned altar also means the overturning of all false religions. As the truth of the Gospel goes out among the nations, people turn from their false worship and worship the One True God and Savior. It is completing and finishing as the name teaches. When He comes again, all who have continued to worship false gods will be ashamed for they have exchanged the worship of the true God for false gods.

"... The LORD alone will be exalted in that day, but the idols He shall utterly abolish." Isaiah 2:17-18 [NKJV]

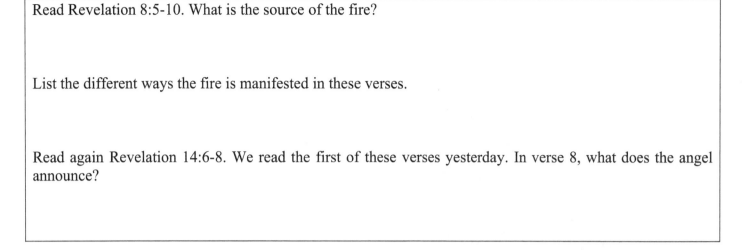

Read Revelation 8:5-10. What is the source of the fire?

List the different ways the fire is manifested in these verses.

Read again Revelation 14:6-8. We read the first of these verses yesterday. In verse 8, what does the angel announce?

Before we look at this more closely, remember our very first week in this study? Babylon was first the city of Nimrod. It was also home to the first documented false religion. Now let's look at Revelation.

> "And on her [*a woman representing Babylon*] forehead a name *was* written:
> MYSTERY,
> BABYLON THE GREAT,
> THE MOTHER OF ALL HARLOTS
> AND OF THE ABOMINATIONS OF THE EARTH."
> Revelation 17:5 [NKJV]

Since Scripture calls going after false gods and the worship of idols, harlotry, what do you think the designation, "mother of all harlots" signifies?

> "Then one of the seven angels who had the seven bowls came and talked with me, saying to me, 'Come, I will show you the judgment of the great harlot who sits on many waters.'" Revelation 17:1 [NKJV]

> "After these things I heard a loud voice of a great multitude in heaven, saying, 'Alleluia! Salvation and glory and honor and power *belong* to the Lord our God! For true and righteous *are* His judgments, because He has judged the great harlot who corrupted the earth with her fornication; and He has avenged on her the blood of His servants *shed* by her." Again they said, "Alleluia! Her smoke rises up forever and ever!'" Revelation 19:1-3 [NKJV]

Finally, judgment is poured out upon all false religion, its altar is overturned and its works are destroyed. This is also the completing or finishing referred to in the sign.

Day Four – Draco – The Dragon Cast Down

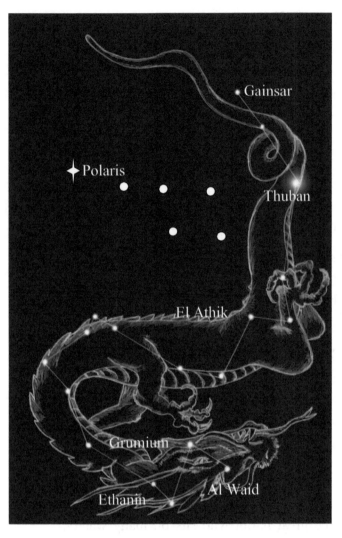

"So the great dragon was cast out,
that serpent of old,
called the Devil and Satan,
who deceives the whole world;
he was cast to the earth,
and his angels were cast out with him."
Revelation 12:9 [NKJV]

Read Isaiah 27:1. This is the "fugitive serpent" [*may be translated "fleeing serpent" in your translation*] under the foot of Hercules. It is the dragon cast down.

Draco is a Latin translation of the Greek, Drakon, meaning "dragon." According to Rolleston the Greek name Drakon is a translation from the more ancient Hebrew Dahrach which means, "to tread."

In Psalm 91:13, the Psalmist says, "On lion and asp thou treadest, Thou trampest young lion and dragon." [YLT]

The meaning of the name, Draco, is **he will be tread upon**, not the other way around. We have already seen this truth in Hercules, who is pictured treading on Draco's head.

Read the two previous verses, Psalm 91:11-12. Who quoted these verses in the New Testament? (Hint: see Matthew 4.)

Here is an example of Satan's subtlety. He quoted just the verses in Scripture that achieved his aim, and left off where he did to distort truth. Had he continued he would have been quoting prophecy of his own defeat. He frequently employs this method. Whenever Scripture is taught, we should bring our Bibles to read along; context is so important. Be sure and check everything out by its context. This brings us to the names of the stars in this constellation.

There are several ancient star names:
- In the head is Al Waid, Arabic, "to be destroyed" or Rastaban, Hebrew, "head of the subtle"
- Also in the head is Ethanin, Hebrew, "the long serpent or dragon"
- The alpha star in the coil is Thuban, Hebrew, "the subtle"

- El Athik, "the fraudful"
- Giansar, "the punished enemy"
- In the Jaw, Grumium, "the subtle"
- Not designated is El Asieh, "the bowed down."

Notice how many times these stars tell us that this dragon is subtle, in the head, the body, and the jaw. The repetition must be necessary. So let's spend some time here. First, let's look at the word "subtle." Its meaning has evolved over time and is hardly used in modern translations of the Bible because it does not necessarily connote something negative today.

In Young's Literal Translation, Genesis 3:1 says, "And the serpent hath been subtile above every beast of the field …" [YLT] (You can tell this is an old translation by the spelling of subtle.)

> What word does your translation use instead of subtle?

The King James uses a form of subtle in 2 Corinthians 11:3.

> "But I fear, lest by any means, as the serpent beguiled Eve through his subtilty, so your minds should be corrupted from the simplicity that is in Christ." [KJV]

> Write the word your translation uses here for subtlety.

Newer translations have chosen to use words for subtlety more closely in line with the original meaning. We must be on guard against the wiles [subtlety, craftiness] of Satan. It is clear that the warning given by the early prophets who named the stars in Draco, is still a concern for us today, though we have so many more advantages than the earlier saints.

> He is "the punished enemy" according to the star name, Giansar. How is this portrayed in the starry revelation?

If you are familiar with the astronomical reality called the procession of the equinoxes, you may recognize another way in which the dragon is shown as already punished or cast down from a spot he desired to hold. The brightest star, Thuban, near his coil was the North Star from 4000 to 1900 BC. Due to the wobble of the earth as it rotates (discussed in lesson 2), our North Pole gradually moved until another star in Ursa Minor was closer in alignment and so became the new North Star. Today the drift southward for Draco has progressed through two more stars in Ursa Minor until it has come to the most distant star from Draco in Ursa Minor, Polaris. He, as represented by Draco, has fallen from his high place already.

> Read Isaiah 14:12, 13. What is Lucifer/Satan's boast?

In Draco's drift southward we can see that there is a sense where the opening lines, about how he has fallen from heaven are shown to be true every single night. A line of his boast directly correlates with his former place as having the North Pole star in his constellation in the sky.

What is that line?

We know that this punished enemy has already been cast down. He no longer occupies his former place as chief among the angels. But there is a future fulfillment of being cast down as well. In Revelation he is cast out of heaven completely.

> "And war broke out in heaven: Michael and his angels fought with the dragon; and the dragon and his angels fought, but they did not prevail, nor was a place found for them in heaven any longer. So the great dragon was cast out …" Revelation 12:7-9 [NKJV]

Read in your Bible Revelation 12:10-12. Praise is the result of this action.

What benefit to the saints is gained by the dragon being cast down?

List the three things that accomplished victory over the dragon for the saints from verse 11.

The final manner of victory is in not fearing death. We talked about this in Scorpio's sign. Satan held us captive by our fear of death, but that fear was defeated in Christ's death and resurrection.

> "Therefore rejoice, O heavens, and you who dwell in them! Woe to the inhabitants of the earth and the sea! For the devil has come down to you, having great wrath, because he knows that he has a short time." Revelation 12:12 [NKJV]

The star Al Waid, says this enemy is "to be destroyed." We see him cast down, and he has a short time, but his ultimate destruction is yet future.

What does he do with that time in Revelation 12:13, 17?

He goes to make war, but his defeat is sure. It is both a warning and a consolation to us.

This concludes the first of the Three Books in the heavenly revelation. We began with the Seed of the woman. We saw the sacrifice and the labor of that seed as He lived among us. We also saw the crown and victory over all His enemies that He procured. Finally, we have seen Him returned, unrivaled in praise and honor, judging all rivals to His authority and casting down the dragon from heaven.

Day Five – Book I– The Redeemer, His Person and His Work – Review

Book I, as compared to the other two Books in the heavens, is the most preoccupied with proclaiming the prophecy of Genesis 3:15. Before we review the Book, we want to look a little closer at an aspect of this prophecy we did not have time to discuss earlier.

The prophecy begins, "And I will put enmity between you and the woman, and between your seed and her Seed …" [NKJV] This is a very curious phrase "her seed," since nowhere else in Scripture is a woman described as having "seed." Everywhere this term is used it is of the man, not the woman.

- Speaking to Abraham, "In your seed all the nations of the earth shall be blessed …" Genesis 22:18 [NKJV]
- Regarding Onan, "And Onan knew that the seed should not be his …" Genesis 38:9 [KJV]
- Speaking of Israel, the seed is spoken as of many descendents in Numbers 24:7.
- To David, "Your seed I will establish forever …" Psalm 89:4 [NKJV]
- To Israel, "O seed of Abraham His servant …" Psalm 105:6 [NKJV]
- "… I will sow the house of Israel … with the seed of a man" Jeremiah 31:27 [NKJV]
- "Now to Abraham and his Seed were the promises made …" Galatians 3:16 [NKJV]

Even though Abraham is promised that the chosen Seed would come through his wife, Sarah, and not Hagar, there is no mention of "Sarah's seed" or any woman's – only here in Genesis 3:15. We believe Genesis 3:15 then, is the first revelation through prophecy that the promised Seed will be born of a virgin.

Using this information, along with the rest of the prophecy in Genesis 3:15, look back over the constellations from Book I and put the ones that expand on its individual parts listed below.

- Seed of a woman

- Enmity between the woman's Seed and Satan's

- Seed mortally bruising the serpent or Satan (there are 3)

- Heel [foot] of the Seed wounded by serpent or Satan (there are 3)

o While you are looking at the wounded heel, we want you to notice an amazing consistency. Which
  leg of the Seed is pictured as bruised? _____ Is it consistent?

Look back over the 16 constellations in Book I and answer the following questions.

Which constellation was your favorite and why?

Did any constellation, together with Scripture, teach you anything new? If so, which one did?

Did any constellation surprise you in what it taught?

Book I has already told the whole redemptive plan of God. It has included the complete Gospel: the virgin birth, the humanity and divinity of Christ, His willing sacrifice of Himself for the propitiation of our sin, His labor and victory over sin, and the truth that He did not remain dead but will return for the salvation of His own and the ultimate defeat of Satan. Wow! Is there anything left for Book II and III? YES, there is so much more still to come. In Book II, the prophecy in the stars speaks primarily of the redeemed – the blessings obtained for them, the present reality for the redeemed and their future hope. It is an exciting Book. We have been so moved that the Lord has preserved in the stars specifically what He has done and will do for us.

Lesson Six - Chapter One – The Blessings Obtained

Day One –Capricorn – One Offering for the Many

Today we open a new scroll. We will find some of the same themes from Book I along with new ones. But even the repeats will contain new ideas. As the coming days will make abundantly clear, this second Book or Scroll is largely concerned with what the Coming One's sacrifice has meant for the redeemed, that is us. We are continually in awe to find that God has put in the night sky, for all to see, just what He has done and will do for us.

Capricorn – One for the Many

"… I came that they may have life, and have *it* abundantly."

John 10:10 [NASB]

We begin the scroll with a strange creature. A half goat and half fish creature is found in all the ancient Zodiacs. Capricorn is the Latin for goat, but that is only half the story.

- The Egyptians called it Hu-penius, "the place of sacrifice."
- The Hebrew name is Gedi, "the kid or cut-off."
- The Arabic is Al Gedi; having the same meaning as the Hebrew.

As we shall see when we progress through today's study, this picture represents an amazing summary of the subject and theme of this second scroll. The Egyptians and Hebrews got it half-right. So let's start with that half, the front half of the picture, the goat.

What function did the goat serve under the Law of Moses? For help read Leviticus 16:5-10.

Several different kinds of animals are appropriate sacrifices under the Mosaic Law: bulls, sheep, goats, turtledoves, and pigeons. All could be an offering for sin; however, the goat is most strongly connected with the sin offering for the people. As you saw in the description of the holy feast called the Day of Atonement, two goats served as a sin offering and atonement for the sins of the people. The first was sacrificed for the sins of the people. Upon the other, called "the scapegoat," the sins of the people were confessed and it was sent into the wilderness to carry away their sins. The constellation speaks of a sin offering.

The star names agree with this idea:

- Al Gedi, the alpha star, means "the kid or cut off." (Since goats were sin offerings, the idea of cut off is nearly synonymous with goat.)
- Debih, the beta star, is "the sacrifice slain"
- Deneb al Gedi, "the judge/the kid or sacrifice"
- Sa'ad al Naschira, "the record of the cutting off."

What a story these star names tell, and what a parallel to the Day of Atonement. As we noted, one goat is slain,"… and Aaron shall bring the goat on which the LORD's lot fell, and offer it *as* a sin offering." Leviticus 16:9 [NKJV] This parallels Debih. The other goat is cut-off (a term denoting being excluded from the community), "The goat shall bear on itself all their iniquities to a uninhabited land …" Leviticus 16:22 [NKJV] and parallels Sa'ad al Naschira. However, as Hebrews 10:4 says, "For it is impossible for the blood of bulls and goats to take away sins." [NASB] The goats are a picture and stand in for the work that Jesus Christ would do.

Read Heb 10:12, 13:11-13 and Isa 53:8, 10. Explain from these verses how Jesus fulfills both roles as the sacrificed goat and the scapegoat.

Christ's single sacrifice fulfills the role of both goats in the Day of Atonement. Let's study the picture more closely. Describe the position of the head and legs of the goat.

So even in the aspect of this picture we see a dying or at least suffering goat. We can then recognize Christ and His sacrificial work in the front half of this constellation. It is more difficult to discern the meaning of the second half. We will need to depend heavily on the written Revelation to unveil its meaning.

But first, describe the back half of this constellation.

While the front depicts a sacrificial animal, a goat going down to death, the back is that of a fish, full of life and vigor.

In ancient times, fish were neither raised nor bred but abundant nonetheless. This idea, linking fish to abundance is found in ancient Hebrew. The masculine for fish, *däg*, has as its root the word, *dägä*, which means, "to multiply or increase." The Hebrews used the word *däg* for fish because they are so wonderfully prolific according to Gesenius' Lexicon. You will be seeing a lot more fish in the continued study of this book and we believe they are meant to symbolize multitudes or abundance. But abundance of what? For that answer we must search Scripture.

We find the word "many" in Mark 10:45, a verse that also speaks of Christ's sacrifice. To what does "many" refer?

Abraham was promised a seed greater than he could number in Genesis 15:5. "Then He brought him outside and said, 'Look now toward heaven, and count the stars if you are able to number them.' And He said to him, 'So shall your descendants be.'" [NKJV]

In Revelation 7:9 is a fulfillment of the promise to Abraham. What are we told in this verse about the multitude before the throne?

This is a sometimes-overlooked truth about the heart of God. His heart has always been to bless all His children, not just the nation of Israel. This desire was expressed to Abraham, that he should be the father of an innumerable people and that they should be "many nations." Now we see the fulfillment of God's desire in the description of His people around the throne.

Imagine that you wished to represent the multitudes that belong to him in picture form. The ancient prophets, as we see, used a fish. What would you use?

It is difficult for us to imagine a better animal to represent abundance or multitudes. But we also see something else in the vigor of the fish.

> "But the free gift *is* not like the offense. For if by one man's offense many died, much more the grace of God and the gift by the grace of the one Man, Jesus Christ, abounded to many. ... For if by one man's offense death reigned through the one, much more those who receive abundance of grace and of the gift of righteousness will reign in life through the One, Jesus Christ. ... Moreover the law entered that the offense might abound. But where sin abounded, grace abounded much more, so that as sin reigned in death, even so grace might reign through righteousness to eternal life through Jesus Christ our Lord." Romans 5:15, 17, 20-21 [NKJV]

Again we see that Christ's act was for "many." What is also abundant besides the number saved by Christ's sin offering?

What an amazing picture this constellation is. Initially we found it very puzzling. Now we see this picture as an amazing demonstration of great wisdom so well expressed, not in words, but in art. We have the sin offering going down to death and from its body, not disconnected but a part, is vigor or life for many. We, the multitudes that belong to Him, have received abundant life and grace from the death of the Perfect Sin Offering. How else could one depict this truth in art? In this one picture is a summary of the entire second Scroll in the heavens.

Of this salvation the prophets have inquired and searched carefully, who prophesied of the grace *that would come* to you, searching what, or what manner of time, the Spirit of Christ who was in them was indicating when He testified beforehand the **sufferings of Christ and the glories that would follow**. 1 Peter 1:10-11 [NKJV emphasis added]

Day Two –Sagitta – Destroying

"He has bent His bow and set me up as a target for the arrow. He has caused the arrows of His quiver to pierce my loins."

Lamentations 3:12-13 [NKJV]

This is the second smallest constellation in the sky. For this constellation, which is the small arrow in the top left corner of this picture, we need context to discern its meaning. We do not have any ancient star names to help us out. It is known today by the Latin word for arrow, "sagitta." The ancient Hebrew name, Scham, "destroying or desolate" gives us the most help in understanding its meaning.

The constellations surrounding this arrow help us first know what it is not. Knowing the archer, Sagittarius is near the arrow, some might imagine it is an arrow from His bow.

Explain why this could not be.

Sagitta has no apparent shooter, no source for its flight evident within the pictures in the sky. It flies in the mid heavens apparently of its own accord. The ancient Greeks recognized that this arrow was not shot by Sagittarius. They saw it as the arrow that wounded the eagle immediately to its southwest as do we. In this, they saw into the ancient truth. It is a truth shrouded in mystery.

To begin, consider how an arrow is distinctive from other weapons of war available in the centuries before Christ. List those distinctions.

For our purposes, the most important distinctive characteristic of an arrow, compared to other weapons of war, is the ability to shoot it from a place of concealment. This also matches our heavenly arrow, whose source is not seen.

"For look! The wicked bend *their* bow,
They make ready their arrow on the string,
That they may **shoot secretly** at the upright in heart."
Psalm 11:2 [NKJV emphasis added]

Who sharpen their tongue like a sword,
And bend *their bows to shoot* their arrows – bitter words,
That they may shoot **in secret** at the blameless; ...
Psalm 64:3-4 [NKJV emphasis added]

Continue reading in Psalm 64. We see here that God, Himself is described as shooting arrows. It is also implied that His arrow can be shot from concealment – "suddenly they shall be wounded."

What is a distinction between God's and the arrows of the wicked? (Compare verses 3 and 7)

God does not use a multitude of arrows, His arrow does not miss.

We feel that Sagitta, which has wounded the eagle, is shot by the invisible hand of God the Father.

Read Genesis 22:1-18. Both revelations, the heavenly and the written, declare that the sacrifice of Christ was the free will offering of Himself and represents the bruising of the heel by the serpent. But there is a final player typified by Abraham in this story.

Now we see the involvement of all the actors in this great drama, the Son, the serpent and the Father. Abraham had demonstrated willingness to make in faithful obedience, the sacrifice that God the Father actually completed.

"For God so loved the world, that He gave His only begotten Son ..." John 3:16 [NKJV].

As Abraham assured his son on the way up the mountain, God the Father did provide a Lamb. And by His own hand, He slew Him.

"Yet it pleased the LORD to bruise Him; He has put *Him* to grief. ..." Isaiah 53:10 [NKJV]

We believe receiving an arrow from the hand of God the Father is a unique experience of Christ the Son. It is not something we should expect to suffer. Because He took that arrow, we never need to.

There is much we can understand about the suffering of Christ on the cross. The suffering in His physical body, the suffering of scorn and ridicule from those who looked on, and the suffering of the shame of such a death, with all these we can identify. But whatever happened in the darkness that shrouded the cross from the eyes of all, this is a mystery. It was in this darkness that Jesus cried, "My God, my God why have you forsaken me." And not much later, "It is finished." In that darkness, the Son of God must have been pierced by the arrow of the Father. What exactly He experienced no one can say. And so this strange little arrow, flying in the midst of the heavens with no obvious shooter, and no explanation in its stars is a fitting picture of this mystery.

Day Three –Aquila – The Smitten

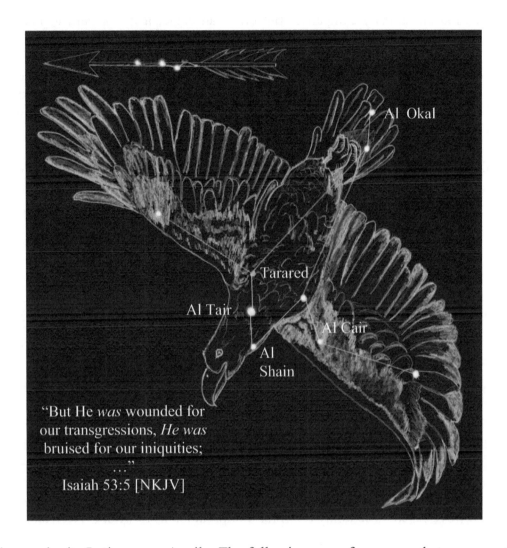

This eagle is known by its Latin name, Aquila. The following are a few verses that compare the eagle with the Lord.

> "You yourselves have seen what I did to the Egyptians, and *how* I bore you on eagles' wings, and brought you to Myself." Exodus 19:4 [NASB]

> "As an eagle stirs up its nest, hovers over its young, spreading out its wings, taking them up, carrying them on its wings, *So* the LORD alone led him[His people], And *there was* no foreign god with him." Deuteronomy 32:11-12

What do you notice about these verses? More specifically, when the Lord's actions are compared to an eagle, what kind of attributes does He apply to Himself?

The eagle today is most frequently used as a predatory symbol of strength. In Scripture, the Lord has chosen to use it for Himself in connection to His nurture and rescue. It is somewhat surprising.

Since in Scripture God has already compared Himself to an eagle, it is not hard to imagine this eagle as another picture of the work of the Redeemer.

In the first constellation of this sign, we saw the front of the goat bowed down toward death. We saw in it that the coming Seed was the sin-offering. Now in the following two constellations, the ancient prophets have expounded on that theme; declaring to us that the Seed, represented here as the falling eagle was slain by the arrow of God.

There are several star names and they all serve to confirm that this eagle is falling, wounded:
- The alpha star located in the eagle's neck is Al Tair, Arabic, "the wounding"
- The beta star in the throat is Al Shain, Arabic, "the bright" from the Hebrew, "scarlet colored"
- Tarared, "wounded or torn"
- Al Cair, "the piercing"
- Al Okal, in the tail, "wounded in the heel"

The star in the tail is another reminder that this revelation preserves which ancient prophecy?

It begs the question, what else but the promise given by God in the garden could be the inspiration for such a repetition?

Notice that all the stars speak in unison. Hopefully, if you were not sold yesterday that the arrow had wounded this eagle, today's look at the eagle's stars has convinced you.

In Isaiah 53, we found five phrases that appear to teach this "tender shoot", or Christ, suffered at the hand of God the Father. However, there is certainly room for interpretation as to whom "He" sometimes refers.

Read this passage and write each of the phrases below.

We find in Isaiah that the Savior was wounded both as a result of the Father's and His own determination.

What does this passage say the Savior suffered at the hands of men?

How hard it is to know that with all He has done for us, we have not esteemed Him as we should. For, as Isaiah 53:5 points out, He took upon Himself the chastisement that was ours. We should have been the one struck by the arrow of God, but because of His sacrifice, we will never feel God's wrath.

> "Therefore, having been justified by faith, we have peace with God through our Lord Jesus Christ. … Much more then, having now been justified by His blood, we shall be saved from wrath through Him." Romans 5:1, 9 [NKJV]

Thank you Jesus!

> "Let us therefore come boldly to the throne of grace, that we may obtain mercy and find grace to help in time of need." Heb 4:16 [NKJV]

Day Four – Delphinus – The Dead One Rising Again

"… I am the resurrection and the life. He who believes in Me, though he may die, he shall live."

John 11:25 [NKJV]

The dolphin, known as Delphinus, has no ancient star names to help us interpret it. We are not certain that a dolphin was placed here by the ancient prophets. However, we do feel that whatever was placed here was intended to convey victory over death by the Savior through resurrection.

This uncertainty does give us a chance to note that, in the study of the starry revelation, there is much room for interpretation. Not everyone who sets to understanding this ancient art draws the exact same conclusions. Additionally, unlike the written Word which has been carefully preserved, the heavenly revelation has most certainly been corrupted. Sometimes the corruption is obvious, as with Coma, and we can trace back and find the original. Other times, the corruption may be so ancient itself that we cannot find any references to any other picture. This should make us thankful for the Word, which God has carefully preserved so that we can put our trust in it. What is most exciting about our study of the constellations is that they point us to that Word; they lead us on a broad survey of the redemption story contained in it, and often, they direct our view of it from a new angle.

The ancient names for this constellation are:
- Dalaph, Hebrew, "pouring out of water"
- Dalaph, Arabic, "coming quickly"
- Scalooin, Arabic, "swift (as the flow of water)"
- Rotaneb, Syriac and Chaldea, "swiftly running"

The Persian star picture has a fish and a stream of water. The Egyptians had a vessel pouring out water. But this is so similar to next week's constellation we will save it to explore next week.

From the ancient names and pictures we can be sure that water figured into the sign, and possibly a fish. Today the sign is always pictured as a dolphin or fish leaping from the water, with its head up, full of life and vigor. The dolphin is known for its swiftness, anciently called "the arrow of the seas". A dolphin conveys well the repeating idea of swiftness in the ancient names. They have a broad geographic distribution and are recognized by most people groups. They have been seen as possessing duality: as both a fish and a mammal and as inhabiting the water but breathing air.

Study the picture of the dolphin in contrast to the two other animal pictures in this chapter: the goat's head and the eagle.

List all the ways the dolphin contrasts with them.

The head of the dolphin finds a match in the fishy tail of the goat since both belong to the seas and both are drawn lively, pointing upward and full of vigor. The contrast and similarity with these pictures helps us interpret this sign.

The goat sacrificed and the eagle falling down to death from the arrow of God is followed by life springing up from the depths represented in this dolphin. We see this as a representation of the resurrection. It is fitting to conclude this chapter with the resurrection of Christ – life for the multitudes is obtained first by the resurrection from the dead of the Savior. Book I, concerned itself mostly with the conflict and defeat of the enemy. So the Messiah's triumphal return to take His vengeance on him is fitting. In Book II, where His redeemed are a central theme, His resurrection becomes the important completion of the story.

Read 1 Corinthians 15:13-18. How important is the resurrection of Christ to us?

We think there are parallels in the way Paul has expressed the significance of Christ's resurrection and the picture of Capricorn. Read 1 Corinthians 15:20-23.

How might the expression, "in Christ all will be made alive" be artfully depicted in Capricorn?

We believe Christ "the first fruits" is portrayed in Delphinus. This is the picture of one unique "fish" risen from the waters. As a note of interest, Christian art, beginning in the second Century AD, used dolphins as a symbol of resurrection.

Lions are recognized as the king of beasts and eagles the king of birds; in the same way, dolphins have been seen as the king of fish. The fishy tail in Capricorn, living and vibrant represents the abundant life gained for the multitudes by Christ's death. The king of fish, rising from the water would then represent the multitude's king. Delphinus declares Jesus Christ "the first fruits" from the dead.

From the ancient names of Delphinus, there is a repeated idea we have not yet explored.

Look back at the ancient names and meanings and write here the repeated theme.

It was, at first, a difficulty to connect quickness with the meaning of this constellation. We have seen, and will see often again in the coming signs, the idea of swiftness connected with Christ's return. But how does it fit here?

As we pondered this, a verse from the old King James Version suddenly came to mind.

> "But God, who is rich in mercy, for his great love wherewith he loved us,
> Even when we were dead in sins, hath quickened us together with Christ, (by grace ye are saved;)" Ephesians 2:4-5. [KJV]

What does your version use instead of "quickened" in these verses?

Notice that in old English the word for making alive or reviving was the same word to convey the idea of speed. This has changed and modern versions no longer use the word "quicken" to express the idea of reviving or making alive. But one has to wonder why, in the not so distant past, the same word was used for both ideas together. There are no clues to help us in the original Hebrew or Greek, both used a common word meaning, "to make alive or revive." The Word teaches that when we come to Christ, He quickens us – makes us alive who were dead in sin.

Now notice how Psalm 71:20 reads in the KJV.

> "Thou, which hast shewed me great and sore troubles, shalt **quicken** me again, and shalt bring me up again from the depths of the earth." [KJV emphasis added]

What two things does the Psalmist know will be done for him by the Lord?

So God reviving our life, though we were dead in our sins, can be what is referenced by the names conveying the meaning quickness. And the above verse brings another possibility. That is the second promise of the above verse, our resurrection.

In relation to speed, how does 1 Corinthians 15:51-52 describe our resurrection?

At the time Paul wrote this, we do not believe there were any instruments that could measure so short a time period as, "the twinkling of an eye." But that is just how quick we shall be quickened. How amazing. We had not considered before that the concept of quickness can be applied to both His making us alive in our old bodies and the final redemption of these bodies in resurrection.

Read Job 19:23-27. Until this study, the following verses had been a mystery. Job is likely the oldest book in the Bible. He was a contemporary of Abraham. Moses, who wrote the first five books of the Bible, would not be born for over 400 years. The mystery is how he knew so much about his own resurrection. Maybe he understood it from what the heavens declare. (Psalm 19:2)

> This strange goat-fish, dying in its head, but living in its after part – falling as an eagle pierced and wounded by the arrow of death, but springing up from the dead waves with the matchless vigour and beauty of the dolphin – sinking under sin's condemnation, but rising again as sin's conqueror – developing new life out of death, and heralding a new springtime out of December's long drear nights – was framed by no blind chance of man. The story which it tells is the old, old story on which hangs the only availing hope that ever came, or ever can come to Adam's race. To what it signifies we are forever shut up as the only saving faith. In that dying seed of the woman we must see our sin-bearer and atonement for our guilt, or die ourselves unpardoned.[1]

How privileged we are to live on this side of the first coming of Christ. The concepts taught in this first chapter of the starry revelation for most of those living before Christ must have been mysterious. But for us, who've come to Christ and know about His sacrifice and resurrection, they are familiar. Even the prophets who spoke as they were moved by the Spirit longed to understand what has for us become familiar.

> "Of this salvation the prophets have inquired and searched carefully, who prophesied of the grace *that would come* to you, searching what, or what manner of time, the Spirit of Christ who was in them was indicating when He testified beforehand the sufferings of Christ and the glories that would follow." 1 Peter 1:10-11 [NKJV]

---

[1] Dr. Joseph Seiss, The Gospel in the Stars or Primeval Astronomy, E. Claxton & Co, Philadelphia, PA, 1882, pg 71.

Day One – Aquarius--The Pourer Forth of Blessings

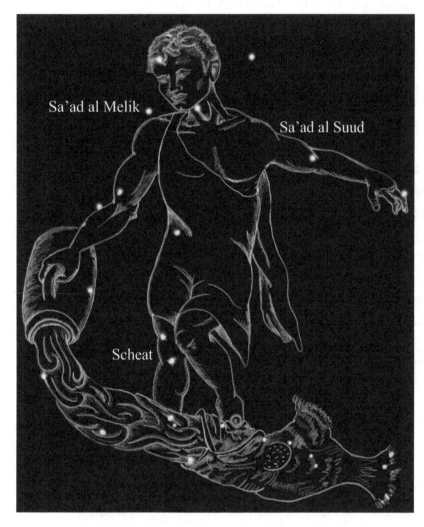

"For I will pour water on him who is thirsty,
and floods on the dry ground;
I will pour My Spirit on your descendants,
and My blessing on your offspring"

Isaiah 44:3 [NKJV]

This constellation has been well preserved and consistent across antiquity. Aquarius is Latin meaning, "the pourer forth of water."

Other ancient names for this constellation are:
- Hupei Tirion, Coptic, "the place of pouring out"
- Deli, Hebrew, "water urn"
- Hydrokoeus, Greek, "the pourer forth of water"

The alpha star is just above the shoulder holding the urn:
- It is Sa'ad al Melik, "the record of the pouring forth."
- The beta star in the opposite arm is Sa'ad al Suud, "who went and returned or poured out."
- Scheat, in his leg, "who goes and returns."

All the names speak together in concert. All but one, Scheat, which we will examine later, speak of pouring out water, which is also well preserved in the picture.

Take a second look at the various names for the sign, minus the Hebrew name. What or who is the subject of the sign?

Summarize the truths you saw last week in Capricorn through Delphinus.

In Capricorn we saw the blessings obtained through the sin offering slain and His subsequent resurrection from the dead. The blessings were obtained for the multitudes that are His.

The blessing obtained in Chapter One, are poured out for the redeemed, in Aquarius. The stars, in this section of the sky, are preoccupied with what Christ's sacrifice has meant for the redeemed, blessings poured out. In addition, we see from the picture that our Redeemer is not stingy with the blessings He has obtained for us.

How does this picture show this?

Manilius, the first century poet and astronomer in his poem Astronomica wrote,

> "He holds the cup or little urn in his hand, inclined downwards; and is always pouring out of it; as indeed he out to be, to be able from so small a source to form that river, which you see running from his feet, and making so large a tour over all this part of the globe. And so the urn flows on which seems to have been a proverbial expression among the ancients, taken from the ceaseless flowing of this urn …"[1]

And so the urn flows on….should remind us that the source of blessing is really not small but according to His riches in glory. (Eph 1:18; 3:16; Phil. 4:19; Col. 1:27)

This picture is a good reminder for anyone who might be tempted to believe that God is stingy with His blessings. Such a notion is the whispering of the deceiver. In the garden, he took this tack with Eve. Read Genesis 3:1.

Never mind that God had planted a paradise from which they have every need met and can enjoy the fruit of many trees. The tempter chose to focus on what they may not have, "Is it true that you cannot eat from every tree?" In other words, "Is it really true that God has denied you the fruit of some perfectly good trees?" Now Eve's focus shifts from all that God has provided, to the one tree from which she could not eat.

---

[1] Spence, Rev. Mr. Joseph, *Polymetis: Or, An inquiry concerning the Agreement Between the works of Roman Poets and the Remains of the Antient Artists being an attempt to illustrate them mutually from one another*, (London, 1755) page 172

So we don't fall into the same trap, let's look at all the blessings He has already poured upon us, who are His redeemed.

Read Eph. 1:1-14, list all the blessings God has given you.

These are great gifts indeed: sonship, acceptance, forgiveness, grace given in wisdom and prudence, knowledge of His will, an inheritance that is guaranteed, and the Holy Spirit. Notice a couple of words in this passage that describe the abundance of the blessings.

"Who has blessed us with **every** spiritual blessing" verse 3
"The forgiveness of transgressions, **according to the riches** of His grace" verse 7
"Which He **lavished** upon us" verse 8 [NASB emphasis added]

Today's lesson should be a wonderful refreshing in the Word for you, a reminder that Christ has and will drench you with the blessings He has obtained.

Read Isaiah 41:17-18 – What is the Lord saying in these verses by pointing out He will make rivers in desolate heights, the wilderness pools of water, the dry land springs of water?

Now read Isaiah 55:1-2. A good opportunity is provided here to think about what things we may buy that do not satisfy. List what has come to your mind.

It is interesting how verse 2 ends, telling us to listen carefully to God and to eat what is good. We are told to let our souls delight in abundance. Remember how Christ answered Satan when tempted to turn stones into bread after 40 days without food.

> "Man shall not live by bread alone, but by every word that proceeds from the mouth of God." Matthew 4:4 [NKJV].

How perfect a parallel to Isaiah 55:2. What is said before we are told to eat what is good?

What does this tell us is the food we should eat so our souls delight in abundance?

It is also intriguing that He commands us to listen carefully to Him. How often, in reading God's Word, do we listen carelessly? He says to listen carefully, for His Words revive the soul, but much is missed in a careless reading.

Another parallel to this final phrase in Isaiah 55:2 is John 4:32, where Jesus says, "I have food to eat of which you do not know." [NKJV] Look back in John 4 for the context of these words of Jesus.

What do you think His food was?

Let's continue with encouragement from the Word.

Stay in John 4 and read verses 10-14. Besides having special food, He also offers special water. It possesses much the same quality as the food we already examined.

What is special about it?

This same water is spoken of in Revelation 21:6.

> "And He said to me, 'It is done! I am the Alpha and the Omega, the Beginning and the End. I
> will give of the fountain of the water of life freely to him who thirsts.'" [NKJV]

Now look back at the star Scheat. It is found in the leg of Aquarius – such a fitting place – because it means, "who goes and returns." You may have noticed that the depiction of Aquarius in this study has him performing two actions at once.

What are they?

Hopefully, the picture is drawn well enough that walking quickly was what you saw as the second action portrayed in the picture. The second action is inspired by the meaning of the star, Scheat and one not always portrayed in depictions of Aquarius. It is also an important truth for the most significant meaning of this sign.

Read John 16:5 and 7. According to Christ, what must He do and what will we receive as a result?

The depiction of Aquarius matches the following Scriptures well, this cannot be a coincidence.

"Until the Spirit is poured upon us from on high ..."
Isaiah 32:15 [NASB]

"For I will pour water on him who is thirsty,
And floods on the dry ground;
I will pour My Spirit on your descendants,
And My blessing on your offspring"
Isaiah 44:3 [NKJV]

"And it shall come to pass afterward
That I will pour out My Spirit on all flesh;
Your sons and your daughters shall prophesy,
Your old men shall dream dreams,
Your young men shall see visions.
And also on *My* menservants and on *My* maidservants
I will pour out My Spirit in those days."
Joel 2:28-29 [NKJV]

How is giving the Holy Spirit described in all these verses?

One final point, the star, Scheat, teaches He will not only go away, but will return also.

"Now when He had spoken these things, while they watched, He was taken up, and a cloud received Him out of their sight. And while they looked steadfastly toward heaven as He went up, behold, two men stood by them in white apparel, who also said, 'Men of Galilee, why do you stand gazing up into heaven? This *same* Jesus, who was taken up from you into heaven, will so come in like manner as you saw Him go into heaven.'" Acts 1:9-11 [NKJV]

Day Two – Piscis Australis – The Blessings Received

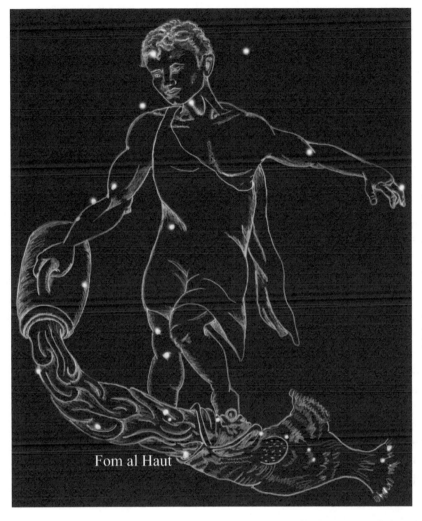

Fom al Haut

"I *am* the LORD your God,
Who brought you out of the land of Egypt;
Open your mouth wide,
and I will fill it."

Psalm 81:10 [NKJV]

The second constellation is inextricably linked to the first. It is known as Pisces Australis, Latin meaning, "the southern fish." It is 'southern' because there are two other fish quite near and above it.

Again, we continue with a theme in the pictures beginning in Capricorn. In fact, so many pictures in this portion of the night sky are connected with water, the ancients called this part of the sky, "the sea."

What does the Fish symbolize?

This picture finds a perfect parallel in the oracle of Balaam regarding Israel found in Numbers 24:7. This passage, because it is prophecy, is a bit veiled. But it so perfectly parallels the message communicated in this star picture, it is worth unveiling. In Balaam's prophecy regarding Israel, he says "his seed shall be in many waters." "His" refers to Israel. Seed refers to Israel's offspring – more exactly those who inherit the promises made to Israel's patriarchs – Abraham, Jacob, and David. Paul, in Galatians 3:26-29 best explains the seed "in many waters."

What do you think is meant by "his seed shall be in many waters?"

The promises given to Abraham will be shared by people from many nations.

The prophecy of Balaam matches this picture in meaning, "seed in many waters" or many from many nations will receive the blessings poured out.

We only have one star named in this constellation, Fom al Haut, "the mouth of the fish." While the names of the fish and the star names do not reveal much about the meaning of this constellation, we have enough context and the written revelation to help us uncover all we need to know about its meaning.

What do you notice about the stream of water and the mouth of the fish?

The great flow of water certainly represents the abundance of blessing, and the fish's mouth must be open wide to receive them. This fish succeeds in receiving all. No water is shown to flow past its open mouth. And so we can receive all the blessings God has for us, provided our mouths are open wide to Him. As the arrow of God is sure to hit its mark, so too, the blessings He bestows will all reach the mouth of His people. If you feel God's blessings are passing you by, you may need to seek in Scripture and with God in prayer as to why that might be. Can your mouth be closed to receiving from God? Can we be looking in the wrong direction with a mouth open in expectation, and thereby unable to receive God's blessings? We think either or both can be true.

> "He who walks righteously and speaks uprightly
> He who despises the gain of oppressions,
> He who gestures with his hands, refusing bribes,
> Who stops his ears from hearing of bloodshed,
> And shuts his eyes from seeing evil:
> He will dwell on high;
> His place of defense *will be* the fortress of rocks;
> Bread will be given him,
> His water *will be* sure."
> Isaiah 33:15, 16 [NKJV]

In the above passage, God's blessings are conditioned upon several things. Look again and underline them. This is a common theme in Scripture, from the beginning to the end, Look up Psalm 36:7-10 and Revelation 22:12-17 and note what the blessings of God are contingent upon.

Turn to Jeremiah 2:13. This is a great contrast to the other passages we have been studying. What are the two evils committed by God's people?

How does a fountain of water contrast with a cistern of water?

What do you think is meant in the metaphor, "hewn themselves cisterns?"

From the context, we believe the Lord is talking about chasing after other gods and making idols. The people of Israel had put their trust in other things. In so doing, they were missing out on the blessings of God.

What might be the temptation leading a person to make a large container to hold water, rather than relying upon a fountain of water?

The Lord is the source of everything we need. A variety of temptations can and will come to turn us from relying upon the Lord alone as our source. The Lord says other things are "cisterns that can't hold water." What a trade, the fountain of living water for a broken barrel that cannot even hold water much less produce an endless supply. And by seeking these broken barrels our mouths are turned in the wrong direction and unable to receive the blessings of God.

Among the blessings of the Holy Spirit poured out, discussed yesterday, is the seal and surety of the promise. Read 1 Corinthians 12:13.

How does its metaphor match this constellation?

We hope the lessons of the past two days have been a great encouragement to you. What a powerful encouragement Aquarius has been to us. We were amazed to find written without words in the night sky, the surety that our Savior has secured blessings that He pours out upon us.

Day Three –Pegasus – Deliverance Coming Quickly

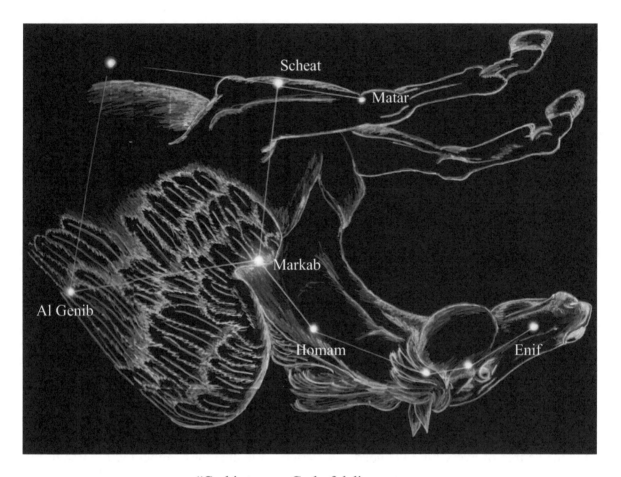

"God is to us a God of deliverances;
And to GOD the Lord belong escapes from death."
Psalm 68:20 [NASB]

This horse with wings can be traced back to ancient Zodiacs. It is pictured upside down because it appears this way in the sky. It is the eighth largest constellation in the sky and easy to find by the giant square of stars in its body. It is one of only three constellations that is incomplete – the back half of this horse is never pictured.

The origins of its name are interesting since Latin for horse is *equus*, and the Greek word is *ippos*. As you likely noticed, most of our current constellation names are simply Latin words for what they are. Not so with Pegasus. So what is the origin and meaning of the name? In the Egyptian Zodiac we find the name, Pe ka, under this picture which is very similar to the first part of Pegasus and must have influenced the current name. But there is no certainty to the Egyptian meaning of Pe ka. We also know that the Hebrew word for horse is *sus*, which matches the final syllable of the name. Likely our current name has inherited its last syllable from Hebrew. Many etymologists believe "pega" comes from the Greek word *pegai*, meaning "a spring" and *pegazo* meaning "spring forth or gush forth." This fits our horse very well. First, horses do spring into action – imagine the beginning of a horse race. And as you'll see, the second meaning of the word spring "a source of water" also fits the meanings of Pegasus well.

There are two stars whose names include references to water:

- Homam the star in the neck means, "water"
- Matar in the leg means, "who causes to overflow"

This third supporting constellation in Aquarius, though it is a flying horse, is still connected with the theme of water. Even though this is a horse with wings with no obvious connection to water, the ancient Phoenicians and Greeks, who either lost or corrupted the original meaning of the constellation, understood this connection.

- The ancient Phoenicians used this horse as the figurehead for their ships.
- The Egyptians connected this constellation with boats also.
- The Greeks invented myths around this constellation that kept the connection between this flying horse and water. According to their myth, Pegasus was born out of the ocean. He **sprung** out of the ocean when the blood of Medusa mingled with it. Also, the fountain of Hippocrene, meaning "horse's fountain," was created by Pegasus when he pawed at the earth until the spring came forth. Again these fables around this horse are most likely the imaginations of men replacing and corrupting an ancient truth in this constellation.

We believe the Greeks have mangled the message of deliverance contained in Pegasus. In the myth surrounding Hippocrene, "the horse's fountain," they have exchanged the worship of the true Deliverer for an image. Professing to be wise, they became fools.

Read the following and list what the Lord has done in each.

- Genesis 21:14-20

- Exodus 17:1-7

- Judges 15:18-19

This is what Pegasus proclaims; God will come to our rescue! He is our fountain of living water (Jeremiah 2:13). He delivers His servants, in the above three instances, by a miraculous provision of water. And while that is bound up in the meaning of Pegasus, we believe His promise of deliverance, in whatever way His help is needed is what He has promised.

> "You have seen what I did to the Egyptians, and *how* I bore you on eagles' wings and brought you to Myself." Exodus 19:4 [NKJV]

- The zeta star, Enif, is a variant spelling of the Hebrew, anaph, meaning, "branch or bough." This word is only used seven times in the Old Testament, but has the idea "to cover." The covering, the branches of a tree spreading out is connoted here (Ezekiel 36:8).
- The brightest star, Markab is also Hebrew, "returning from afar."
- The beta star, Scheat, also the name of a star in the leg of Aquarius, means "who goes and returns."

Taken together, it is clear that this horse is meant to represent a work of Christ. It is He who covers; it is He who goes and returns from afar. When He returns, he will do many things.

> What two things will He provide in Revelation 22:1-2?

Were not both of these things implied in the star names Homam, Matar, and Enif? Again we see how the mythology of the Greeks is a perversion of ancient truth.

Let's move on now to the broader promise of deliverance. A horse with wings is a comforting reminder of His deliverance.

> What attributes of a horse, especially a horse with wings, are reassuring when you think about deliverance?

Did speed or a similar word make your list? This is one of the main ideas of this picture – His deliverance is in time. Read Deuteronomy 33:26-27 and Psalm 18:6-7, 9-10. Besides being a marvelous match for this constellation, these verses also imply the swiftness of His help.

> What phrases express this?

We still have one star whose name we haven't looked at, that is Al Genib. It is located in the wing and means, "who carries." What a lovely promise! Look again at Exodus 19:4, quoted above.

Isaiah 46 contains a beautiful appeal from the Lord to his wayward people that emphasizes the significance of Al Genib. He is God who carries.

To understand this chapter some background may be needed.

1. *Bel* is a Babylonian word for "lord" or "master" used for their gods, especially their chief god.
2. Nebo is another god of Babylon and Assyria.
3. It was customary during this time, for the gods of the vanquished to be carried on carts to the kingdom of the conquerors.

Now look at Isaiah 46:1-2. What three things do you notice about these gods?

1. Rather than carrying they are _____ .

2. They are a _____ (even to beasts).

3. They, "have themselves _____ ."

We will come back to verses 3-5, but first look at Isaiah 46:6-7

1. What is the origin of these gods?

2. How do these gods come to occupy their place?

3. Once in their place, what is true about them?

We know none of the ideas above are new. But the One True God contrasted against these idols is beautiful. This exercise is worth doing. Now go back and read Isaiah 46:3-4. He has contrasted himself with each point he has made about the false idols of Babylon.

1. Rather than being carried, He _____ .

2. Rather than being a burden, He _____ .

3. Rather than being made by a man, He has _____ .

4. Rather than going with His followers into captivity and being unable to move answer or help in the day

    of trouble, He _____ .

Verse 5 naturally follows, "To whom will you liken Me, and make *Me* equal and compare Me, that we should be alike?" [NKJV]

It is breathtaking that anyone should exchange this God – a God who carries from birth to old age – for a lie, but it has happened over and over again throughout the course of human history.

Wasn't today's study another powerful encouragement? We will end with a few more verses that speak of His deliverance.

"*The righteous* cry out, and the LORD hears,
And delivers them out of all their troubles.
The LORD *is* near to those who have a broken heart,
And saves such as have a contrite spirit."
Psalm 34:17-18 [NKJV]

"I will lift up my eyes to the hills –
From whence comes my help?
My help *comes* from the LORD,
Who made heaven and earth."
Psalm 121:1-2 [NKJV]

"Blessed be the Lord, who daily bears our burden,
The God *who* is our salvation.
God is to us a God of deliverances;
And to GOD the Lord belong escapes from death."
Psalm 68:19-20 [NASB]

Day Four – Cygnus – The Blesser Surely Returning

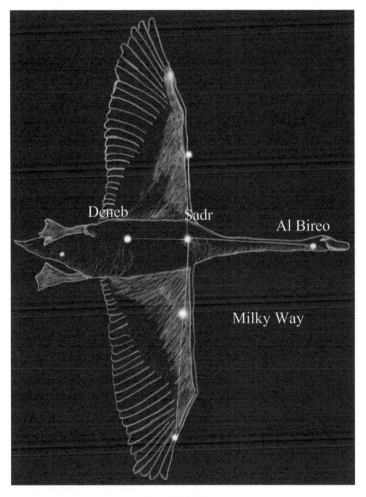

"And behold, I am coming quickly, and My reward *is* with Me,
to give to every one according to his work."

Revelation 22:12 [NKJV]

This is a stunningly beautiful constellation and easy to find in the night sky. Cygnus, Latin for swan, is also known as the Northern Cross. Its 6 brightest stars form a cross, though not the perfect cross formed by the stars in the famous Southern Cross.

It has an ancient name Tes-ark, Egyptian, "this from afar."

There are five ancient star names:
- Deneb is the alpha star. Its meaning is, "judge"
- Al Bireo, Arabic, "flying quickly"
- Sadr, "who returns in a circle"

Two are faint in the tail, and not shown in our picture:
- Azel, Hebrew, "who goes and returns quickly"
- Fafage, "gloriously shining forth"

Swiftness is a theme as the swan is pictured flying quickly down the Milky Way. In it are two stars that speak of a quick return. This beautiful swan is another representation of the work of Christ. He is the One who was once here, who has gone away and will return again.

"And if I go and prepare a place for you, I will come again and receive you to Myself; that where I am, *there* you may be also." John 14:3 [NKJV]

The idea of quickly returning, either in the representation of the picture or in the names of the stars within it or both, is repeated often in the heavenly revelation. We have seen it in Boötes, Sagittarius, Delphinus, Pegasus, and now Cygnus. We will see it again in the heavens.

Why do you think the swiftness of His return is so often repeated by the prophets?

Additionally, the stars tell us that He, who is returning, will judge. We have looked at Him as the judge of the nations in Boötes. But how does Christ as judge relate to us, the redeemed? Look again at our theme verse for Cygnus.

"And behold, I am coming quickly, and My reward *is* with Me, to give to every one according to his work." Revelation 22:12 [NKJV]

His judgment is not in relation to eternal life or death for us. To what is this judgment related?

Read 2 Corinthians 5:10 and Romans 14:10-12. This is a sobering thought. The One who blesses us will return and ask us to give an account of what we have done in this body- He has blessed us to do His work.

Read 1 Corinthians 3:10-15. According to these verses, what is judged?

What are the possible results of this judgment?

What is guaranteed?

In verse 15, though the judgment does not go well for the one whose work is entirely burned up, he is still saved – yet so through fire. He will be saved, but will suffer the loss of all his work. Like one who escapes his burning home, he is saved but the result of his labor is lost.

It is interesting that a swan was chosen to represent the return of the Blesser for a couple of reasons: first, of the four birds (two of the birds are eagles) chosen for these sky pictures this is the only bird that migrates. (The dolphin in Capricorn is the only other animal in our night sky that also migrates.) It is this habit of the swan that gives us a clue to the meaning of the star located at the central axis of this constellation, Sadr, "who returns in a circle."

Look at Psalm 19:6. "Its [the sun's] rising *is* from one end of heaven, And its **circuit** to the other end; and there is nothing hidden from its heat." [NKJV emphasis added]

The sun, which is a metaphor of Christ, is described as going and returning in a circle.[1]

How does the migratory habits of animals compare to the rising and setting of the sun?

Since the migration of swans follows the changing of seasons, we can know when they will return before they actually come again by the signs of the changing seasons. The Lord has expected those who are His redeemed to be able to recognize the signs of His returning as well.

Read 1 Thessalonians 5:1-6. Who will be surprised at the "Day" and who should be expecting its coming?

What is the final warning?

Now turn to Luke 21:29-36. Regarding the signs of His coming kingdom, what metaphor does Jesus use?

This is what is meant by Sadr. He returns as in a circle – there are signs that fortell His return. We who are waiting for Him, like all of us who look for summer, should know His coming is soon by the signs.

What is the warning in this passage?

We want to be sure that all are aware of these signs, since He expects us to know them.

Read Matthew 24:3-30. List as many signs of His coming as you find.

Our Blesser is One who returns in a circle so we can recognize the signs of His coming and prepare ourselves for it. He does not come suddenly without warning for those who are His.

---

[1] The whole universe, as we experience it from our vantage point, is circles within larger circles. The smallest circle is the 24 hour day. The circle of our orbit around the sun – creates the repeating year of 365 days. There is an even larger circle created by the earth's wobble. It is a circle of just under 26,000 years.

"But of that day and hour no one knows, not even the angels of heaven, but My Father only."
Matthew 24:36 [NKJV]

Though we should be able to recognize that His time is close, no one knows the date. Those who try to predict the year or the day are pretending to know something that Christ has said they cannot.

We said above that there were a couple of reasons the swan is an interesting choice to represent the return of the Blesser. The second interesting attribute of the swan is their ability to fly at extreme altitudes, far beyond the sight of the earthbound. Swans were observed by an airplane pilot at 27,000 feet. They were flying over the Atlantic Ocean between Iceland and the European continent.[2]

It should be a comfort, that though we cannot see Him now, we are still certain of His return.

---

[2] Whiteman, Lilly, "The High Life," *Audobon Magazine*, 2001, Web. 30 Aug 2011.
    http://audubonmagazine.org/birds/birds0011.html

Day One –Pisces and the Band – The Conflict of the Redeemed

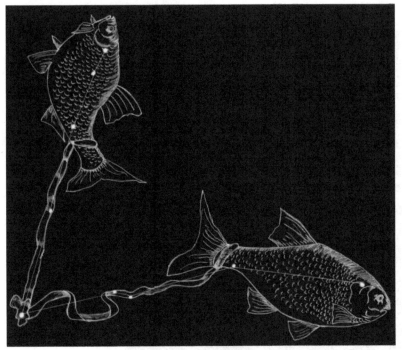

"…In the world you will have tribulation;
but be of good cheer,
I have overcome the world."

John 16:33 [NKJV]

Pisces is Latin for, "the fish." Before we look closely at this sign, it is important to note its context. In Capricorn, the first Chapter of Book II, we saw that our Redeemer has secured for us blessings through His death and resurrection. In the second Chapter, Aquarius, the blessings obtained were poured out. We have received His Holy Spirit, we are promised deliverance and rewards. The next is Pisces, the third Chapter of Book II. Like the third Chapter of Book I, this chapter speaks of conflict. In Book I, the third Chapter was Scorpio, the conflict of the Redeemer. In Book II, Chapter 3, is the conflict of the redeemed.

The ancient Hebrew name for this constellation is Dagim. Remember the ancient Hebrew word for fish *däg*, has as its root, *dägä* which means, "to multiply or increase." The Syriac name, Nuno, has a similar meaning to the Hebrew; "the fish lengthened out (as in posterity)." We know these fish represent the multitudes that are His. The Egyptian name, Pi-cot Orion or Pi-cot Hori agrees with our interpretation. It means, "the fish of Him that cometh."

Before we say anything more, we want you to study the picture for yourself. We have included the surrounding constellations because we believe they all help interpret the meaning of this constellation.

Describe the picture on the next page, citing as many details, in relation to Pisces as you can.

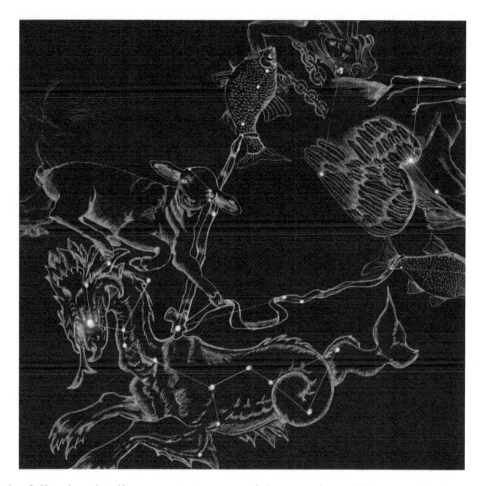

We will refer to the following details as we try to unravel the meaning of this constellation.

- The band tied to the tail of each fish and attached to the neck of the sea monster
- The fish's apparent inability to otherwise escape the sea monster
- The two fish and their separate directions and the constellations to which they point
- The lamb's foreleg that cuts across this band

As we write this lesson we feel a special connection with it. We are both right in the midst of earthly trials. We have been encouraged in these trials by every chapter we have written thus far. If you are in the midst of trying circumstances right now, we want to reach across the pages of this study and impart to you that joy is available to you from the hand of the Lord, even in trials.

> "My brethren, count it all joy when you fall into various trials, knowing that the testing of your faith produces patience. But let patience have *its* perfect work, that you may be perfect and complete, lacking nothing." James 1:2-4 [NKJV]

We want you to know that there can be joy through trials, especially when you are being filled up daily with Him and His Word. What a great privilege to be journeying through this study at the very time when our joy is so dependent upon it.

How do we know that worldly troubles are what is meant in this constellation? The two fish are bound with the band to the sea monster. The band is considered a separate constellation. But it is inextricably tied to understanding pisces. It is evident in the picture that these fish wish to escape an oppressor. The sea monster to which the fish are tied is another representation of Satan. We believe this representation of Satan as a sea monster is more specifically to identify him as the instigator behind this world's system.

> "We know that we are of God, and the whole world lies *under the sway of* the wicked one."
> 1 John 5:19 [NKJV]

We will study the sea monster further next week, and develop our case better there.

If we've been redeemed, if the Redeemer has overcome the world and the adversary, if every blessing He has procured for us He has also poured out for us to drink, why isn't life easy? Why do we face trials?

We'll look to the Written Revelation and let you answer. For each verse or verse set, write a reason for the earthly trials of His redeemed.

1 John 3:1, 13 and John 15:19

Romans 8:17 and 1 Peter 2:20, 21

Romans 5:3-5, 1 Peter 5:9-10 and Hebrews 12:7, 10-11

James 5:10-11

The conflict can take many forms. It can come in the form of suffering that is a natural part of life in this fallen place or it can come in the form of persecution for the name of Christ. In either and all cases, these trials or chastisements are an important, necessary part of the journey of His redeemed. Many great benefits are gained only by walking through these struggles.

> "Concerning this thing [a thorn in the flesh] I pleaded with the Lord three times that it might depart from me. And He said to me, 'My grace is sufficient for you, for My strength is made perfect in weakness.' Therefore most gladly I will rather boast in my infirmities, that the power of Christ may rest upon me. Therefore I take pleasure in infirmities, in reproaches, in needs, in persecutions, in distresses, for Christ's sake. For when I am weak, then I am strong."
> 2 Corinthians 12:8-10 [NKJV]

There is still more to the conflict of the redeemed. Read 1 John 2:15-17, and 2 Timothy 4:10.

> What is this additional conflict faced by the redeemed?

This is a daily battle. We live in this world and daily face the desires of this flesh and the siren voices of this world system. We are bombarded from nearly every direction with the world's notion of what will make us happy. But these are all lies, and we must resist their call or crash upon the hidden rocks. The following are sobering verses.

> "What causes quarrels and what causes fights among you? Is it not this, that your passions are at war within you? You desire and do not have, so you murder. You covet and cannot obtain, so you fight and quarrel. You do not have, because you do not ask. You ask and do not receive, because you ask wrongly, to spend it on your passions. You adulterous people! Do you not know that friendship with the world is enmity with God? Therefore whoever wishes to be a friend of the world makes himself an enemy of God." James 4:1-4 [ESV]

God's grace, and our eyes fixed in the proper place can bring victory for the redeemed in this battle. Read Titus 2:11-14.

> How does God's grace help us?

There are so many more apropos verses but we must move on.

There are two ancient star names in the fish that we must talk about because they serve as encouragement. They are not identified above because they do not appear any longer on modern star charts. Their names are:
- Okda, Hebrew, "the united"
- Al Samaca, Arabic, "the upheld"

1 Peter 5:9 touches on Okda, "… knowing that the same sufferings are experienced by your brotherhood in the world …" [NKJV] These fish are united in suffering.

Even more encouraging is Al Samaca, "the upheld." God has promised to aid and keep us in our trials.

> "The steps of a *good* man are ordered by the LORD,
> And He delights in his way.
> Though he fall, he shall not be utterly cast down;
> **For the LORD upholds *him with* His hand.**
> I have been young, and *now* am old;
> Yet I have not seen the righteous forsaken,
> Nor his descendants begging bread."
> Psalm 37:23-25 [NKJV emphasis added]

"For You are my hope, O Lord GOD;
You are my trust from my youth.
By You I have been upheld from birth …"
Psalm 71:5-6 [NKJV]

"Fear not, for I *am* with you;
Be not dismayed, for I am your God.
I will strengthen you,
Yes, I will help you,
I will uphold you with My righteous right hand."
Isaiah 41:10 [NKJV]

Tomorrow we will continue with the meaning of Pisces and the Band.

Day Two –Pisces and the Band – Continued

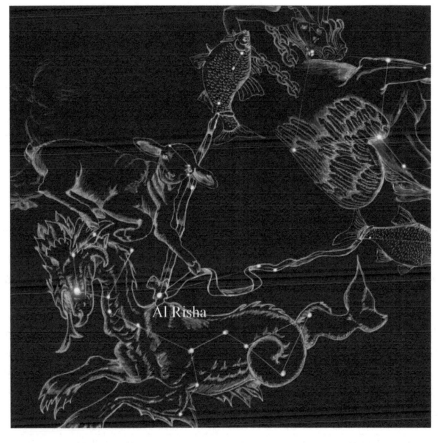

"For You, O God, have tested us;
You have refined us as silver is refined;
You brought us into the net;
You laid affliction on our backs."

Psalm 66:10-11 [NKJV]

This is the conflict: though we belong to Him who cometh, while we remain in the flesh, we face the temptations and pull of this world.

The brightest star in Pisces and the Band is the star in the knot on the neck of the sea monster. Its name is Al Risha and means, "the band or bridle."

This is our present reality. Though we have so many blessings already poured out, though we belong to our Redeemer who has overcome, this is also a time where our hearts are tested. It is a time where we might face want, where we will need to trust in the Lord's provision despite our circumstances.

"He led you through that great and terrible wilderness, *with its* fiery serpents and scorpions and thirsty land where there was no water; He brought water for you out of the rock of flint. In the wilderness He fed you with manna that your fathers did not know, that He might humble you and that He might test you, to do you good in the end." Deuteronomy 8:15-16 [NASB]

Why is the journey through the wilderness necessary, according to the verse above?

In the wilderness, if we wait on Him, God can and will do mighty things--things thought to be impossible. We might walk through the wilderness so that we learn to trust in Him. And His miraculous provision teaches us humility. Otherwise we might think it is by our own strength that we have achieved success.

Yesterday, when you looked at this picture, we discussed the following details:
- The band tied to the tail of each fish and attached to the neck of the sea monster
- The fish's apparent inability to otherwise escape the sea monster

Today we will deal with these two details:
- The two fish and their separate directions
- The lamb's foreleg that cuts across this band

Earlier in Book II, one fish symbolized the multitudes who are His. Yet here are two fish. So why two? There are a lot of conflicting theories on the meaning of the two fish. Before we state our understanding of the two, why not make a guess yourself?

Why do you think there are two fish?

We believe the use of two fish and their relative positions in the sky, are purposeful choices and therefore have meaning. The two must be a purposeful choice. There could easily have been one fish or three fish swimming together.

Look again at the picture. These two fish swim nearly perpendicular to each other. Consequently, in relation to each other, they represent all points of the compass. The fish closest to the lamb is called the Eastern fish, but it is also north of the other. So this fish could be said to represent northern and eastern directions. The fish closest to Aquarius is called the Western fish and is also south of its partner. The use of two fish, presented as they are, allows all four directions to be represented.

Read the following passages: Psalm 107:1-3; Matthew 8:11; 24: 31; and Luke 13:29. What is a likely meaning in how these two fish are presented?

The multitude of His redeemed is from every place on this planet, or as Scripture states: from all four corners of the earth. Though they are scattered in every direction throughout the world, He will gather them together to bring them into His kingdom. We believe this is the broad meaning of the two fish.

Scripture has more to teach about whom these two might specifically represent.

Read Ephesians 2:11-16. What two groups of people are spoken of in these verses?

Though the Lord has called a distinct people group to Himself, the Jewish people, His plan was always to draw not only from one people group or place, but from every tribe, tongue and nation a multitude for Himself.

Several times in Book III you will find a pair to represent His redeemed. We believe each time these pairs represent this same idea.

Let's move on to our final detail, the lamb's foreleg across the band.

Doubtless, there is little mystery as to the significance of the foreleg of the lamb over the bands. The lamb is a familiar picture of Christ.

What do you see is the meaning behind His foreleg across the bands?

We see two meanings. One is in the future.

Read Jeremiah 30:8 and Ezekiel 34:27 and interpret the meaning of the lamb's foreleg across the bands.

Ultimately, the bands will be cut, the journey through the wilderness will be over, our tears will be wiped away, and we will realize the good end He has for us!

But there is also a present meaning for the leg over the band.

Read 1 John 5:3-5 and explain the present meaning.

Though we are bridled to this world because we must walk in it, and the god of this world can plague us, or attempt to do so, he doesn't have unlimited control. Christ has set us free, He has overcome and if we seek after Him, the devil has no power over us.

This is a wonderful promise. We know Satan desires to drag us down without mercy to the very depths, but the Lamb guards us from his darkest purposes and liberates us from his influence altogether.

Psalm 107 is the same message as Pisces. The first three verses were quoted earlier. To finish today's lesson, read this Psalm. The Psalmist speaks of God's faithfulness through all of life's troubles. In each conflict, the redeemed are ultimately rescued.

"Whoever is wise will observe these *things*,
And they will understand the lovingkindness of the LORD"
Psalm 107:43 [NKJV]

Day Three – Andromeda – The Chained

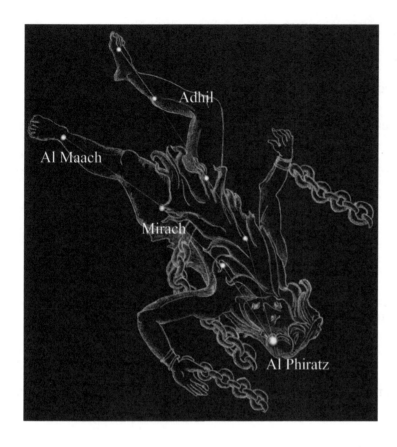

"Let my eyes flow with tears night and day,
and let them not cease;
for the virgin daughter of my people has been
broken with a mighty stroke,
with a very severe blow."

Jeremiah 14:17

Here is a mysterious picture. Today it is called, Andromeda, which is Greek meaning, "set free from death."
- Her Hebrew name is Sirra, "the chained" and Persea, "the stretched out."
- In the Egyptian temple of Denderah she is called Set, meaning "set up as queen."

Today astronomers wonder at this constellation. The Greek fable of Andromeda, which we will look at, is very familiar. However it is well established that this sign existed long before the Greeks. The original inspiration for this picture was unknown to them. As you shall see, the answer is found in Scripture

The star names all speak in unison:
- Al Phiratz, the alpha star in the head in Arabic means, "the broken down"
- Mirach, the star in the hip in Hebrew means, "the weak"
- Al Maach, in the foot is Arabic, "struck down"
- Adhil, in the other leg is Arabic, "the afflicted"

Every part of this constellation speaks with a singular voice. Though the Egyptian name, Set, appears to bear a different testimony, you will see that all agree, since originally Andromeda was set up as a queen.

146

Take a moment to describe the woman in the constellation.

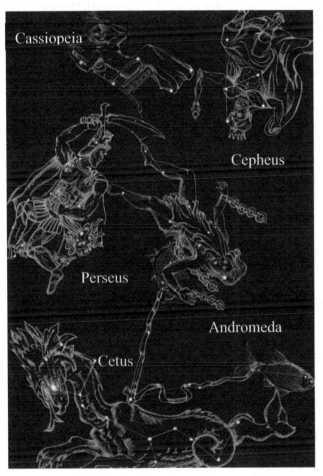

As we have seen time and again, the Greeks have developed fables around these star pictures that are a corruption of original truth. The original is still discernible, however. Briefly, the fable goes that Andromeda was a beautiful princess, the daughter of Cepheus and Cassiopeia. Because of Cassiopeia's boast about her beauty, Andromeda was bound to the rocks at the edge of the sea to be devoured by Cetus, the sea monster. Ultimately, Andromeda is rescued by Perseus. A quick look at the proximity of all these constellations is informative.

With the proximity of all these constellations in the sky, the Greek fables around Andromeda are not a difficult stretch. There is much that is right about her story, and there are some particulars misunderstood and corrupted. The Greeks ignored Pisces – the two fish – in this fable even though one swims directly into Andromeda's side.

Like the rest of the constellations, Andromeda is not a specific person. She is a symbol for something else. She is the subject of Jeremiah's lament. On the next two pages, you will find the entire first chapter of Lamentations.

Underline the many ideas we have found in this constellation for her, either through star names, old fables or the picture. Here is a list of words or ideas to underline together with their synonyms: **Daughter, Princess, Beauty, Naked, Bound or Chained, Captive, Afflicted, Weak, Struck Down, Broken Down, Stretched Out.**

Lamentations 1 [KJV]

"How doth the city sit solitary, that was full of people how is she become as a widow she that was great among the nations, and princess among the provinces, how is she become tributary [a slave]

"She weepeth sore in the night, and her tears are on her cheeks: among all her lovers she hath none to comfort her: all her friends have dealt treacherously with her, they are become her enemies.

"Judah is gone into captivity because of affliction, and because of great servitude: she dwelleth among the heathen, she findeth no rest: all her persecutors overtook her between the straits.

"The ways of Zion do mourn, because none come to the solemn feasts: all her gates are desolate: her priests sigh, her virgins are afflicted, and she is in bitterness.

"Her adversaries are the chief, her enemies prosper; for the LORD hath afflicted her for the multitude of her transgressions: her children are gone into captivity before the enemy.

"And from the daughter of Zion all her beauty is departed: her princes are become like harts that find no pasture, and they are gone without strength before the pursuer.

"Jerusalem remembered in the days of her affliction and of her miseries all her pleasant things that she had in the days of old, when her people fell into the hand of the enemy, and none did help her: the adversaries saw her, and did mock at her sabbaths.

"Jerusalem hath grievously sinned; therefore she is removed: all that honoured her despise her, because they have seen her nakedness: yea, she sigheth, and turneth backward.

"Her filthiness is in her skirts; she remembereth not her last end; therefore she came down wonderfully: she had no comforter. O LORD, behold my affliction: for the enemy hath magnified himself.

"The adversary hath spread out his hand upon all her pleasant things: for she hath seen that the heathen entered into her sanctuary, whom thou didst command that they should not enter into thy congregation.

"All her people sigh, they seek bread; they have given their pleasant things for meat to relieve the soul: see, O LORD, and consider; for I am become vile.

"Is it nothing to you, all ye that pass by? behold, and see if there be any sorrow like unto my sorrow, which is done unto me, wherewith the LORD hath afflicted me in the day of his fierce anger.

"From above hath he sent fire into my bones, and it prevaileth against them: he hath spread a net for my feet, he hath turned me back: he hath made me desolate and faint all the day.

"The yoke of my transgressions is bound by his hand: they are wreathed, and come up upon my neck: he hath made my strength to fall, the LORD hath delivered me into their hands, from whom I am not able to rise up.

"The LORD hath trodden under foot all my mighty men in the midst of me: he hath called an assembly against me to crush my young men: the LORD hath trodden the virgin, the daughter of Judah, as in a winepress.

"For these things I weep; mine eye, mine eye runneth down with water, because the comforter that should relieve my soul is far from me: my children are desolate, because the enemy prevailed.

"Zion spreadeth forth her hands, and there is none to comfort her: the LORD hath commanded concerning Jacob, that his adversaries should be round about him: Jerusalem is as a menstruous woman among them.

"The LORD is righteous; for I have rebelled against his commandment: hear, I pray you, all people, and behold my sorrow: my virgins and my young men are gone into captivity.

"I called for my lovers, but they deceived me: my priests and mine elders gave up the ghost in the city, while they sought their meat to relieve their souls.

"Behold, O LORD; for I am in distress: my bowels are troubled; mine heart is turned within me; for I have grievously rebelled: abroad the sword bereaveth, at home there is as death.

"They have heard that I sigh: there is none to comfort me: all mine enemies have heard of my trouble; they are glad that thou hast done it: thou wilt bring the day that thou hast called, and they shall be like unto me.

"Let all their wickedness come before thee; and do unto them, as thou hast done unto me for all my transgressions: for my sighs are many, and my heart is faint."

This is just one chapter of Lamentations. This subject fills many more pages of the prophets.

What do we know from Scripture that the picture of Andromeda represents?

According to Lamentations, why was she chained, broken down and stretched out?

It is amazing that this prophecy existed in the night sky long before the nation of Israel or the city of Jerusalem existed. Let's examine what the Greeks got right.

- Andromeda is a princess and a daughter – but not of Cassiopeia as we will see next week. Notice how often she is called daughter in Lamentations. This is repeated elsewhere in the prophets (Isaiah 52:2). You likely found the word "princess" in the first paragraph of Lamentations as well.
- She also was "set" as a queen in the days of her early kings, especially under Solomon, who made her the most prosperous kingdom of its time.
- She is made captive and desolate due to her many transgressions. This even includes her boasting. Hezekiah, a king of Judah showed the Babylonians, the enemies that captured and burned Jerusalem, all his treasures as a kind of boast (2 Kings 20:13-17).
- Ultimately she will be rescued.

> "'For the LORD has called you
> Like a woman forsaken and grieved in spirit,
> Like a youthful wife when you were refused.'
> Says your God.
> 'For a mere moment I have forsaken you,
> But with great mercies I will gather you.
> With a little wrath I hid My face from you for a moment;
> But with everlasting kindness I will have mercy on you,'
> Says the LORD your Redeemer."
> Isaiah 54:6-8 [NKJV]

This is the present conflict of His people. Jerusalem has yet to realize the full deliverance promised her.

According to Luke 21:24, how long will Jerusalem be in conflict?

From the fall of Jerusalem by the hand of Nebuchadnezzar, king of Babylon, in 586 BC through the time of Jesus Christ to today, 2011 AD, with various reprieves, Jerusalem has been trampled by the Gentiles. That equals roughly 2,597 years and counting. But in the Lord's timing, that is "a mere moment" according to Isaiah 54:8.

The obvious question is: Does Andromeda have anything to do with us? We say yes. We are told that Israel serves as an example for us (1 Corinthians 10:6, 11-12). Israel is a bride, and so is the Church (Eph. 5:25-32). Israel was chosen and so is the Church (Eph. 1:4). So it begs the question, if the Church falls into the same apostasy can the same thing that happened to Israel/Jerusalem happen to the Church? We'll leave that for you to ponder.

Additionally, look what Paul says in Romans.

> "I say then, have they [Israel] stumbled that they should fall? Certainly not! But through their fall, to provoke them to jealousy, salvation *has come* to the Gentiles. Now if their fall *is* riches for the world, and their failure riches for the Gentiles, how much more their fullness! ... For if their being cast away *is* the reconciling of the world, what *will* their acceptance *be* but life from the dead?" Romans 11:11-12, 15 [NKJV]

It has been a sobering three days. We have looked at the conflict of the redeemed. We have been assured that our days here will include various tests and tribulations. We have also seen the present conflict and suffering of God's holy city. Tomorrow is a better day! The stars will direct our attention to the Redeemer.

Day Four –Cepheus – The High King

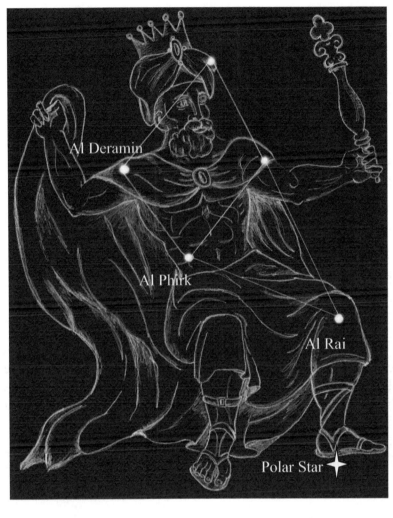

"It is He who sits above the circle of the earth,
And its inhabitants *are* like grasshoppers,
Who stretches out the heavens like a curtain,
And spreads them out like a tent to dwell in."

Isaiah 40:22 [NKJV]

Cepheus is a picture of the high and lofty king. His left foot is planted on the Polar Star, the North Star. From our vantage point, this star sits atop the center of the giant dome of the sky. What a perfect way to convey the truth that He sits high above all things. Around this star, all other stars turn. That is why the alpha star Al Deramin, is also known as Al Derab, "to go around." We believe the constellation is so placed to aid us in discerning the meaning.

Before digging into the meaning of this constellation, we wish to clarify that the picture itself is not meant to be a representation of what God looks like or who He is. This picture like all the rest, conveys some aspect of His work or His person. Taken all together, these pictures tell the story He wishes to reveal to us without words. No single picture in the sky seeks to represent Him; how could it? This picture teaches that He is the High King seated above all creation.

Remember our context – we are in Pisces, the conflict of the redeemed. We have seen that His redeemed face trials and tribulations in this life, that we are bridled to the system of this world as we struggle in this flesh. We have also seen the great discipline of the Lord on His own people and city in the constellation of Andromeda.

In this context, why do you think the ancient prophets follow the conflict of the redeemed with our Redeemer portrayed as a King sitting upon His thrown high above the earth?

Let's look to the Word for help. We have already quoted from Isaiah 40:22. Turn to Isaiah 40 and read verses 12-31. See if anything else comes to your mind to help answer the above question. If so, go back and add those things to your answer.

We have found the following truths in reading Isaiah 40:12-31.

Isaiah 40:12-14 – There is no one else like Him, He is above every other thing, unequalled in power and knowledge. How does this help or comfort you in trouble?

Isaiah 40:27 – Being above all things He has a great vantage point from which to see all things, there is nothing hidden. How does this knowledge help or comfort you in trouble?

Isaiah 40:28-31 – He is able to help us from His lofty place in ways only available to Him, who else can do these things? Again, record how this should be your comfort.

Isaiah 40:18-20, 23 – If He is above all things, nothing is hidden from Him and He is able to provide help in ways only available to Him. Why would we put our trust in any other place than our High King? This is the thrust of this chapter. God is compared to idols, princes, and judges. All pale in comparison to His power, might, and wisdom. Idols must be formed, judges and princes He brings to nothing. The final appeal is that He gives power to those who wait for Him.

How are we tempted to put our trust in other things rather than waiting for His help?

Isaiah 40:15, 17, 22, 27 – He is high and in the midst of our trouble, He can seem unreachable. What truth do you know from Hebrews 4:14-16 that assures us that He isn't unreachable?

In Isaiah 40, the feeling by the redeemed that the High King is far away and not coming quickly enough is only barely intimated. But look through the Psalms and see the very common lament that asks Him not to stay far off but to come and deliver us:

"This you have seen, O LORD;
Do not keep silence.
O Lord, do not be far from me.
Stir up Yourself, and awake to my vindication ..."
Psalm 35:22-23 [NKJV]

In both the Psalms and the prophets you will find this theme. It is a commonly shared feeling among all His redeemed in the midst of their troubles.

Read Isaiah 40:31 and 64:4. What is the promise from our Redeemer?

Before moving on, we have to share these verses of comfort.

"For He looked down from the height of His sanctuary;
From heaven the LORD viewed the earth,
To hear the groaning of the prisoner,
To release those appointed to death."
Psalm 102:19-20 [NKJV]

"For thus says the High and Lofty One
Who inhabits eternity, whose name *is* Holy:
'I dwell in the high and holy *place*,
With him *who* has a contrite and humble spirit,
To revive the spirit of the humble,
And to revive the heart of the contrite ones.'"
Isaiah 57:15 [NKJV]

There is more to see in the constellation in its names and the names of its stars:
- The Egyptians called him: Pe-ku-hor, "this one comes to rule.
- He was called Hyk by the Ethiopians, which means, "king."
- Today the constellation is called by its Greek name: Cepheus which is likely derived from Hebrew: *keph* – "rock especially hollow of rock like a cave" or *kaph* – "hand, palm, a branch shaped like a hand (palm branch) especially hollow of the hand"

The Hebrew root for the name Cepheus links Andromeda to it. Read Isaiah 49:14-16.

What has He said to answer Zion's complaint that the Lord has forgotten them?

There are three star names still preserved in this constellation:
- The alpha star has two possible names:
  - Al Deramin, Arabic, "right hand or arm"
  - Al Derab, Arabic "to go around"
- Al Phirk, in the waist, is Arabic, "to redeem or snatch away"
- Al Rai, in the leg, is Arabic, "who breaks"

The alpha stars names have very literal meanings since Al Deramin meaning right hand or arm is located in the right arm of Cepheus. Read Psalm 138:7 and 139:9-10

The verses above are just a small sampling of a recurring theme – our Redeemer saves and

upholds   us   with   _____   _____

_____ .

Al Phirk – we find this root in Psalm 136:24. It means to break or snatch away and in the King James Version is translated in this verse, "redeems." "And hath redeemed us from our enemies …" [KJV]

Finally, we have Al Rai, "who breaks." In the context of our chapter, we think this relates to the redeemed. Read Jeremiah 31:28.

Does our Redeemer also break His redeemed?

In Jeremiah 31:28, we see the Lord's promise to Zion. Yes, He watched over them to break and to afflict, but what else does He promise?

In regards to us, we have already seen that as a good Father, He disciplines us, and sometimes this means breaking us. Read Genesis 32:24-32.

Who did Jacob wrestle with?

How did his opponent disable him?

Why did he disable him?

What was the result for Jacob (verse 31)?

It appears that this joint was never healed. Jacob's will was so strong, that to teach him to submit to God, God physically "broke" him.

> "The sacrifices of God *are* a broken spirit,
> A broken and a contrite heart –
> These, O God, You will not despise."
> Psalm 51:17 [NKJV]

> "The Lord *is* near to those who have a broken heart,
> And saves such as have a contrite spirit."
> Psalms 34:18 [NKJV]

154

God draws near to what kind of person?

For the redeemed, a broken and contrite heart is only achieved under the watchful discipline of our loving King and Father.

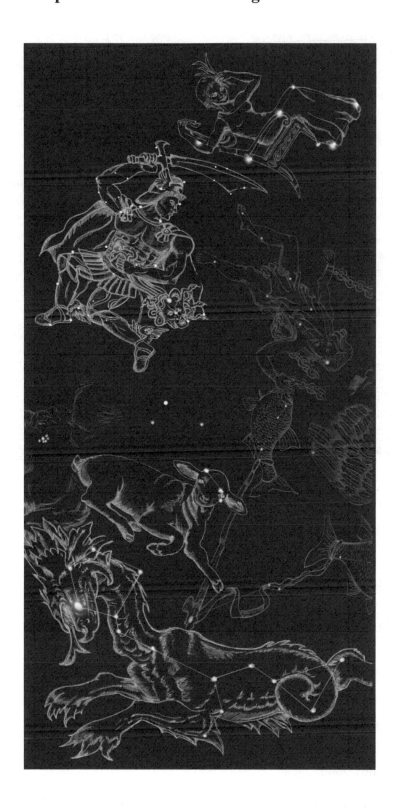

Day One – Aries – The Lamb's Reign

With Aries, we begin the final chapter of Book II – The Redeemed. Today it is often pictured as a ram. However, its most ancient names call for a lamb. Given its obvious connection to the Lamb of God, we have represented it as a lamb in our picture.

The ancient names:
- Telah, Hebrew, "the lamb"
- Al Hamal, Arabic, "the sheep, gentle, merciful"
- Baraziggar, ancient Akkadian, "altar of righteousness [right making]"
- Aries, Latin, "the ram"
- Tametouris Ammon, Coptic, "the reign of Ammon"

The star names:
- The alpha, El Natik, Arabic, "wounded or slain"
- The beta, Al Sheratan, Arabic, "the bruised or wounded"
- Mesartim, Hebrew, "the bound"

All speak to truth about our Redeemer with which we are familiar. Only the Coptic, or Egyptian, seems out of step, "the reign of Ammon."

The Coptic name is explained by their history. The Theban Egyptians, at the time when the sun entered the constellation Aries, decorated their doors with branches, garlanded a ram with wreathes of flowers, carried it in a procession, then sacrificed the ram. This was the annual festival of Ammon, who was their chief god and represented by a ram. In the sacrifice of the ram, the Egyptians believed they were not just paying tribute to this chief god, but that Ammon, himself, was actually sacrificed. Since they saw Ammon as a ram, ram's were sacred and never sacrificed except at this festival.[1] In this pagan practice is a great deal of error. But we can see also the shadow of original truth.

The Jewish Passover Feast also occurred in spring and was the first of seven feasts ordained by God. It was marked by the sacrifice of a male lamb.

Read Romans 5:6. What does this passage say about the time that Christ died?

When was Jesus, the Lamb of God, to whom the Passover Lamb pointed, crucified? (Read John 18:38-39 if you are not sure.)

The Passover occurred in the springtime between March 23rd and April 19th. For all possible dates of the crucifixion of the Lamb of God, the sun was in the constellation of the lamb, Aries. The Lord of the Heavens, when He speaks of "the right time" can order this to be so in more ways than we often imagine.

"The sun in Aries" or any sign, means that the sign is in the same path together with the sun. It is not visible to us during its time "in the sun" because its rising and setting are at the same time as the sun's. So the sun's light obscures the light of its stars.

Turn to Matthew 27:45. What happened from noon to three while the Lamb of God hung upon the cross?

This darkening of the sun during the middle of the day is recorded in Matthew, Mark and Luke and is spoken of by early church fathers. Some compared it to a solar eclipse because its effect was the same; though it could not possibly be an eclipse for two reasons. First of all, no eclipse lasts 3 hours, their duration lasting less than 5 minutes. Secondly an eclipse is not possible at Passover. Passover is celebrated at the full moon; solar eclipses are only possible during a new moon. It was, then, a miraculous event, in which the sun was obscured.[2] It was not a dark storm or cloud covering either because the early church fathers, who spoke of it, as well as other Roman chroniclers, attest to the stars becoming visible in the heavens. An early church father, Eusebius, says:

> "'However in the fourth year of the 202nd olympiad, an eclipse of the sun happened, greater
> and more excellent than any that had happened before it; at the sixth hour, day turned into

---

[1] Sir James George Frazer, *The Golden Bough* (New York London: Macmillan and Co), pg 510.
[2] Parker, John (1897). "Letter VII. Section II. To Polycarp – Hierarch. & Letter XI. Dionysius to Apollophanes, Philosopher.." *The Works of Dionysius the Arepagite*. London: James Parker and Co., pp. 148-149, 182-183.

dark night, so that the stars were seen in the sky, and an earthquake in Bithynia toppled many buildings of the city of Nicaea.' These things the aforementioned man (says)."[3]

Don't miss this! As the sun reached its zenith during the middle of the day on the day Christ was crucified, it was suddenly darkened. The three brightest stars of Aries shown in its place over the cross of Christ. These star names mean: "the slain," "the bruised," and "the bound". The ancient name for Aries, Barziggar, "the altar of right making," was declared by the heavens over the cross of Christ. As the Psalmist says, "The heavens declare the glory of God, and the sky above proclaims His handiwork." Psalm 19:1 [ESV]

We can speculate on the purposes of the miraculous obscuring of the sun, but certainly among them must be the Heavenly Father speaking through the testimony of these stars, saying, "Behold! The Lamb of God who takes away the sin of the world!" It is this dying man who was wounded [Al Sheratan], slain [El Natik] and bound [Mesartim], who is the Passover Lamb [Telah], the merciful and gentle [Al Hamal], the One who makes righteous [Barzigger] and He, though He dies, who will ultimately reign [Tametouris]. The stars spoke as a banner and a testimony at both His birth and His death. And really, how could they keep silent?

There is even more to this constellation. We will look at it in the context of our heavenly scroll, Book II – The Redeemed.

Aries begins the final chapter of this book and, as with all final chapters in the heavenly revelation, it is a chapter that declares the Lord's triumph. Remember that Book I ended with Sagittarius, the archer whose arrow is aimed directly at the heart of Scorpio; and Lyra, "His praise ascending;" and Ara, "His wrath poured out" and Draco, "the dragon cast down." It is a chapter that speaks of the Lord as conqueror. We will also see this in the last book, Book III. But this middle book, Book II, is a book whose theme is the redeemed. So keep this in mind when thinking about this apparent problem.

How is the Lamb, whose stars all speak of His wounding, a picture of His final triumph?

We believe this final chapter is a lamb because it is not about the Lord's vengeance on His enemies – it is about His rescue of His redeemed. The atoning sacrifice of the Lamb is the foundation for our rescue. Book II, has been book-ended between two sacrificial animals; the sin offering in the goat, Capricorn, and the Lamb, Aries.

> "… though He was a Son, *yet* He learned obedience by the things which He suffered. And having been perfected, **He became the author of eternal salvation** to all who obey Him." Hebrews 5:8-9 [NKJV emphasis added]

> "For in Him dwells all the fullness of the Godhead bodily; and you are complete in Him, who is the head of all principality and power. In Him you were also circumcised with the circumcision made without hands, by putting off the body of the sins of the flesh, by the circumcision of Christ, buried with Him in baptism, in which you also were raised with *Him*

---

through faith in the working of God, who raised Him from the dead. And you, being dead in your trespasses and the uncircumcision of your flesh, He has made alive together with Him, having forgiven you all trespasses, having wiped out the handwriting of requirements that was against us, which was contrary to us. And He has taken it out of the way, having nailed it to the cross. Having disarmed principalities and powers, He made a public spectacle of them, triumphing over them in it." Colossians 2:9-15 [NKJV]

Our rescue is not possible without the sacrifice of the Lamb. For our robes must be washed white in the blood of the True Passover Lamb, that His wrath will pass us over and we will be delivered from the wrath to come. (Ro. 5:9) And for the now, Romans 5:17 says the ones who receive the abundance of grace and gift of righteousness shall reign in life.

Spend some time in Revelation, the final book in the written revelation, and you will find that our Savior is more frequently referred to as the Lamb than any other designation. In fact, He is called the Lamb or Lamb of God 27 times in this book. The Gospel of John is the only other book where He is directly called the Lamb of God. The Book of Revelation, which is chiefly concerned with the final revelation of Christ, chooses to refer to Him most frequently as the Lamb or Lamb of God. And so, however mysterious it is, the chapter of triumph for Book II begins with the Lamb.

Day Two –Cassiopeia – The Enthroned

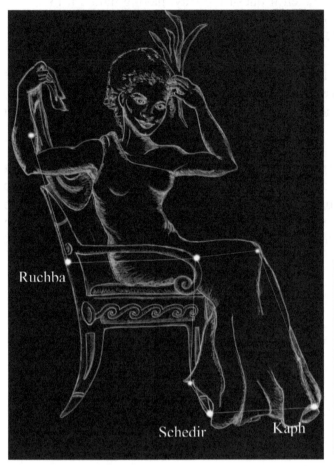

Ruchba

Schedir   Kaph

"For thus says the LORD:
'Just as I have brought all this great calamity on this people,
so I will bring on them all the good that I have promised them.'"
Jeremiah 32:42 [NKJV]

The configuration of stars in this constellation makes a giant W. Cassiopeia has an easily recognizable shape, making it an easy constellation to find in the Northern Hemisphere's night sky.

Briefly describe what you notice about this woman.

The Greeks saw her as a queen and as the mother of Andromeda, the chained woman. The ancient names also declare her as a queen:

- Set, Egyptian, "set up as queen"
- Ruchba, Arabic, "the enthroned"
- Dat al cursa, Chaldee, "the enthroned"
- Cassiopeia, Greek, "she on the throne, beautiful"

A woman seated on a throne with the branch of a palm in her hand, while fixing her hair is the consistent manner in which she has been pictured. The Greeks, however, corrupted the truth in making her the mother of Andromeda. We will discover who this queen is, and how she is actually related to Andromeda.

Let's look to the Word. In the passages below, underline the words or phrases that relate to Cassiopeia and circle the words or phrases that remind you of Andromeda.

Awake, awake! Put on your strength, O Zion;
Put on your beautiful garments, O Jerusalem, the holy city!
For the uncircumcised and the unclean shall no longer come to you.
Shake yourself from the dust, arise;

Sit down, O Jerusalem!
Loose yourself from the bonds of your neck,
O captive daughter of Zion!
For thus says the LORD:
'You have sold yourselves for nothing,
And you shall be redeemed without money.'"
Isaiah 52:1-3 [NKJV]

"To console those who mourn in Zion,
To give them beauty for ashes,
The oil of joy for mourning,
The garment of praise for the spirit of heaviness;
That they may be called trees of righteousness,
The planting of the LORD, that He may be glorified.
"I will greatly rejoice in the LORD,
My soul shall be joyful in my God;
For He has clothed me with the garments of salvation,
He has covered me with the robe of righteousness,
As a bridegroom decks *himself* with ornaments,
And as a bride adorns *herself* with her jewels."
Isaiah 61:3, 10 [NKJV]

"For Zion's sake I will not hold My peace,
And for Jerusalem's sake I will not rest,
Until her righteousness goes forth as brightness,
And her salvation as a lamp *that* burns.
The Gentiles shall see your righteousness,
And all kings your glory.
You shall be called by a new name, which the mouth of the LORD will name.
You shall also be a crown of glory in the hand of the LORD,
And a royal diadem in the hand of your God.
You shall no longer be termed Forsaken,
Nor shall your land any more be termed Desolate;
But you shall be called Hephzibah[My Delight is in Her], and your land Beulah [Married];
For the Lord delights in you,
And your land shall be married.
For as a young man marries a virgin,
So shall your sons marry you;
And *as* the bridegroom rejoices over the bride,
So shall your God rejoice over you."
Isaiah 62:1-5 [NKJV]

Who does this constellation represent?

How is she related to Andromeda?

Briefly tell her story according to what you learned last week in studying Andromeda and what you have seen about her today.

Cassiopeia speaks to the final glory of His city and people. Though she was punished, imprisoned, and made desolate, God has not forsaken her. He will remember His promises to Jerusalem and her people and He has made her a beautiful city, glorious and righteous. She will sit as queen among all the nations.

In the final passage, what is Zion called in addition to a queen? (Isaiah 62:4-5)

Read Isaiah 54:4-7, 11-12. What is the chief metaphor used for God and Israel?

Andromeda who was put to shame in her youth and widowed, receives mercy from her Maker and Redeemer who is also called her husband. What a beautiful picture of God's mercy. Andromeda was cast down for her sins, but God has promised to redeem her because He has married Himself to her. In the final verses her walls, gates, and foundations are described as adorned with beautiful stones. Underline all the parallels to Isaiah 54 found in Revelation.

> "Then, I, John, saw the holy city, New Jerusalem, coming down out of heaven from God, prepared as a bride adorned for her husband. … Then one of the seven angels … talked with me, saying, 'Come, I will show you the bride, the Lamb's wife.' And he carried me away … and showed me the great city, the holy Jerusalem, descending out of heaven from God, having the glory of God. Her light *was* like a most precious stone, like a jasper stone, clear as crystal. … The construction of its wall was *of* jasper; and the city *was* pure gold, like clear glass. The foundations of the wall of the city *were* adorned with all kinds of precious stones …" Revelation 21:2, 9-11, 18-19 [NKJV]

Cassiopeia, the constellation, represents God's promises to Zion. See how she straightens her hair and her robe as if readying herself as a bride. She sits expectantly on her throne. In her hand she carries the branch of a palm, which is a special symbol of victory and especially God's victory that brings salvation.

The star names are:
- Schedir, Hebrew, "the freed"
- Ruchba, Arabic, "the enthroned"
- Kaph, Hebrew, "palm of hand or palm branch"

Cassiopeia is Andromeda freed. We have also seen the Hebrew word *kaph* before in our study of Cepheus. "See, I have inscribed you on the palms [*kaph*] *of My hands*; Your walls *are* continually before Me.'" Isaiah 49:16 [NKJV]

What a lovely picture of redemption. Can we, who are a part of His church, find ourselves in this picture as well? We believe so.

Read Eph. 5:25-27. How does this description of the church match the star picture?

We see these similarities:

- We find a reference to Aries – "Christ loved the church and gave Himself for her."
- We find parallels to Cassiopeia
  - the church and Christ's relationship is compared to a husband and wife's.
  - the church is being prepared for union with Christ
  - the church is being made glorious
  - those who overcome in the church are promised to rule on thrones (Rev. 3:21; 5:10)

The promise in Cassiopeia is a promise to both the Old and New Testament people of God. She is pictured as fixing her hair. She is currently in process of being made worthy. She sits in anticipation because her wedding is still future. This is the present and future reality for us the members of His church.

Day Three – Cetus – Leviathan Bound

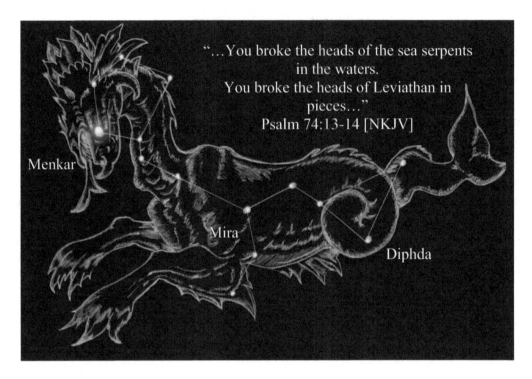

Cetus has been such an integral part of Chapter Three, Pisces, we feel like we have already looked at him. The constellation itself is giant, being the fifth largest in the sky. He is in step with a prominent theme in Book II, that of water. He is recognized as a sea monster or sea dragon.

From what has already been said about Cetus, who or what does he represent?

His ancient Egyptian name is Knem, "the subdued." As the subdued he is under the feet of the Lamb. All his names make the same declaration.

The star names are:
- Menkar, the alpha star, means "The bound or chained enemy"
- Diphda, the beta star, means "overthrown or thrust down"
- Mira, "the rebel" – this is a very interesting star, we will discuss further.

Isn't this like our present reality? What does 1 John 2:17 say about this world system?

The process of destruction for this world system is already begun, the end already determined. But it often does not look or feel that way. Satan is already defeated by the Lamb, but he still retains power. In the present, he is restrained and subdued by the sovereignty of God. Besides his ultimate defeat, there is still a future sense in which he will be subdued further than he is now.

Before we move on, we wish to note deliberate patterns in the construction of the story in the sky. In the final chapter of Book I, we saw Draco – the dragon cast down. The final chapter of Book II, contains Cetus – the enemy subdued and bound. You will see this pattern continued in the final chapter of Book III. Also, keeping with the pattern, each of these three constellations, are among the largest in size of all constellations in the sky, another proof of a single design – not a haphazard conglomeration of unrelated mythological creatures.

Isaiah 27:1 could have been discussed earlier in Draco, but we have saved it for now.

> "In that day the LORD with His severe sword, great and strong,
> Will punish [judge, visit] Leviathan the fleeing [fugitive] serpent,
> Leviathan that twisted [perverted] serpent;
> And He will slay [kill, destroy] the reptile [dragon] that *is* in the sea."
> Isaiah 27:1 [NKJV]

The words in brackets above are all alternative words the translator could have used – words we wish they had chosen.

Provide the adjectives used for the three repetitive descriptions of the dragon.
1. Leviathan the _____ _____
2. Leviathan the _____ _____
3. the dragon _____ _____ _____

Isaiah 27:1 has three repetitions and descriptions of the dragon matching the three main pictures of him in the sky: Draco, Cetus, and Hydra. This passage speaks of the three-step defeat of Satan and so does the heavenly revelation.

Without the book of Revelation this verse may well have been impossible to understand. But Revelation makes clear that Satan suffers a three-fold defeat.

We saw the first of these when we studied Draco, "Leviathan the fugitive serpent." When he was cast out of his place, he went about as a fugitive. Do you remember Job? When God asks Satan where he has been, he replies that he was going back and forth on the on the earth (Job 1:7). This sounds like a fugitive to us. And when he is cast out of heaven in Revelation 12:7-9, 12, he goes about the earth as a fugitive in rage.

Book II, the final chapter, contains Cetus, the second leviathan of Isaiah 27:1, "Leviathan the perverted serpent."

Read Revelation 20:1-3. What happens to Satan?

Look back to chapter 19 in Revelation, as far back as you need. What event precedes binding Satan in the bottomless pit?

This is the second step of Satan's defeat. Amazingly, this is such a perfect match for the construction of the heavenly revelation. Satan, the god of this world, as he is portrayed in Cetus, loses not his life but his place as the prince of the air. He is bound in the pit so he cannot influence the world.

Keep in mind that Cetus has words for its name and the name of its stars like subdued, bound, chained, overthrown, thrust down, and rebel.

List ways Rev. 20:1-2 matches these ideas.

This is still not the final defeat for Satan. What does Revelation 20:3 say will happen and when?

In these passages, Satan is called the deceiver of nations. It could also be said, he perverts the nations. He is "Leviathan the perverted serpent."

Before moving on, there is something else to point out from Isaiah 27:1. Regarding these first two Leviathans, it says the Lord will "punish" them. This word does not mean destroy. But before speaking of the third dragon, the prophet uses another word, "slay." But you have to wait for the final chapter of Book III to see it.

We have not yet spoken of the unusual star in the neck of Cetus, Mira, "the rebel." It was the first variable star discovered. As a variable star, it does not shine with a consistent brightness. Its light can increase in brightness then dim to a point where it completely disappears from visibility to our naked eye then returns and increases in intensity. This appears to match the Revelation story. Satan will have his way for a time of great tribulation, but with the return of the Lamb, he will be overthrown and cast into the bottomless pit where he will have no influence at all. At the end of 1,000 years, he will be released for a short time.

We believe Cetus also represents another one, whose coming, is in accordance with the working of Satan (2 Thessalonians 2:9).

Read Revelation 13:1-10. Where does the beast come from?

Mira, the star meaning, "the rebel" also describes this beast. List how this beast is a rebel.

His end is already foretold in Revelation 13:10. "He who leads into captivity shall go into captivity; he who kills with the sword must be killed with the sword. ..." [NKJV]

"For God *is* my King from of old,
Working salvation in the midst of the earth.
You divided the sea by Your strength;
You broke the heads of the sea serpents in the waters.
You broke the heads of Leviathan in pieces ..."
Psalm 74:12-14 [NKJV]

Day Four – Perseus – The Breaker of Every Bond

"You went forth for the salvation of Your people, for salvation with Your Anointed.
You struck the head from the house of the wicked, by laying bare from foundation to neck."
Habakkuk 3:13 [NKJV]

Our final constellation of Book II is easily recognized as triumphant. We do not know much about how this constellation was anciently represented, except that the Hero carried a devilish head, and a large sword. More recent renderings of this constellation (1500s AD forward) show the Hero wearing a helmet and breastplate. These may or may not be faithful to the ancient renderings. The Greeks included the winged shoes in their fables about Perseus. We do not know for sure which came first, the winged shoes or the fables. We have included the winged shoes and helmet since this book already includes many winged creatures representing our Redeemer. Earlier in Book I, wings were an unexpected part of a few pictures, Virgo, and the lyre. Also, the Greeks imagined Pegasus, the winged horse as belonging to Perseus, so what need did he really have of winged shoes?

In any case, we find a strong parallel for this picture and the "Commander of the army of the LORD," found in Joshua 5. The parallel is in both the context of this picture and its soldierly presentation.

Read Joshua 5:1-8. What was the first instruction the Lord gave Joshua after the people crossed the Jordon?

We see a parallel between this circumcision of the Israelites before taking the Promised Land and Cassiopeia. In Joshua, the circumcision of all the men is a renewal of the covenant of Abraham, and obedience to that covenant after spending many years in bondage to Egypt (the world) and wandering in the desert. This matches the message in Cassiopeia. She is the bride being made ready for her marriage and to receive the glorious promises the Lamb has for her. She must undergo a circumcision of the heart before being ready to receive the promises.

"In Him you were also circumcised with the circumcision made without hands, by putting off the body of the sins of the flesh, by the circumcision of Christ." Colossians 2:11 [NKJV]

In the same way, the children of Israel, before receiving the Promised Land, had to make themselves ready through circumcision.

> Read Joshua 5:9. After Israel obeyed the command to circumcise every male, what does the Lord say?

Keep this verse in mind because it has an even greater parallel to this sign that we will discuss later.

Here is another parallel to the starry revelation. The reproach Israel formerly suffered as slaves, is rolled away by the Lord. This matches the story of Andromeda, who suffered reproach for her sins, and Cassiopeia who is made perfect by the Lord and her reproach forgotten.

This also parallels Pisces and Cetus. In Scripture, Egypt is often a symbol for the sinful world. Israel was in bondage to that empire and bore both the sorrow and shame of it. However, the Lord told Joshua that on the day they were circumcised, He rolled away the reproach of Egypt from them.

> There is still more. What event happens next in Joshua 5:10?

Amazing! We now find Aries, the lamb, in this section as well. Aries parallels the Passover in both its picture and the time of year it finds its place in the sun.

Now read Joshua 5:13-15. Here is the One who calls Himself, the Commander of the army of the LORD.

> What two clues in the passage tell us this is the Lord Jesus, Himself and not an angel?

We believe this passage helps explain the constellation, Perseus. He should be recognized as the Living Commander of the heavenly army.

- The Egyptians called him, Kar Knem: "he who fights and subdues."
- The Modern name Perseus is Greek.
- The Hebrew name for this sign, Peretz, "the breaker" is the likely origin of the Greek name.

The Hebrew name for the constellation is used in Micah 2:12-13.

> "I will surely assemble all of you, O Jacob,
> I will surely gather the remnant of Israel; …
> They shall make a loud noise because of *so many* people.
> The **one who breaks open** [*peretz*] will come up before them;
> They will break out, pass through the gate, and go out by it;
> Their king will pass before them,

171

With the LORD at their head."
[NKJV emphasis added]

What a beautiful match to this constellation. This is the One who goes ahead and breaks open the way for His people.

In the passage below, underline the phrases that match Perseus, either portrayed in the art above or in what you have learned about him.

"He [the LORD] saw that *there was* no man,
And wondered that *there was* no intercessor;
Therefore His own arm brought salvation for Him;
And His own righteousness it sustained Him.
For He put on righteousness as a breastplate,
And a helmet of salvation on His head;
He put on the garments of vengeance for clothing,
And was clad with zeal as a cloak.
According to *their* deeds, accordingly He will repay,
Fury to His adversaries, recompense to His enemies …
'The Redeemer will come to Zion,
And to those who turn from transgression in Jacob,'
Says the LORD."
Isaiah 59:16-18, 20 [NKJV]

Read Isaiah 63:1-5 where we also find parallels to this constellation. What ideas or descriptions in these verses remind you of it?

The final phrase in verse 4, could be the title of this last chapter of Book II – "The Year of My Redeemed Has Come."

The rest of the names in this constellation:
- The alpha star is Mirfak, "who helps."

"I looked, but *there* was no one to help …
Therefore My own arm brought salvation for Me;"
Isaiah 63:5 [NKJV]

- Al Genib, in the helmet, "who carries away" Read Isaiah 49:25.
- Athik, in the foot, "who breaks"

The ancient names for the head carried by Perseus are:
- Rosh Satan, Hebrew, "the head of the adversary"
- Al Oneh, Arabic, "the subdued"
- Al Ghoul, Arabic, "the evil spirit"

"And I will put enmity
Between you and the woman,
And between your seed and her Seed,
He shall bruise your _____,
And you shall bruise His heel."
Genesis 3:15 [NKJV]

The beta star in Perseus, is in this head and is called: Al Gol, "rolling around."

- The root for the star name, Al Gol is the Hebrew *galal*. It is found twice in Joshua 5:

"Then the LORD said to Joshua, 'This day I have **rolled away** [*galal*] the reproach of Egypt from you.' Therefore the name of the place is called **Gilgal** [*ghilgal* derived from *galal*] to this day." Joshua 5:9 [NKJV emphasis added]

The idea here is that the shame Israel bore as slaves in Egypt, and **more importantly**, the fact that they had forgotten their covenant and conformed to the world (Egypt), had been removed from them. This star, which is tied to the idea of removing our reproach, being found in the head of the adversary reminds us of Revelation 12:10, "… for the accuser of our brethren, who accused them before our God day and night, has been cast down." [NKJV] We see in the severed head, the accuser or reproacher removed.

Day Five –Book II – The Redeemed – Review

It has been quite a journey so far. Before we move into Book III, our final book, let's look back at what we have already seen in Book I:

- The Redeemer is from the seed of the woman and the God/man.
- He made propitiation for us by laying down His own life.
- While in the flesh, He was engaged in a mighty conflict. In it, He was wounded but He mortally wounded His enemies.
- He will return in power.

Now it is your turn. Summarize Book II. (It might be helpful to think of entire chapters as we did above.)

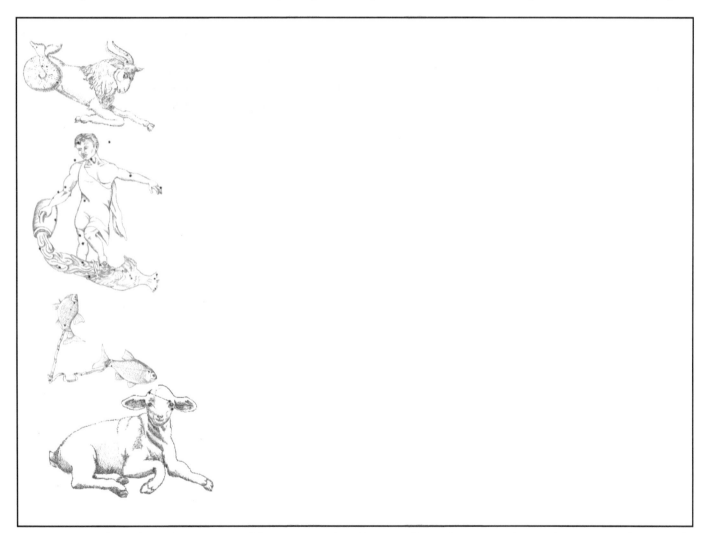

When we reviewed Book I, we noted its constructive themes: Genesis 3:15 – the seed (seen as "the branch," the wounding of the seed, the seed crushing His enemies.) We see Book I as the most preoccupied with the Redeemer as the seed of the woman or as a man, though all three books present Him this way.

Now, let's look at the constructive themes of Book II: water creatures and sky creatures.

List the constellations of water in Book II.

List the constellations of the sky.

A couple could be placed in both: Cygnus, the swan, and Pegasus (he has a stars meaning water, or matching the idea of water; he has "springing forth" in the meaning of his name and possesses wings)

This shows very purposeful construction. Such a careful and detectable construction creates unity for all 16 of the constellations found here. It points to authorship, and a single cohesive idea or story. It also adds to the case we wish to make that truth preceded fable. The Greeks, in their imaginations were only clever enough to link five constellations together. According to their myths, the rest tell completely separate and unrelated stories. In their approach, the whole structure is not recognized and the pictures are just a chaotic collection. It is easy to see the superiority of the truth to their fables.

What was your favorite constellation from this book and why?

We have a final book to discover. Book III contains from the very first chapter events still future. Because of this, it is the most mysterious of the books; but it can also be the most exciting and eye opening. Among its constellations are some of the most well known in the heavens: Ursa Major (containing the Big Dipper), Ursa Minor (the Little Dipper) and Orion. After their study, you will never see any of them the same.

Book III - The Redeemer, His Glory

Lesson Ten - Chapter One – The Coming Judge

Day One –Taurus – The Judge Comes Suddenly

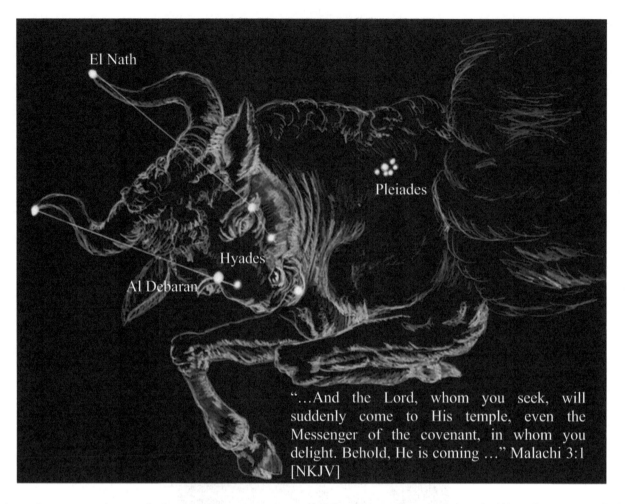

El Nath

Pleiades

Hyades

Al Debaran

"…And the Lord, whom you seek, will suddenly come to His temple, even the Messenger of the covenant, in whom you delight. Behold, He is coming …" Malachi 3:1 [NKJV]

This is a fearsome picture is it not? Dare anyone stand in front of a charging bull? It is a very different picture from the first Chapter of Book I – Virgo – or the first Chapter of Book II – Capricorn (though a bull is also a sacrificial animal). Book III, even from its first sign, will not revisit the First Coming of Christ, of which He says,

> "And if anyone hears My words and does not believe, I do not judge him; for I did not come to judge the world but to save the world." John 12:47 [NKJV]

Instead, we begin with His Second Coming in fury and just judgment of the world.

Describe today's picture.

The hind end of Taurus is never pictured. In fact, the hind end of Taurus is overlapped by Aries.

The stars, by their position in the head and horns, preserve this bull in the act of charging. It is always drawn in this attitude.

Most have probably seen "The Running of the Bulls" in the streets of Spain, where 200 to 300 people are injured annually. Those who are in the bull's path must scatter out of the bull's reach or be thrust through by its horns or trampled under its feet.

Read the below passages describing Christ's return. It contains imagery similar to a stampeding bull. Underline any parallels you find.

"Behold, the day of the LORD comes,
Cruel, with both wrath and fierce anger,
To lay the land desolate;
And He will destroy its sinners from it. …
I will punish the world for *its* evil,
And the wicked for their iniquity;
I will halt the arrogance of the proud,
And will lay low the haughtiness of the terrible.
I will make a mortal more rare than fine gold …
Therefore I will shake the heavens,
And the earth will move out of her place,
In the wrath of the LORD of hosts
And in the day of His fierce anger.
It shall be as the hunted gazelle,
and as a sheep that no man takes up;
Every man will turn to his own people,
And everyone will flee to his own land.
Everyone who is found will be thrust through,
And everyone who is captured will fall by the sword."
Isaiah 13:9, 11-15

"I have trodden the winepress alone,
and from the peoples no one *was* with Me.
For I have trodden them in My anger,
And trampled them in My fury;
Their blood is sprinkled upon My garments,
And I have stained all My robes.
For the day of vengeance is in My heart,
And the year of My redeemed has come. …
I have trodden down the peoples in My anger,
Made them drunk in my fury,
and brought down their strength to the earth."
Isaiah 63:3-4, 6

These verses speak of a God of wrath. He comes suddenly, like a charging bull, so that many do not escape but are trampled in His anger.

179

> Why is He angry? Look back through the verses and list His reasons.

His anger is just.

"Now I saw heaven opened, and behold, a white horse. And He who sat on him *was* called **Faithful** and **True**, and in **righteousness** He judges and wages war." Revelation 19:11 [NKJV emphasis added.]

As you examine the passages below, which attribute of His judgment (the bolded words from Revelation 19:11) explains His wrath?

Isaiah 35:3-4 _____

Romans 1:18-24 _____

Romans 1:25 _____

Colossians 3:5-6 _____

2 Thessalonians 1:4-7 _____ and _____

Revelation 6:9-17 _____

This ancient constellation was called:
- Isis, "who saves" or Apis, "head or chief" by the Egyptians
- Shur, Hebrew, "bull coming, ruling." All the rest are derived from the Hebrew name:
    o Tor, Chaldean
    o Al Thaur, Arabic
    o Tauros, Greek and Taurus, Latin

Star names:
- The alpha star is Al Debaran, Chaldee, "leader, governor"
- The beta star is shared with the last constellation in the set. It is El Nath, Arabic, "the wounded or slain"

Star cluster in the shoulder:
- Pleiades, Greek, "congregation of the judge"
- Succoth, Syriac, "booths"
- Chima, Hebrew, "heaped up, accumulation"

Star cluster in the face:
- Hyades, origin not known, but may be from Hebrew root edah meaning, "congregated." This is a feminine noun.

The names of the constellation, along with the alpha star speak with a united voice. This is a picture of the Leader who comes to judge and rule.

The pair of star clusters, the Pleiades and the Hyades, are both called the congregation of the judge. Notice the name, Succoth, means "booths." Taurus is visible in the night sky during the Jewish festival of Booths. The Greeks corrupted the meaning of these two star clusters making them sisters and daughters of the gods. But they offer no explanation as to why these are placed in the body of the bull. Scripture makes sense of who these clusters represent and why they are placed where they are.

In the following passages, list who these star clusters actually represent and why are they in the body of the bull.

1 Thessalonians 4:14

1 Thessalonians 5:9

Jude 14, 15

Revelation 19:11, 14

They remind us of the two fish, Pisces. That the congregation pair is within the body of the bull is a perfect picture of being in Jesus as 1 Thessalonians 4:14 states. This is not a position earned by merit or great works. You can find yourself a part of the congregation of the judge by being in Jesus.

How does 1 Thessalonians 4:14 say one can be in Jesus?

If you have placed your trust in the death and resurrection of Jesus, you have been placed in the congregation of the Judge. Wow! How exciting. When He returns, He will bring us with Him and we will dwell with Him and Him with us. This is the meaning of the Jewish Feast of Tabernacles or Booths and the ultimate goal of His redemptive plan.

Day Two – Oarion – The Judge Comes As Light

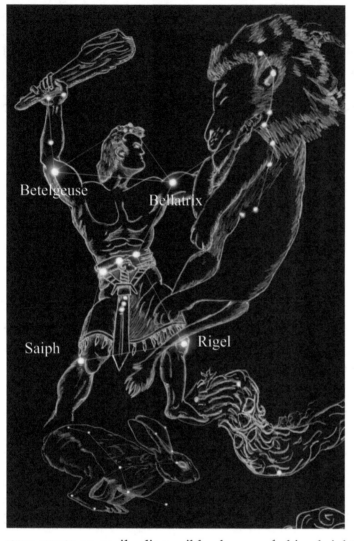

"The glory of the LORD shall be revealed,
And all flesh shall see *it* together;
For the mouth of the LORD has spoken."

Isaiah 40:5 [NKJV]

Today we will look at one of the most well known, conspicuous and beautiful of the 48 constellations. It is among the select few constellations that can be seen by the entire inhabitable world. It is known, today, by the name Orion; thought to mean "giant or hunter." But it was previously spelled Oarion – still bearing its Hebrew root – oar – meaning "light." The name Oarion, according to Frances Rolleston, means, "Coming forth, as light."[1]

The Egyptians called him Ha-ga-t, "this is he who triumphs."

In the Denderah Zodiac, the hieroglyph under Oarion's picture spells, Oar.

The ancient Akkadian name is Ur-ana, "the light of heaven."

His glory as the Light of the world is the prominent meaning of this constellation. Its seven principal stars create an easily discernible shape and shine brightly enough in the sky to be seen even before the sky has gone completely dark. In the written revelation, we find that His coming is likened to light and glory breaking forth. The Hebrew word for light is used in a passage that reminds us of Oarion.

"Arise, shine;
For your light (oar/owr) has come!
And the glory of the LORD is risen upon you.
For behold, the darkness shall cover the earth,
And deep darkness the people;
But the LORD will arise over you,
And His glory will be seen upon you."
Isaiah 60:1-2 [NKJV]

---

[1] Rolleston, Frances. "Mazzaroth by Frances Rolleston." *Philologos*. Web. 30 Aug. 2011. http://philologos.org/__eb-mazzaroth/201.htm

This passage is a perfect fit for the constellation, Oarion. It dominates the winter sky, a time ruled by long hours of darkness especially for those in the upper northern latitudes. How wonderful light is, even the thought of it, in the midst of darkness.

> "The people who sat in darkness have seen a great light, and upon those who sat in the region and shadow of death Light has dawned." Matthew 4:16 [NKJV]

> "Then Jesus spoke to them again, saying, 'I am the light of the world. He who follows Me shall not walk in darkness, but have the light of life.'" John 8:12 [NKJV]

Oarion, in its representation of our Lord as Light has already dawned on the world in His first coming. Yet, the prophecy in Oarion still has a more perfect fulfillment in His second coming. Read Psalm 50:1-3, Habakkuk 3:3-6, and 2 Thessalonians 2:8.

From these, list below the headings how the Coming One is described and what He will do.

His Description	What He Does

Read Joel 2:30-31 and Matthew 24:29. What precedes His coming?

Other passages teaching this truth are Isaiah 13:9-10 and Joel 3:14-15.

The unnatural darkness that precedes His coming, together with the bright light of His coming will certainly be terrifying for those who did not believe in Him. It is a worthwhile exercise to imagine what His coming might be like. An unnatural and deep darkness followed by the breaking forth of His light and glory. Scripture also teaches that this light breaking forth will be at an unnatural time – when the sun is setting.

> "It shall come to pass in that day
> *That* there will be no light;
> The lights will diminish.
> It shall be one day

183

> Which is known to the LORD –
> Neither day nor night.
> But at evening time it shall happen
> *That* it will be light."
> Zechariah 14:6-7 [NKJV]

Will the light of His return be like a great headlight that does not completely eliminate the darkness and can be seen coming from afar or like a flood light that is switched on suddenly and eliminates all darkness immediately? Matthew 24:27 may shed some light on this.

How do you imagine the light of His return?

We have pictured Oarion with part of the next constellation in Chapter One, Eridanus – the river of fire, seen flowing from his left foot. We have also included the hare, Lepus, who is "the enemy" and part of Chapter Two. Though they are separate constellations, these play a part in interpreting the details of Oarion's message. We want you to take a turn at uncovering more of what Oarion declares about the Lord's coming, but first let's look at some more helpful information.

We have several star names for this constellation. Below are the most useful for interpreting the story in this sign:
- The alpha star in the right shoulder, Betelgeuz or Betelgeuse, means "coming of the branch." It is also the tenth brightest star in the sky.
- The beta star in the left leg, Rigel, means "foot that crushes" and is the seventh brightest star.
- Bellatrix, "quickly coming or swiftly destroying"
- Saiph, in the right leg is "bruised" (this is the very word used in Genesis 3:15)

Now take a look at this constellation. We know that the light and glory of His coming are a great part of its message. But there is more.

What else do you see going on in this picture?

Did you notice a similarity between Oarion and Hercules?

Both these sky pictures show every limb occupied. For Oarion:
- The foot with the star signifying bruised is [_____] by the "enemy," the hare; while in Hercules it is lifted as if bruised.
- The left foot, with the star meaning, "foot that crushes" is [_____]. In Hercules the left foot was placed over the head of the dragon.
- The right arm of Oarion holds a raised club, while the left arm holds [_____].

184

- In Hercules the right arm also holds a raised club, the left arm holds the dead lion but also offers the tree of life.

Let's take a look at a few of these details. The prophecy in Genesis 3:15 is pictured by the star name in his right leg (bruised), and the enemies head under the left "foot that crushes." The defeated lion is another picture of the enemy. We found a dead lion in the hands of both Hercules and Oarion. Satan has been compared to a lion in Scripture.

> "Be sober, be vigilant; because your adversary the devil walks about like a roaring lion, seeking whom he may devour." 1 Peter 5:8 [NKJV]

Therefore, Oarion not only speaks to Him coming forth as light, but to His defeating His enemies, signified by the dead lion held in his hand and the hare whose head is under his foot. It also reminds us that this is the One who was bruised. Tomorrow, when we look at the river, Eridanus, we will see that judgment is another message in the sign.

Did you notice the hilt of the sword that hangs from Oarion's belt? Look there now. What is on the hilt?

This is an amazing detail. We are not sure how the ram's head found its way into star atlases dating to the 1800s, but we had to include it in our picture. It reminds us that this glorious conqueror is also the Lamb of God.

Three stars are named in Oarion's belt:
- Mintaka – "the belt"
- Alnilam – "the belt of pearls"
- Alnitak – "the girdle"

These stars lie along the celestial equator (a great circle on the imaginary celestial sphere on the same plane as the earth's equator). This places this constellation in a position in the heavens where it can be seen by the entire inhabitable world.

The belt or girdle of a warrior was his chief ornament and was often highly decorated. Likewise the belt of Oarion is decorated by these lovely stars. The belt served the purposes of girding up a warrior's clothing and holding his sword and in some cases his shield. It was highly prized everywhere in the ancient world. It is among the great gifts given by Jonathon to David (1 Samuel 18:4). It is the first piece of armor we are to take up in Eph. 6. In speaking of the Branch, Isaiah says in 11:5, "Righteousness shall be the belt of His loins, and faithfulness the belt of His waist." [NKJV]

We are going to explore the meaning of His belt further so record the ornaments of His belt in the above verse.

In Job 38:31, God asks Job if he can loose the belt of Oarion. To take a warrior's belt is a terrifically dangerous task against any formidable foe. It is an impossible task against the Light of heaven. Consider the spiritual significance of this question posed to Job.

In the Lord's rhetorical question He has answered the burning question of the righteous sufferer. While we suffer, we are tempted to question either God's righteousness or His faithfulness. Job did.

> "It *is* all one *thing*;
> therefore I say, 'He destroys the blameless and the wicked.'"
> Job 9:22 [NKJV]

Can the Lord's faithfulness and righteousness ever be taken from Him? If righteousness and faithfulness are the ornaments of His belt, we are assured He ever remains faithful and righteous.

Yesterday, we saw that because of these same attributes He will come to deliver His people and take vengeance on His enemies.

Let's conclude today with a look at Isaiah 40:10 which seems to describe what we find in the first three constellations of this chapter.

> Behold, the Lord GOD shall come with a strong *hand*, (*Oarion holding the dead lion*)
> And His arm shall rule for Him; (*Oarion's right arm holding high the club*)
> Behold, His reward *is* with Him, (*Taurus coming with His congregation*)
> And His work [recompense] before Him. (*Eridanus, the river of fire that flows from Oarion's foot*)
> [NKJV]

Day Three – Eridanus – The River of the Judge

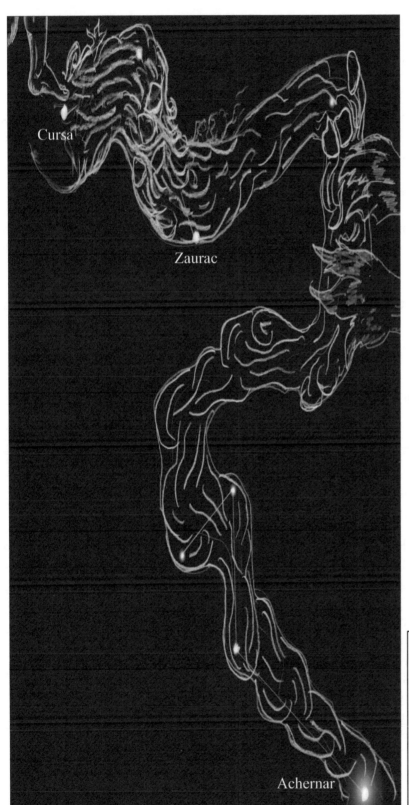

"For behold, the LORD is coming out of His place … The mountains will melt under Him, and the valleys will split like wax before the fire, like waters poured down a steep place."

Micah 1:3-4 [NKJV]

This is a giant constellation, the 7th largest in the sky. As we saw yesterday, it begins under Oarion's "foot that crushes" and travels a crooked coarse down – as though it flows down from heaven to the earth – far into the Southern Hemisphere. Its brightest star is Achernar, which means "end of the river." Achernar is in the deep southern sky and never rises above 33°N, roughly the latitude of Dallas, Texas. Achernar is best seen from the southern hemisphere in November; it is circumpolar below 33°S (Sydney Australia). Likely this star was not a part of the ancient constellation and this river has been lengthened on our modern star atlases to include this star. Our picture is very distorted in its attempt to portray Eridanus' length.

Other stars in the constellation:
- Cursa, the beta star, "bent down"
- Zaurac, Arabic, "flowing"

What do you think might be the message of this great river, which flows from Oarion's foot?

187

This river in the sky is a river of fire, the Judge's fire. Eridanus' connection with fire has been preserved in the ancient myths. "Dionysiaca" by Nonnus, a Greek poet who lived at the end of the fourth or early fifth century, is a long epic poem. Below is an excerpt from his work.

"I will drag down from heaven the fiery Eridanos whose course is among the stars, and bring him back to a new home in the Celtic land: he shall be water again, and the sky shall be bare of the river of fire." [Nonnus, Dionysiaca 23.380][1]

This constellation has three other constellations immediately adjacent to it: Oarion, from whom it flows, Lepus, (the hare) who is being chased into it, and Cetus (the sea monster) the feet of whom the river bends out of its way to envelop. As Scripture teaches, Satan will not escape judgment upon the Lord's return. He will be captured and bound in the great abyss.

Interestingly, in the constellation of Eridanus, astronomers have found an unexplainable "cold spot" hypothesized to be the largest void in the universe. It is called Eridanus Supervoid, and would be 1,000 times larger than any other known void. Astronomers believe the Eridanos Supervoid is 500 million to 1 billion light years in diameter and completely void of galaxies, stars, light, gas, or dark matter. In other words it is a giant hole or abyss in the universe.

Yesterday you read Psalm 50:1-3. The next three verses teach us about Eridanus. Read Psalm 50:3-6. What phrase in these verses describes Eridanus?

How do these verses teach that the Lord's fury is not indiscriminate but is righteous?

Remember we quoted Psalm 50:6 in our second day of study? Now it is easy for us to see that the heavens do declare His righteousness and depict God Himself as judge!

Consuming fire flowing before the Lord at His coming is throughout Scripture. But, today, it is very often overlooked. So, we have included a wealth of Scripture in today's lesson.

As you read the next several passages, highlight or underline every phrase which relates to fire or its effects. (You may also want to circle phrases that remind you of Oarion.)

"A fire goes before Him,
And burns up His enemies round about.
His lightnings light the world;
The earth sees and trembles.
The mountains melt like wax at the presence of the LORD,

---

[1] Atsma, Aaron J. "ERIDANUS : River God of Hyperborea in N. Europe ; Greek Mythology ; Constellation : ERIDANOS." THEOI GREEK MYTHOLOGY, Exploring Mythology & the Greek Gods in Classical Literature & Art. Web. 02 Sept. 2011. http://www.theoi.com/Potamos/PotamosEridanos.html

At the presence of the Lord of the whole earth.
The heavens declare His righteousness,
And all the peoples see His glory."
Psalm 97:3-6 [NKJV]

"Wail, for the day of the LORD *is* at hand!
It will come as destruction from the Almighty.
Therefore all hands will be limp,
Every man's heart will melt,
And they will be afraid.
Pangs and sorrows will take hold of *them*;
They will be in pain as a woman in childbirth;
They will be amazed at one another;
Their faces *will be like* flames."
Isaiah 13:6-8 NKJV]

"Behold, the name of the LORD comes from afar,
Burning *with* His anger,
And *His* burden *is* heavy;
His lips are full of indignation,
And His tongue like a devouring fire.
His breath is like an overflowing stream,
Which reaches up to the neck,
To sift the nations with the sieve of futility …
The LORD will cause His glorious voice to be heard,
And show the descent of His arm,
With the indignation of *His* anger
And the flame of a devouring fire,
With scattering, tempest, and hailstones. …
For Tophet[place of sacrifices by fire to Molech] *was* established of old,
Yes, for the king [Molech – a false god] it is prepared.
He has made *it* deep and large;
Its pyre *is* fire with much wood;
The breath of the LORD, like a stream of brimstone,
Kindles it."
Isaiah 30:27-28, 30, 33 [NKJV]

"For behold, the LORD will come with fire
And with His chariots, like a whirlwind,
To render His anger with fury,
And His rebuke with flames of fire.
For by fire and by His sword
The LORD will judge all flesh;
And the slain of the LORD shall be many."
Isaiah 66:15-16 [NKJV]

"The mountains quake before Him, the hills melt,
And the earth heaves at His presence,

Yes, the world and all who dwell in it.
Who can stand before His indignation?
And who can endure the fierceness of His anger?
His fury is poured out like a fire,
And the rocks are thrown down by Him."
Nahum 1:5-6 [NKJV]

"… when the Lord Jesus is revealed from heaven with His mighty angels, in flaming fire taking vengeance on those who do not know God, and on those who do not obey the Gospel of our Lord Jesus Christ." 2 Thessalonians 1:7b-8 [NKJV]

"But the day of the Lord will come as a thief in the night, in which the heavens will pass away with a great noise, and the elements will melt with fervent heat; both the earth and the works that are in it will be burned up." 2 Peter 3:10 [NKJV]

Scripture is not shy in speaking of the Lord's wrath. His wrath or anger is spoken of 401 times.

In the face of all the terror and fiery fury of His coming, it is appropriate to ask again, "Who can stand before Him and endure the wrath of His anger?" (Nahum 1:6)

Day Four – Auriga – The Great Shepherd

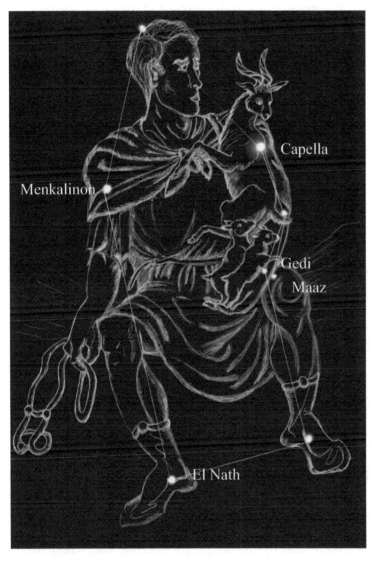

"and to wait for His Son from heaven, whom He raised from the dead, *even* Jesus who delivers us from the wrath to come."

1 Thessalonians 1:10 [NKJV]

This constellation answers the question we've been asking in previous constellations. Who can stand when He appears? Before we delve more deeply into that question and the wonderful message of this sign, let's do the work of first discovering the meanings of the various names within Auriga.

The names for this constellation are:
- Auriga, – /uh-RY-guh/ – Latin, "charioteer"
    - Though the Greeks and Romans have taken this picture to be a coachman or charioteer, they have continued to picture the man carrying a goat and her kids. The incongruity of a charioteer, without chariot or horses, but carrying a she-goat and her kids has somehow escaped them. Likely they adopted the idea of a charioteer by mistaking the bands in the man's hand for a bridle.
    - Frances Rolleston states that the name, Auriga, comes from a Hebrew root – ra-ah – meaning "shepherd." A shepherd is a more appropriate understanding for this man who cradles the goat and her kids.[1]

---

[1] Rolleston, Frances. "Mazzaroth by Frances Rolleston." *Philologos*. Web. 30 Aug. 2011. http://philologos.org/__eb-mazzaroth/201.htm

- Trun, Egyptian, "scepter or power"
    - In the temple of Denderah, this constellation is pictured differently. The man is carrying a scepter rather than goats. However, the scepter has the head of a goat at the top and the symbol of the cross at the bottom. The Egyptians equated the symbol of the cross with life. So even though Auriga is presented differently by the Egyptians, some of the same idea is preserved.

Star names:
- The alpha star is in the body of the goat, Capella, Latin, "she-goat" This star was previously called Alioth, Hebrew, "she-goat" Capella is the sixth brightest star in the sky.
- The beta star is Menkalinon, Chaldean, "band or chain of the goats"
- El Nath, in the right foot, Arabic, "wounded"
- Gedi, Hebrew, "kids"
- Maaz, "flock of goats"

It is clear from the star names why, though it is incongruous to have a goat and her kids in the arms of a charioteer, they have remained there. The names of the stars would not let this be changed. The names, the picture, and the star names communicate, not a charioteer, but a shepherd. Auriga is the Good Shepherd who lays down His life for His sheep.

> "I am the good shepherd. The good shepherd **gives his life** for the sheep." John 10:11 [NKJV emphasis added.]

Which star name reminds us that this is the "Good Shepherd" of John 10:11?

These are not sheep in Auriga; they are decidedly goats; the star names confirm it. Our answer to the difficulty this may pose for some of us who are used to thinking in terms of the judgment described in Matthew 25 – separating the sheep and goats – is answered in Appendix C.

We love this passage in regard to the picture of the bands held by the shepherd, and the star, Menkalinon, that refers to them.

> "I led them with cords of kindness,
> with the bands of love,
> and I became to them as one who eases the yoke on their jaws,
> and I bent down to them and fed them."
> Hosea 11:4 [ESV]

What do you think might be meant by Auriga holding the bands in his right hand, while the goats are unbridled and cradled in his left?

The quote from Hosea was speaking of the Lord leading Israel from Egypt. The redemption of Israel from Egypt is a picture of the ultimate redemption He has planned for all His people. Our past, pictured in Pisces, had us chained to the world just as Israel was in bondage in Egypt. But the Lord has drawn us to Himself with gentle cords of love and removed the yoke from us.

When you look at the whole constellation set together, what do you notice about the gaze of the she-goat and her kids?

Auriga, to be truly appreciated, should be examined in the context of all the constellations of this chapter. The first three constellations contain the fury of His coming – but this final constellation is not terrifying.

We read Isaiah 13:14 in Taurus. Read this passage again.

How would you describe Auriga?

How does Isaiah 13:14 contradict the constellation Auriga?

Read Psalm 37:28. How is the contradiction answered?

For those who do not obey the Gospel of Jesus Christ, the Day will be one of great severity, but for those who belong to Him, kindness and rescue.

Look again at Psalm 50:3-6. What does this passage say He will speak aloud when He comes?

This gathering of His saints is found in both the Old and New Testaments. Find in the Old Testament Zechariah 10:8 and Isaiah 27:12.

In Isaiah, how does the Lord call His saints?

In the New Testament find Matthew 24:30-31 and 1 Thessalonians 4:16-17.

What sounds accompany the calling of the saints?

Auriga expands on an idea already presented in Taurus. In Taurus were two congregations of the judge. In Auriga, the goat and her two kids are gathered safely to His arms.

When do these signs in the heavens and Scripture speak of this happening? (1 Thessalonians 4:16, 17)

Read 2 Thessalonians 1:6-10. Compare the reaction to His appearing of "those who believe" in 2 Thessalonians 1:10 and "the tribes of the earth" in Matthew 24:30.

Auriga is a picture of the severity and lovingkindness of our God.

"Therefore, since we are receiving a kingdom that cannot be shaken, let us have grace, by which we may serve God acceptably with reverence and godly fear. For our God *is* a consuming fire." Hebrews 12:28-29 [NKJV]

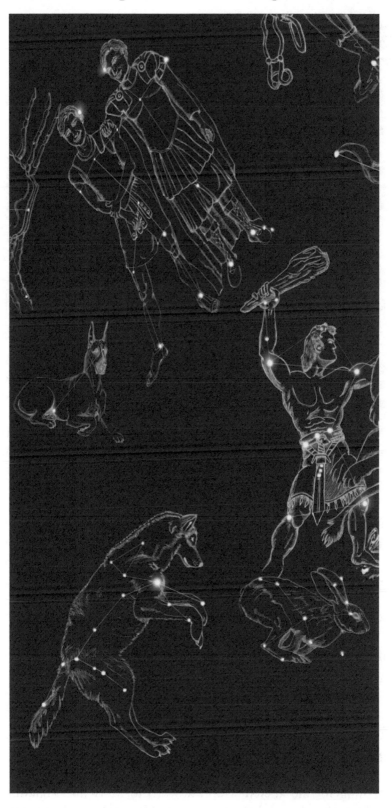

Day One – Gemini--The United

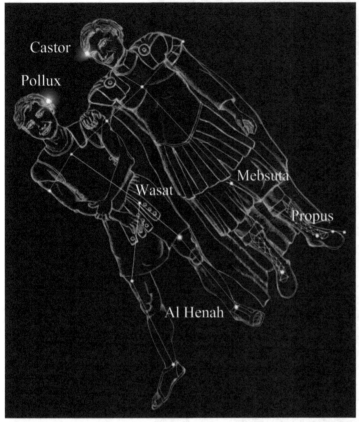

"For if we have been united together in the likeness of His death, certainly we also shall be *in the likeness* of *His* resurrection."
Romans 6:5 [NKJV]

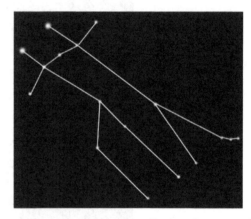

From antiquity, this constellation has consistently been recognized as a sky couple. The brightest stars look like two standing stick figures joined together at the shoulders and are easily seen even through some light pollution. Although there is no question that this constellation represents two people, so much corruption has mingled with it making it difficult to discover its meaning. In fact, we will greatly depart from E.W. Bullinger's interpretation, though it has merit.

The Greek's have thoroughly created confusion around this constellation, even in their drawings of Gemini. They have drawn this constellation as two cupid-like babies. There is nothing in the meaning nor in the tall stick figures their stars make to support such a depiction. I have drawn Gemini from scratch to reflect our understanding of the sign. I reject the more common cupid-like depiction of twin boys.

The antiquity of this constellation is well established though the Greeks claimed to have invented it. Its names are:

- Clusus or Claustrum Hor, Egyptian temple of Denderah, "the place of Him who cometh"
- Pi-Maki, Coptic, "the united"
- Thaumim, Hebrew, "to be doubled"
- Al Tauman, Arabic, "united"

The modern name is Dioskouroi, (mentioned in Acts 28:11) Greek, "sons of Zeus" or Gemini, "the twins"

The Greeks took the meaning for the ancient Hebrew word to be twins. Thaumim is from the root ta'am found in Exodus 26:24, "They [two boards] shall be coupled [ta'am] together at the bottom and at the top by one ring." [NKJV] It is not necessary to understand these two figures in the sky as twins, but more likely as two who are joined or twinned. This distinction is important for interpreting the meaning of Gemini. It also aids us in understanding how the Greek's foolish corruption of the sign began.

All the ancient meanings of this constellation teach that this picture represents a uniting or joining. But of what or who? For answers we look to two ancient star names in each person of Gemini.

- Stars in the man on the left:
  - Wasat, near waist, Arabic, "set or appointed"
  - Al Henah, left foot, Arabic, "hurt or afflicted"
- Stars in the man on the right:
  - Mebsuta, "treading under foot"
  - Propus, in left foot, Hebrew, "the branch spreading"

These ancient star names shall be more heavily relied upon in our interpretation than the modern Greek names for the two brightest stars in Gemini. We do not have ancient names for these two stars, only Greek and their Latin translations. Although we are sure these names have seeds of ancient truth attached to them, we cannot be sure upon what truth the Greeks formed their foolish imaginations.

The beta star in the head of the man on the left has a pair of modern names:
- Pollux, Latin, from the Greek Polydeuces or Polydeukes "many dukes or leaders"
- Hercules, Greek, "the mighty one or coming to labor"

The alpha star in the head of the man on the right has also had a pair of modern names:
- Apollo, Greek, "ruler/judge"
- Castor, Greek. Its root meaning is not known.

After all that explanation, let's summarize what we have.
We have two figures united – this uniting or doubling is the consistent and key idea.
- The figure on the left has these ideas with it: set (very possibly to place in authority), hurt or afflicted, and possibly from Greek – ruler or many leaders
- The figure on the right has these ideas with it: treading under foot, the branch spreading, and most likely from Greek – ruler

Based on this information, can you make any guesses to the meaning of Gemini? Who or what is joined? Remember to consider its context; we have just studied the wrath of His coming and the rescue of those who belong to Him. We are now in the chapter characterized by grace from the pattern established in Book I (Libra) and Book II (Aquarius).

What do you think is the meaning of Gemini?

All the star names can apply to our Savior: for the one on the left – He is set or appointed as ruler and was afflicted in His first coming; for the one on the right – He shall tread under foot, He is the branch, His Kingdom shall spread and He is the ruler. This is E.W. Bullinger's interpretation of the constellation; His two-fold nature – God and man, His two fold work – suffering and glory and His two fold coming – humiliation and triumph. We favor a different interpretation we believe better advances the story, better represents the idea "united" and better matches the theme of grace.

We find a "uniting" in the following passages.

In Romans 6:5, how are we are united with Christ in two ways?

In Romans 8:15-18, what are we called?

What do you think this means practically speaking?

In Hebrews 2:10-12, who are all from one?

The Lord Jesus says He is not ashamed to call us _____!

What an amazing grace! This is what we have sought to depict in our picture of Gemini: the "Captain of our salvation," as He is called in Hebrews, shares His reward and inheritance with us. He has reached out His right hand to us and made us "joint heirs" together with Him. And though we are undeserving, He has sanctified us and is not ashamed to call us His brothers.

This grace was introduced in Corona – the final constellation of Libra. In Gemini, we see an expansion on its theme.

Consequently, star names that can apply to Christ, can also apply to us – the co-heirs.

Al Henah, "hurt or afflicted," in the left foot of the left twin would then be understood better in the light of Romans 8:15-18 and Matthew 5:10-12.

What is promised to the co-heirs who suffer for and or with Christ?

In Revelation 20:4 a more specific reward is described for what specific affliction?

We also believe that the placement of the star, "hurt or afflicted," in the left foot of the man means this is not the Redeemer. In every other depiction of the Branch, the star bearing the theme bruised or wounded is in the **right** foot. (See Centaurus, Ophiucus, Hercules, Oarion, and Auriga.)

According to Psalm 78:54, He acquired His inheritance with His right side (even possibly His right thigh)

"And He brought them to His holy border,
This mountain *which* His right hand [this word can be translated for any part of the right side]
had acquired."
[NKJV]

The other star in the left "twin" – Wasat, which means [   ] we find several parallel passages.

"To him who overcomes I will grant to sit with Me on My throne, as I also overcame and sat down with My Father on His throne." Revelation 3:21 [NKJV]

"This is a faithful saying:

'For if we died with *Him*,
We shall also live with *Him*.
If we endure,
We shall also reign with *Him*.
If we deny *Him*,
He will also deny us,
If we are faithless,
He remains faithful;
He cannot deny Himself.'"
2 Timothy 2:11-13 [NKJV]

---

1 Corinthians 6:2 adds another concept to being set up to reign in the shared inheritance we have with Him. What is it?

It is also interesting that the Greek star name in this person's head, Pollux, means "many dukes." This fits our interpretation very well. As co-heirs with Christ, Pollux would represent many leaders.

Finally, it is obvious that we have interpreted the man on the right to be a representation of the Captain of our salvation in His return to reign. The star "Mebsuta," "treading under foot" in His left foot is consistent with what He did and will do. It is also consistent with the previous star pictures, which always depict the enemy tread down under the left foot of the Branch.

Propus, "the branch spreading" is fulfilled in the following verses. Explain how this occurs for each verse.

- Isaiah 53:10-11

- Zechariah 6:12-13

- Hebrews 2:10

We hope this constellation has been a reminder to you of the wonderful grace of our Lord Jesus Christ. We also hope you are filled with awe at this grace He has reserved for His brethren.

"Behold what manner of love the Father has bestowed on us, that we should be called the children of God! Therefore the world does not know us, because it did not know Him. Beloved, now we are children of God; and it has not yet been revealed what we shall be, but we know that when He is revealed, we shall be like Him, for we shall see Him as He is. And everyone who has this hope in Him purifies himself, just as He is pure." 1 John 3:1-3 [NKJV]

Day Two – Lepus – The Enemy Confounded

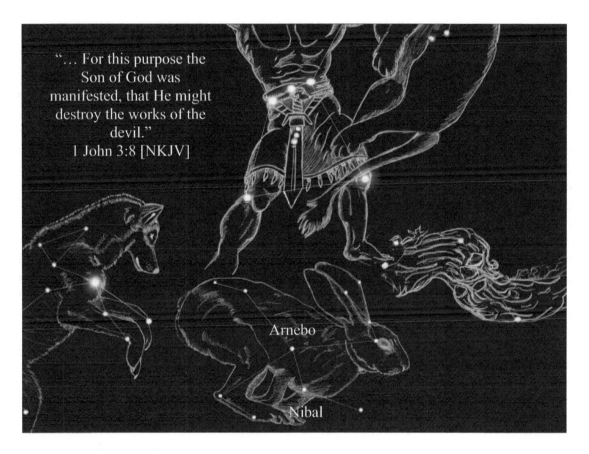

Do not be taken in by this cute furry creature. Its ancient names and star names speak together with a united voice.

The Zodiac in the Egyptian Temple Denderah, pictures instead of a hare, a snake underneath a bird of prey in the process of devouring it. Its name is Bashti-beki, "confounded" and "failing."

- The Persian planisphere also has a snake.
- Latin, Lepus, "hare"
- Greek, Lagos, "hare" the name has a root meaning "slack or languid"

The star names:
- Arnebo, the alpha star is Hebrew, "enemy of Him that cometh" or
  - Arnebeth, Arabic, means the same as the Hebrew
- Nibal, Hebrew, "fool, perverse"
- Rakis (not identified), Arabic, "the bound [with a chain]"
- Sugia, (not identified) "the deceiver"[1]

---

[1] These are names identified by Rolleston, but can't be found on any star maps. This is why they are not identified in the picture. Rolleston, Frances. "Mazzaroth by Frances Rolleston." *Philologos*. Web. 30 Aug. 2011. http://philologos.org/__eb-mazzaroth/202.htm

> Describe the action relating to the hare in the picture and what/who you think this hare represents.

The hare is surrounded by pictures depicting defeat for the great adversary, the dead lion, and the bound sea monster, Cetus. It is under the foot of Oarion, chased by the Prince of Princes (the wolf) and headed toward the fiery river.

Most Americans today have a fond attachment to the hare's cousin, the rabbit. This may make it a difficult leap for some to imagine a rabbit-like creature as something sinister. This has not been traditionally so. Hares have been viewed in widely divergent cultures around the world as tricksters, lazy and pests. They are an unclean animal according to Jewish Law and specifically forbidden as food in Deuteronomy 14:7. A hare representing something undesirable was natural for Jews and many other cultures. Many people today do not have experience with wild rabbits or hares; most only know the domesticated rabbits in pet stores. But, if you have every tried to garden or grow plants in a rural setting where wild rabbits or hares wreak havoc on plants, your fondness for them will quickly adjust itself to one more in sync with the traditional view. Lepus, the hare, represents the deceptive works of folly and false teaching. These works, though evil, may also sometimes appear outwardly attractive. This makes the hare a perfect representation.

You may have noticed a variation of the spelling Nabal in the star names listed above. He is an infamous character found in 1 Samuel 25 whose actions and reputation among all who knew him testified:

> "… he is such a son of Belial [worthlessness, wickedness, destruction] that a man cannot speak to him." 1 Samuel 25:17 [KJV]

> "Please, let not my lord regard this scoundrel Nabal. For as his name *is*, so *is* he: Nabal [folly] *is* his name, and folly *is* with him!" 1 Samuel 25:25 [NKJV]

You can read his story, but his foolish actions recorded in 1 Samuel were:
- He scorned David, the Lord's anointed
- He scorned the protection David had given to his shepherds
- He accused David of wrong doing mocking David's need
- He denied David and his servants their just recompense for aid, meanwhile lavishly entertaining others
- He engaged in revelry and became exceedingly drunk not knowing the danger he had made for himself and his household.

Folly in Scripture is linked to perverseness, laziness, and wickedness. All traits most cultures attributed to the hare. We believe the Nabal of 1 Samuel 25 is a picture paralleling in part this starry picture. The hare represents the fool and especially the false prophets. These are called sons of destruction whose works will be confounded and fail as the ancient name, Bashti-beki, suggests. Nabal was struck by the Lord and died 10 days after these foolish actions.

In Jude and Second Peter are warnings against false teachers. There are many parallels in these passages to either Lepus, with its star names, or Nabal's actions. Read 2 Peter 2:1-3, 12-17 and Jude 4, 8, 10, 14-19. Write below any similarities to Lepus (words connected to Lepus: confounded, enemy, fool, perverse, bound, deceiver) or Nabal (look at the list of his actions on the previous page).

Lepus	Nabal

Remember that Eridanus contains a Supervoid 1 billion light years in diameter, into which this hare in the sky is chased. We are told in 2 Peter 2:17, that this awaits those represented by Lepus, "… for whom is reserved the blackness of darkness forever." 2 Peter 2:17 [NKJV]

The same idea is found Zechariah 13:2 and Jeremiah 23:11-15.

Judgment on false teachers belongs in this Chapter, which speaks of the Messiah's Kingdom because:
1. It is God's grace that He separates us from these false teachers (2 Peter 2:9).
2. He has promised that during His reign lies will not enter His City

"But there shall by no means enter it [New Jerusalem] anything that defiles, or causes an abomination or a lie, but only those who are written in the Lamb's Book of Life." Revelation 21:27 [NKJV]

"Blessed are those who do His commandments, that they may have the right to the tree of life, and may enter through the gates into the city. But outside are dogs and sorcerers and sexually immoral and murderers and idolaters, and whoever loves and practices a lie." Revelation 22:14-15 [NKJV]

The Prince of princes has chased away and guarded against all these.

"Now to Him who is able to keep you from stumbling,
And to present *you* faultless
Before the presence of His glory with exceeding joy,
To God our Savior,
Who alone is wise,
Be glory and majesty,
Dominion and power,
Both now and forever.
Amen."

Jude 24-25[NKJV]

Day Three – Canis Major – The Coming Prince of Peace, The First

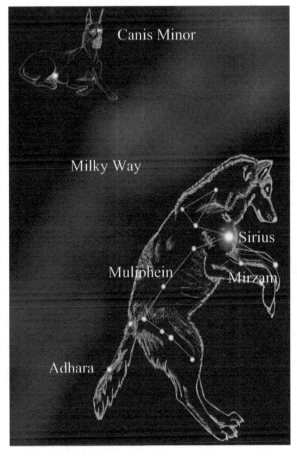

"The LORD will give strength to His people;
The LORD will bless His people with peace."

Psalm 29:11 [NKJV]

The larger of the two final constellations of Gemini is called, Canis [dog] Major because it is preeminent in size and glory compared to its companion, Canis Minor. Both are pictured here. It is the third sub-constellation of Gemini and our subject today.

Canis Major contains the brightest star in all the heavens. Its name is Sirius and has been used interchangeably as the name of the star and the constellation. The meaning of the name, Sirius, is greatly misunderstood. We are confident it is derived from the Hebrew word for prince, sars. This matches the ancient Akkadian name for the same star, Kasista, "leader" and the other names connected to this constellation. As we move forward, we will call this constellation Sirius, because it more accurately reflects its meaning and we do not believe this constellation should be a dog at all.

Other names for this constellation are:
- Al Shira Al Jemeniya, Arabic, "prince of the right hand"
- Apis, Egyptian, "head"

Other star names are:
- Mirzam, "prince or ruler"
- Muliphen, "leader or chief."
- Adhara, meaning "the glorious"

Other names connected to this constellation are:
- Zeeb, the Persian name for this sign, meaning "wolf" We believe a wolf belongs here, not a dog: first, because the ancient Persian name means wolf and, second, because a wolf better represents the idea of a prince than does a dog. Myths that make the two constellations, Canis Major and Canis Minor, the hunting dogs of Oarion have caused the current corruption, which has replaced the wolf with a dog.

The constellation is always drawn in the act of pouncing upon Lepus, the hare. Even the shape of Sirius' stars suggests this idea.

Read Isaiah 9:3-7. The Messiah as Prince of Peace is familiar. What examples of this truth does this passage give?

Scripture has much to say about this Prince of peace that is less familiar than Isaiah 9:6. Read Isaiah 48:22. How is this idea reflected within the four constellations of Gemini?

This is an important concept, and ignored by the world. The world seeks peace but cannot find it. Read Luke 19:41-42. Even Jerusalem, who had the Word of God and was visited by the Prince of peace, did not know the things that make for peace. Recently, we saw a picture of thousands of Buddhists meditating together for peace. But peace is not a fluffy, happy notion achieved just in earnestly desiring it. Scripture teaches that peace is not achieved without other virtues. This is why when Jesus came the first time He said:

> "Do not think that I came to bring peace on earth. I did not come to bring peace but a sword. For I have come to set a man against his father, a daughter against her mother, and a daughter-in-law against her mother-in-law." Matthew 10:34 [NKJV]

Read the following passages and note what is joined with peace:

Psalm 85:10

Isaiah 32:17

Isaiah 60:17

Romans 14:17

Hebrews 7:2 – This is the translation of the name Melchizedek, King of Salem[Jerusalem] – a type of Christ in the Old Testament. What do these verses say is the translation of his name?

We must conclude that there is no peace without righteousness. Sirius, the Prince, must guard against and chase away the wicked as a necessity for peace.

Read 1 John 3:10-13. How do we know that the world does not desire true peace from these verses?

This is why Jesus said, in His first coming, He did not come to bring peace on earth. The world and sometimes the Lord's own people do not love what brings true peace. Those who seek after righteousness will find division even in their own family.

However, when we become His, His kingdom has already come in our hearts, and in our hearts He reigns as the Prince of peace right now. (Luke 17:20-21) He did not come to bring "peace **on earth**," but He did come to bring peace on an individual basis in the present not just the future.

> "Peace I leave with you, My peace I give to you; not as the world gives do I give to you. Let not your heart be troubled, neither let it be afraid." John 14:27 [NKJV]

Read Romans 5:1. Between what two parties is peace established?

Philippians 4:6-7. This passage speaks of peace from _____ .

This verse has the word guard in it, which is an occupation of the constellation Sirius. Sirius guards the Holy City in Messiah's kingdom. In this verse, what is guarded?

Ephesians 4:1-6. Between who is peace established?

We can revel in this present reality and still look forward to a future fulfillment. When the Lord comes, He will establish **peace on earth**, first by destroying the wicked from His kingdom.

From the following passages, note between who or what peace will be established by the Prince of peace.

Ezekiel 37:25-27

Ezekiel 34:25 and Isaiah 65:25

Micah 4:3-4 and Zechariah 9:10

Oh, come quickly Lord! For we long for Your peace on the earth.

> "Behold, a king will reign in righteousness,
> And princes will rule with justice. …
> Then justice will dwell in the wilderness,
> And righteousness remain in the fruitful field.
> The work of righteousness will be peace,
> And the effect of righteousness, quietness and assurance forever.
> My people will dwell in a peaceful habitation,
> In secure dwellings, and in quiet resting places …
> Isaiah 32:1, 16-18 [NKJV]

We will explore tomorrow the companion to this Prince. Since they are companions, some of what you have studied today will be relied upon tomorrow.

Day Four – Canis Minor – The Coming Redeemer, The Last

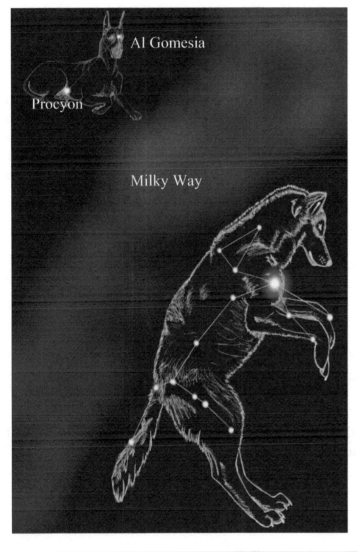

"Thus says the LORD, the King of Israel,
And his Redeemer, the LORD of hosts,
'I *am* the First and I *am* the Last; Besides Me *there is* no God.'"

Isaiah 44:6

The above verse's opening describes the Lord occupying two offices, what are they?

This is what we believe is pictured in the final two constellations of Gemini: The Lord as King/Prince, and the Lord as Redeemer.

Yesterday, we looked at Sirius/Canis Major.

What attributes of this constellation have caused it to be known as Canis Major (or preeminent compared to its companion?

The smaller constellation, Canis Minor, is among the smallest in the sky, only containing 14 stars. Its brightest star, Procyon, is another important star ranking eighth brightest among the heavens. The meaning and picture for this constellation have been almost completely lost. We do not believe a dog was anciently pictured here; we are certain that the modern small breed of dog, shown in pictures of this constellation, is a huge mistake. We think a lamb may have been here – but without the written revelation, who could see a lamb as a companion to a wolf?

Here is what has been preserved:

- The Egyptians called it Sebak, "conquering, victorious"
- The Arabs called it, Al Gomeyra, "who completes and perfects"
- The star Al Gomeisa means, "bearing for others or burdened"

None of these ideas are represented in a small lap dog as it is commonly depicted. The common picture of a small dog is the result of the modern name Canis Minor – small dog and not its ancient meaning.

Canis Minor's most important star, Procyon is believed by modern astronomers to come to us from two Greek words, pro, "before" and kuon, "dog." We do not think so. We believe this is another instance of the Greeks taking an existing Eastern name and substituting their own Greek word in its place on the basis of its sound rather than its meaning. Frances Rolleston asserts that the Hebrew word paraq, "to break away or redeem" is the origin of the modern name Procyon.[1] This Hebrew word is in step with the rest of the preserved names.

Together, what little we have preserved in the sign, points to it representing the Lord as our Redeemer.

In the verse beside the picture, the Lord is first described as King and Redeemer – this parallels the two constellations, Sirius and Procyon. He then says, "I am the First and the Last." The word translated "first" can mean first not only in time, but also in location and rank. The word translated "last" is more specific, meaning last in time and location.

Read a parallel passage, Revelation 22:13. Here the Greek word translated, first, can mean, as the Hebrew, first in time, location and rank; and the Greek word translated, last, also can mean last in time, location and rank.

Regarding the wolf constellation and its companion, the dog, describe how these pictures portray the idea of first and last in all its implied meanings from Revelation 22:13.

When the Lord describes Himself as the "First and the Last," He is speaking of His eternal nature. But, we think we can also draw from this that He is preeminent as King – First in rank. And has made Himself to occupy also a place of lowliness by becoming a servant to all in order to be our Redeemer – becoming last in rank. That is incredible beyond our ability to fathom, God as Last?

Read Matthew 20:25-28. Jesus provided the example of being last. What impact does that have on our lives?

---

[1] Rolleston, Frances. "Mazzaroth by Frances Rolleston." *Philologos*. Web. 30 Aug. 2011. http://philologos.org/__eb-mazzaroth/202.htm

Here is an interesting verse:

> "For I know *that* my Redeemer lives,
> And He shall stand at last on the earth;
> Job 19:25 [NKJV]

It is especially interesting because the translators translated the verse in concert with the most common understanding of the Lord being the First and the Last – that He is First and Last in relation to time. But, this could also read, "stand **as** last on the earth." This would be in concert with another meaning for First and Last – that of rank.

It is clear that the Lord as Prince/King has a companion work as Redeemer. But hasn't His work as Redeemer been finished? So why is this idea repeated now as a companion to His role as ruler?

What work of redemption is still left?

We believe the message in the smaller constellation is illustrated in the story of Ruth. Read Ruth 1:1-5.

What nationality is Ruth? What has she become by verse 5?

Being a Moabite made her an outcast, an alien, and even an enemy as she returned with her mother-in-law to Israel. As a widow in an alien country, she was without hope. Keep your place in Ruth and read Ephesians 2:11-13. These verses demonstrate the predicament faced by all Gentiles even after the time of Christ; a predicament that was very similar to that of Ruth's.

Read Ruth 2:1. Who was Boaz?

This noble, Boaz, "saved" Ruth by allowing her to glean safely in his fields. This gave her the ability to obtain food for herself and her mother-in-law. This was their most pressing and basic need.

How is this a picture of what our Redeemer has done?

But here is the main point. Not only did Boaz provide a means for Ruth's sustenance, he ultimately joined himself to her in marriage, removing her shame as a foreigner and widow and elevating her to the place of a noble's wife. She has been elevated so far she is one of three women, mentioned by name, in the genealogy of Christ (Matthew 1:5).

In the same way, this small constellation teaches that not only has our most pressing need been met by our Redeemer – our need for salvation – but He has joined Himself to us and elevated our status and given us a place together with Him in His kingdom. Turn back to Ephesians, chapter 2 and read verses 13-19.

List all that is gained through Christ's redemptive work.

How inextricably united are these two constellations; we cannot talk of the work of the Redeemer without also seeing the Prince of peace. These are surely companions.

During our first day in Gemini, we saw that the Lord has elevated us to the status of co-heirs with Him. How wonderfully that theme is expanded here.

Before concluding we want to share one more thing. The Hebrew word, checed, is translated using various English words: mercy, kindness, loving-kindness, and goodness among them. It occurs 246 times in the Old Testament. We believe this word sums up the message in the companions, Prince and Redeemer. Michael Card, singer, songwriter and Bible teacher, defines checed this way, "The one from whom I can expect nothing, gives me everything."[2]

"Your mercy [checed], O LORD, *is* in the heavens;
Your faithfulness *reaches* to the clouds.
Your righteousness *is* like the great mountains,
Your judgments *are* a great deep;
O LORD, You preserve man and beast.
How precious *is* Your loving-kindness [checed], O God!
Therefore the children of men put their trust under the shadow of Your wings. They are
abundantly satisfied with the fullness of Your house,
And You give them drink from the river of Your pleasures.
For with You *is* the fountain of life;
In Your light we see light.
Oh, continue Your loving-kindness [checed] to those who know You,
And Your righteousness to the upright in heart."
Psalm 36:5-10 [NKJV]

---

[2] Card, Michael. "Michael Card: Lamenting Is Worship! Part 4 - YouTube." YouTube - Broadcast Yourself. 18 Feb. 2009. Web. 03 Sept. 2011. http://www.youtube.com/watch?v=Ou17lPhzdAI

Day One – Cancer--The Possession Held Fast

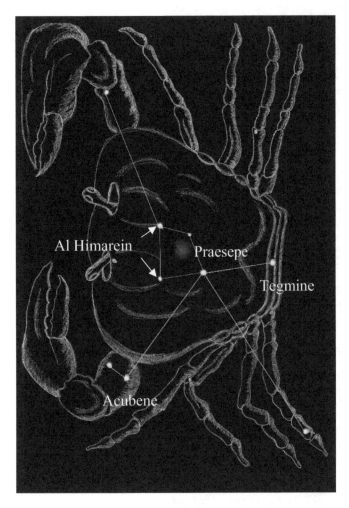

"For the LORD loves justice,
And does not forsake His saints;
They are preserved forever …"

Psalm 37:28 [NKJV]

Turn to John chapter 10. Read verses 7-15 and 26-30. List the actions of the Good Shepherd.

This is the message of the giant sky crab. Any handler of live crabs will attest to the power and tenacity of those claws. But this fearsome trait is, for us, a great comfort. The power and tenacity of those great claws is a picture of how we are kept by our God.

The ancient name of the sign, Sartan – Hebrew – "who holds," is easily traced in the Arabic name Al Sartan and the Syriac name Sartano. The star in the tail, Tegmine, means "holding" as well.

Which verses in the above passage match this idea?

Crabs do not willingly release anything their claws have seized. The harder one tries to free himself from their grip, the tighter their grip becomes. Even though we are a great deal larger and stronger than the largest crab, freeing ourselves from the grip of their claws is extremely difficult. What a picture of our Lord's firm hold on us. And since He is greater than all, no one can take us from His hands.

216

"Who shall separate us from the love of Christ? *Shall* tribulation, or distress, or persecution, or famine, or nakedness, or peril or sword? … Yet in all these things we are more than conquerors through Him who loved us. For I am persuaded that neither death nor life, nor angels nor principalities nor powers, nor things present nor things to come, nor height nor depth, nor any other created thing, shall be able to separate us from the love of God which is in Christ Jesus our Lord." Romans 8:35, 37-39 [NKJV]

How tenaciously we are held by Him. For each of the following verses that speak to this theme, list the additional comforts contained in them.

Isaiah 41:13

Psalm 37:22-24

Psalm 73:23-24

Psalm 94:17-19

The alpha star of Cancer is in the lower claw, Acubene – Hebrew – and means, "the sheltering or hiding place"

"The LORD *is* good,
A stronghold in the day of trouble;
And He knows those who trust in Him."
Nahum 1:7 [NKJV]

Read Nahum 1:1-7 and describe the context of this sheltering.

"Behold, a king will reign in righteousness,
And princes will rule with justice.
A man will be as a hiding place from the wind,
And a cover from the tempest,
As rivers of water in a dry place,
As the shadow of a great rock in a weary land."
Isaiah 32:1-2 [NKJV]

How does this passage speak of our last constellation Gemini?

"A man will be as a hiding place" who is this man?

The Lord is our shelter today to aid and comfort in troubled times. In our present reality, we are not guaranteed freedom from troubles. During His reign, He will shelter His own **from all conflict or trouble,** from wind and tempest, and famine.

The ancient Egyptians and Hindus did not have a crab here, but a scarab beetle. However, there is a connection with this scarab beetle and the crab. The Egyptian hieroglyph has the phonetic value (k)hpr, the adopted pronunciation is Kheper with vowels added. This is also the name of the god associated with the scarab. It is very possible that our English word keeper descends from this god's name. If so, there is a great connection of concepts; He holds us, He keeps us.

> "Now to Him who is able to **keep you** from stumbling,
> And to present *you* faultless
> Before the presence of His glory with exceeding joy."
> Jude 24 [NKJV emphasis added]

Read Psalm 121 and list all the ways you are kept by Him.

Also in Psalm 121, list the attributes of our Keeper by which His preservation is sure.

We noticed a repeated idea in all these passages discussing His holding and keeping us – He keeps our feet from stumbling or slipping.

What do you think this metaphor means? For more insight see the context of Jude 24 and Psalm 73:1-3.

The constellation Cancer does not speak only of Him who holds, though He is the subject of this constellation. It speaks, through the star names, of what or who He holds. A pair of stars in the body is called

218

Al Himarein, Arabic, "the kids or lambs," a common metaphor for His people. We saw this in the first passage of today's lesson.

Additionally, a star cluster in the very center of Cancer, which to the naked eye appears as a mist or cloud, is called Praesepe, commonly understood to mean "manger." But Frances Rolleston says it means "a multitude, offspring." Frances Rolleston's theory is consistent with the Praesepe star cluster; it is multitude of stars.[1] The common name for this cluster of stars is the Beehive Cluster. Either way these names together agree with the ancient Coptic name for Cancer, Klaria, "the cattle-folds."

Tomorrow we will study the next sub-constellations of Cancer, the Greater and Lesser Flock. This is evidence of a narrative. In Cancer, the stars speak of the Keeper of the flocks or cattle. These flocks are then expanded in the first and second sub-constellations of the set.

Though Cancer is a dimly lit constellation, its significant and consistent truth shines brightly from antiquity. It speaks to the firmness and surety of our hope. Our lives, our futures, and our eternal destiny do not rest in our abilities but in Him who is able to keep us for the day of salvation. What a glorious message.

> "For all people walk each in the name of his god,
> But we will walk in the name of the LORD our God
> Forever and ever."
> Micah 4:5 [NKJV]

---

[1] Rolleston, Frances. "Mazzaroth by Frances Rolleston." *Philologos*. Web. 30 Aug. 2011. http://philologos.org/__eb-mazzaroth/202.htm

Day Two – Ursa Minor and Major – His Flocks Led by Their Shepherd

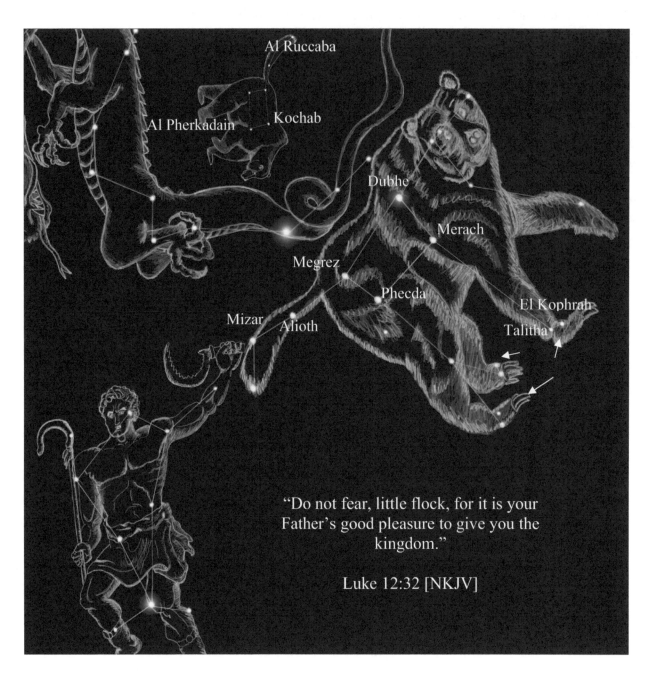

"Do not fear, little flock, for it is your Father's good pleasure to give you the kingdom."

Luke 12:32 [NKJV]

The first two sub-constellations of Cancer are the Greater and Lesser Bears. There is a great deal of controversy over what symbols originally occupied their places in the sky. It is possible they were bears, but their names and meanings appear to have nothing to do with bears at all. What is not uncertain, is that these two constellations represent a pair; one being greater in size than the other; in fact Ursa Major is the fourth largest of the original 48 and Ursa Minor is the fourth smallest. Amazingly, both constellations' primary stars are the same in number, seven, and are virtually the same shape. In addition, the star names in each share similar themes. We are fortunate to have so many names preserved. All these elements have helped preserve the idea that these two represent a pair. We have included in this picture the constellations immediately adjacent to the bears because one, at least, shares in the story. We are uncertain what share the dragon's tail plays, but it simply could not be ignored as we put this picture together.

Before we share the exciting message of these constellations, we are compelled to discuss just a bit of the mystery of these symbols. The Greater Bear, Ursa Major, may be the most well known of all the constellations in the sky. Its seven main stars have shared many widely divergent symbols: the great ladle or Big Dipper; the plough or wagon called Charles Wain; the bier and following mourners; the Seven Sisters or Seven Sages. Yet with all these variations, it has been recognized almost universally as a she-bear (with Ursa Minor recognized as a smaller bear). Even the North American Indian tribes, who did not divide the sky into constellations, recognized these stars as bears.

Included in the mystery is the strange tail. No bear ever had such a tail. We believe the confusion likely began over the phonetic similarities of two Hebrew words: *dohver*, "a fold" and *dohv* "a bear." (The Hebrew spelling of these two words is very different but they carry similar phonetic sounds.) A similar mistake could have come from the Arabic word *dubah* for "cattle" and *dub*, "bear." These two ancient words: *dohver* "a fold" and *dubah*, "cattle" are the origins of the name for the brightest star in these two bears, Dubhe, "a herd of animals." And it is a herd of animals that both are meant to represent, the Lesser and the Greater Flock.

Remember when we started we looked at the constellations mentioned in Job? Turn back to a verse we looked at in the very first week, Job 9:9.

What is the first constellation listed in your Bible in this verse?

The Hebrew word is Ash and is the ancient name for the Greater Flock, its precise meaning is uncertain. The Gesenius' Lexicon has "daughters of the bier" for its meaning. Rolleston defines its meaning more broadly, "the assembled."[1] The Arabs called it Al Naish, which carries the same meaning as the Hebrew. Again, it does not mean bear.

These pictures of long-tailed bears do not communicate the truth as indicated by the star names. To interpret the meaning of these constellations, we must rely on the star names. These names clearly present a single idea:
- Dubhe – the brightest star of both constellations – Arabic, "herd of animals or flock"
- Merach, "the flock or purchased"
- Alioth, "the she-goat" as in Auriga
- Al Cor – a small star, not marked above, very near Mizar – "the lamb"

In the Lesser Flock:
- Al Pherkadain, "the calves or young"

The above star names all speak directly of a flock or herd of animals. The rest of the stars can be applied to that theme and we will explain them as we come to them in the study.

---

[1]Rolleston, Frances. "Mazzaroth by Frances Rolleston." *Philologos*. Web. 30 Aug. 2011, http://philologos.org/__eb-mazzaroth/202.htm#cancer

This is the flock referenced in the body of Cancer, who is held and guarded by the Good Shepherd.

"Know that the LORD, He *is* God;
It is He *who* has made us, and not we ourselves;
We are His people and the sheep of His pasture."
Psalm 100:3 [NKJV]

There is such good news for the members of His flock. From the verses below, list the promises to the flock found in each.

Jeremiah 23:3-4

Jeremiah 31:10-14

Ezekiel 34:24-31

Star Names whose message is also found in the above passages:
- Al Kaid, "the assembly"
- Talitha, "daughters of the assembly"
- Phecda, "visited, guarded or numbered"
- El Kophrah, "protected, covered"

Two star names have the idea of separated in them:
- Mizar, "separate or small"
- Megrez, "separated"

How does the concept, separated, match what we already know about His flock? (Matthew 25:32)

We have an Arabic name for the three pairs of stars in the three downward feet of Ursa Major:
- Kafzah al Thiba, "springs/leaps of the gazelle."
- The pair in the right hind leg is Alula, "the first leap," the pair in left hind leg, Tania, "the second leap," the pair in the right foreleg is "the third leap" marked by Talitha and El Kophrah.

The Arabs saw these stars as marking the place where the feet of a leaping gazelle touched ground. We think the direction of the leaps represents a misunderstanding and should be in the opposite direction.

This concept is also matched well in Scripture.

"The LORD God is my strength;
He will make my feet like deer's *feet*,
And He will make me walk on high hills."
Habakkuk 3:19 [NKJV]

"Then the lame shall leap like a deer,
And the tongue of the dumb sing.
For waters shall burst forth in the wilderness,
And streams in the desert."
Isaiah 35:6 [NKJV]

How beautiful to include these concepts in the night sky. These are an expression of the joy and vitality all His people will enjoy when He leads us to His kingdom.

Two more verses well suited to Kafzah al Thiba use another sense of the word "leap or spring." Look them up and describe how they can also match this name.

Isaiah 61:11

Isaiah 44:3-5

The two final star names are both in Ursa Minor:
- Kochab, "waiting Him who cometh"
- Al Ruccaba, "the turned on or ridden on"

Al Ruccaba is the North Pole star. It is arguably the most important star in the sky. The meaning of its name, "turned on or ridden on" makes sense as the North Pole star since it remains almost stationary while all the rest of the stars in the heavens turn upon it. However, this was not the case five and six thousand years ago, when we believe the ancient prophets likely received its name. Possibly, it was simply prophetic of its future position, or it possibly has spiritual significance as well. If it is the latter, we have not discovered with surety its spiritual application.

Do you have an idea regarding its spiritual meaning?

We think this may be a reference to God's covenant promises because these are what all Scripture seems to turn upon.

Kochab is easier to identify since this concept is prevalent in Scripture and expresses our current condition – in wait for Him to come.

> "… even we ourselves groan within ourselves, eagerly waiting for the adoption, the redemption of our body. For we were saved in this hope, but hope that is seen is not hope, for why does one still hope for what he sees? But if we hope for what we do not see, *we* eagerly wait for *it* with perseverance." Romans 8:23-25 [NKJV]

> "For our citizenship is in heaven, from which we also eagerly wait for the Savior, the Lord Jesus Christ." Philippians 3:20 [NKJV]

> "Therefore be patient, brethren, until the coming of the Lord. See *how* the farmer waits for the precious fruit of the earth, waiting patiently for it until it receives the early and latter rain. You also be patient. Establish your hearts, for the coming of the Lord is at hand." James 5:7-8 [NKJV]

After focusing on what is in store for us, it is so hard to patiently wait to receive them.

There is still a great deal to uncover in these constellations. We will continue tomorrow.

Day Three – Ursa Minor and Ursa Major – The Two Flocks

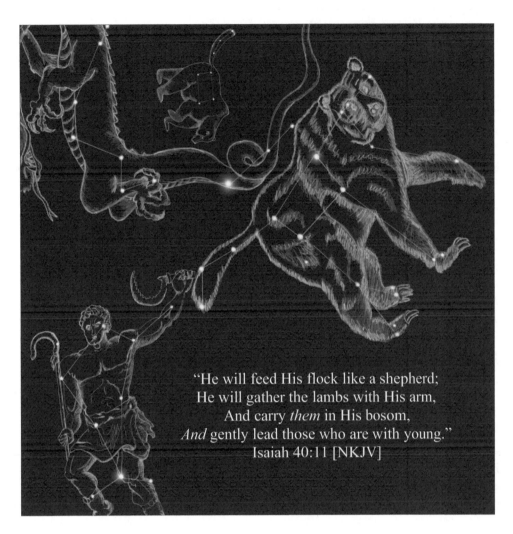

"He will feed His flock like a shepherd;
He will gather the lambs with His arm,
And carry *them* in His bosom,
And gently lead those who are with young."
Isaiah 40:11 [NKJV]

As we press on to the end of this Third Book we are completing the circle of this heavenly scroll; the beginning is mixed up with the end. Today we will be looking again at a constellation we studied in the First Chapter of Book I, Arcturus, more commonly known as Boötes (Ba-OO-tayz).

There is another passage in Job that mentions these constellations, Job 38:32.

"Can you bring out Mazzaroth in its season?
Or can you guide the Great Bear [Ash] with its cubs [sons/young]?"
[NKJV]

Remember the context of this verse; this is in the first answer to Job's complaint spoken by the Lord out of a whirlwind (Job 38:1). Because we have looked into the message of the Mazzaroth itself, the Lord's question can now be comprehended in all its layers of meaning. So let's uncover them.

We now know that "the Great Bear" or Ash is a symbol for what or who?

The reference to "its cubs" or young is probably an acknowledgement that Ash is a great fold or assembly of animals – not a single entity – and probably also a reference to the Lesser fold represented in the smaller bear.

This is a powerful question the Lord has put before Job. In its most literal sense, Job's mouth would be silenced when asked what power does he have over the heavens or their hosts.

But let's consider it in a figurative/spiritual sense since we know these constellations reveal spiritual truth.

What kind of man was Job? (See Job 1:1; 2:3; 23:11-12; 31.)

We think Job would belong in the spiritual Hall of Fame if there was one. Yet, even so, the Lord puts a rhetorical question before him, "Can you guide or lead My flock and its offspring?"

There is another hero of the faith, given a similar task.

Read Numbers 11:10-17. What would Moses' answer be to the question the Lord put before Job?

We can't help but chuckle a little at Moses' complaint here. Especially the end of it, "Just kill me now," – now that's exasperation. We wonder how many of today's shepherds/pastors could relate. If even Moses, who spoke with God face to face as someone who speaks to a friend, felt unable to lead the Lord's flock, who can?

List all the items of Moses' complaint at leading these people.

The verses from yesterday and the verse in today's picture answer Moses' complaint. The Lord has promised He is able to do each one for His flock.

Which complaints are answered in the verse found in the opening picture (Isaiah 40:11)?

> Look up Jeremiah 31:9. Which item from Moses' complaint is accomplished by the Lord?

Now look back at our sky picture. These two flocks, represented by the two bears, have a leader. Their leader is Boötes – which means, "He comes." We discussed this constellation in Book I, Chapter One. The Lord asks Job if he can lead out the two great flocks in the night sky, (Job 38:32). He asks this all the while a constellation is shining in the sky leading the Greater and Lesser Flock. And we know this constellation represents the returning work of Jesus Christ. Job cannot lead so great a multitude, but He can. We think this is the answer for the exasperated shepherd – the Lord is the One who meets the needs of His sheep, only He can carry all their burdens.

Boötes is widely recognized as the herder of these bears however incongruous the idea of herding bears is. So firm is this understanding that the sickle in his hand is ignored and his name is imagined to mean "cow driver". To cover over the apparent incongruity of a herder of animals carrying a sickle, astronomers have added two hounds held by a leash in the hand bearing the sickle. These hounds are supposed to be Boötes' helpers. The loss of the original message has created much confusion. Remember that the sickle fits well in declaring the work of Jesus Christ when He returns. For He will gather the harvest of the earth, those belonging to Himself, as a farmer would gather the wheat at harvest. Then, as the Good Shepherd, He will lead His people to their new home.

A couple of the star names in both Boötes and the two flocks help to unite these three constellations. The brightest star in Boötes, Arcturus, means "traveling with a great company." Another star name in Boötes, Muphride (who separates) has an answering message in the Great Bear's stars: Mizar meaning, "separate" and Megrez meaning, "the separated."

> "I will surely assemble all of you, O Jacob,
> I will surely gather the remnant of Israel;
> I will put them together like sheep of the fold,
> Like a flock in the midst of their pasture;
> They shall make a loud noise because of *so many* people.
> The One who breaks open will come up before them;
> They will break out,
> Pass through the gate,
> And go out by it;
> Their king will pass before them,
> With the LORD at their head."
> Micah 2:12-13 [NKJV]

In light of this it is wonderful to read again John 10:1-10.

Looking back at the picture of the greater and smaller flocks we believe they should be viewed the following way, and not as bears. Imagine the square in each to represent the pen of the folds. Each pen has three stars going out from the pen – these stars represent the sheep going out the gate to follow the Great Shepherd.

Yesterday, we ended our lesson with verses that expressed our eager wait for the One who comes. Boötes is the one who is coming. This is expressed so well in the seasons of these constellations. Both the Lesser and Greater Flocks are circumpolar constellations, meaning they never set but are always present in the sky circling the celestial North Pole. But Boötes is not. During the long winter nights, the flocks are there, but their Shepherd is out of view. As we look at these flocks during those long nights, we know the anxious desiring to see our Shepherd.

> "Give ear, O Shepherd of Israel,
> You who lead Joseph like a flock;
> You who dwell *between* the cherubim, shine forth!
> Before Ephraim, Benjamin, and Manasseh,
> Stir up Your strength,
> *And* come and save us!"
> Psalm 80:1 [NKJV]

We have uncovered the message of these stars but there is still mystery surrounding them worth our attention.

First, it is interesting that both the Greater and Lesser Flocks have seven main stars by which they are chiefly identified. In fact, the seven bright stars of Ursa Major have been given the name Septentriones, Latin. This name has evolved to mean, "north" because the seven stars are in the far north of the sky. Seven also happens to be a significant number in Scripture. It is the number of completion.

The final mystery of this sign is who or what is represented by the two flocks. The idea of two flocks is supported in Scripture.

> "And other sheep I have which are not of this fold; them also I must bring, and they will hear
> My voice; and there will be one flock *and* one shepherd."
> John 10:16 [NKJV]

There are many theories as to who is represented in the two flocks. None of which we feel comfortable in representing as the correct theory. So we will leave you with them to contemplate for yourself.

1. The Lesser Flock is Israel and the rest of the nations are the Greater Flock.
   a. Jesus calls those He is speaking to in Luke 12:32 "little flock."
   b. The star, "separated" is in the Greater Flock which matches Mat. 25:32: All the **nations** will be gathered before Him, and He will **separate** them one from another ..." [NKJV emphasis added]
   c. The Greater Flock has a variety of different animals in the star names, which could be understood to signify a variety of people groups: lambs, goat, gazelle, and the idea of assembly while the Lesser Flock has only one animal type, "calves or young," connected with it.
   d. John 10:16 seems to imply this idea also.

2. The Lesser Flock is all of His who believed before His first appearing, the Greater Flock is all that have come to Him since the sending forth of the Gospel.
   a. The evidence is much the same as above, only the saints that lived before the separation of Israel from the nations, i.e. Adam, Enoch, Noah, Job, etc, would be included in the Lesser Flock with Israel.
   b. Hebrews intimates that those who died in Christ before His coming are completed by we who have come to Him since, "God having provided something better for us, that they [those who died in faith ahead of the promise] should not be made perfect apart from us." Hebrews 11:40 [NKJV]. Those

listed in the passage were both men of faith who lived ahead of Abraham's calling and members of Israel. So they are grouped together as one.

   c. The star Al Ruccaba, "turned on or ridden on" in the Lesser Flock can have spiritual significance, since the blessings given to the Greater Flock turn upon the great Covenants the Lord has made with the early patriarchs, most notable Abraham.

> "Blessing I will bless you, and multiplying I will multiply your descendants … and your descendants shall possess the gate of their enemies. In your seed all the nations of the earth shall be blessed …" Genesis 22:17-18 [NKJV]

3. The Greater Flock is all those who have died in the Lord before His return, the Lesser Flock represents those who remain alive at His return.

> "For if we believe that Jesus died and rose again, even so God will bring with Him those who sleep in Jesus. For this we say to you by the word of the Lord, that we who are alive *and* remain [survive] until the coming of the Lord will by no means precede those who are asleep." 1 Thessalonians 4:14-15 [NKJV]

   a. There is no disputing that the number of those who died and will die before the Lord's final return will exceed the number of those who remain until His coming. The word in the above verse, remain, means "who are left or survive" and implies a small number.

   b. The Lesser Flock follows the Greater Flock – in fact a direct route to follow Boötes is blocked by the tail of the dragon. This seems to parallel a real truth. The verses above teach this order and appear to be the only place where an order of two types is given.

   c. Kochab, "waiting Him who cometh," is in the Lesser Flock and most appropriately applies to those who survive until He returns. There is no similar concept in the stars of the Greater Flock.

   d. The Greater Flock has been called the bier, with the three stars of the tail considered mourners following the coffin. This makes a possible link in this constellation to those who have died.

We are not at all disenchanted that the answer to who is represented by the two flocks is still a mystery. These constellations are prophetic and it is the very design of prophecy, while it remains future, to be mysterious. We believe, even though we cannot arrive at a certain conclusion, it is the Lord's wish that we seek to understand it.

Day Four – Argo – His Possession Traveled Home

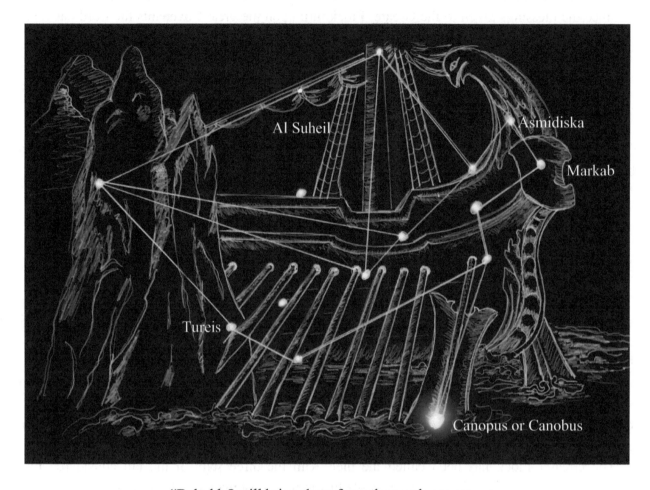

"Behold, I will bring them from the north country,
And gather them from the ends of the earth …
A great throng shall return there."
Jeremiah 31:8 [NKJV]

Argo is an enormous ship and sails in the Milky Way.[1] It is not visible in its entirety anywhere as far North as the continental U.S. Its name probably comes from the Hebrew 'arach, "company of travelers." Its Arabic name is Al Safina, "multitude or abundance."

Argo is the largest of all the constellations. It is so enormous in size that it was dismantled by astronomers and is no longer considered a single constellation. They have divided this ship into four parts, Carina (the keel), Vela (the sails), Puppis (the stern), and Pyxis (the compass – where the mast once was). This dismantling was done for practical purposes because the massive size and number of stars contained within it made it unwieldy for the purposes of designating stars and organizing the sky. How tragic and ignorant it is to dismantle the wonderful message testified by this giant constellation. This is not the only time men have dismantled the truth of God in ignorance when it is convenient to do so.

---

[1] The picture is nearly identical to Johannes Bayer's. The rocks were changed slightly and the men on board were left out. Bayer, Johannes, *Uranometria*, Constellation of Argo Navis, (Augsburg, Germany, Johannes Bayer, Ulm 1723).

The massive size of this constellation is part of the message. The brightest star in Argo is also the second brightest star in the entire heavens. It is Canopus, "the possession" or Canobus, "of Him who cometh." This final sub-constellation of Cancer has continued its theme. Again, the stars tell of His possession.

What do you think is to be understood by making this constellation, containing "the possession," so large?

We have tried to portray its comparative enormous size in our picture of Cancer and all its parts. But that picture should be viewed as approximating the actuality and not mathematically or astronomically accurate in its portrayal.

We see spiritual significance in the contrast of Argo – the largest constellation – and Crux or the Southern Cross – the smallest constellation.

Read Romans 5:12-19 and Isaiah 53:11. What truth is taught by contrasting sizes of Crux and Argo?

What an amazing picture of God's grace; the obedience of One extends grace to a multitude. The death of One procures abundant life for a great and varied throng of people.

Other preserved star names confirm the theme of this great ship:
- Tureis – "the possession"
- Asmidiska – "released who travel"
- Markab (also in Pegasus) – "returning from afar"
- Al Suheil – "all that is bright and beautiful or the desired"

The theme of the Lord gathering His people from all directions is prevalent in Scripture. Turn to Isaiah 43:5-7 and Isaiah 49:8-13 for a sampling.

Where are the people coming from?

Take a look back at our picture because there is something curious about it. Notice that the prow or front of the ship is not visible. This is how the ship is always presented; the prow either is simply not there or is behind the mists of the Milky Way or rocks of a harbor.

What do you think might be the meaning of this consistent presentation?

We agree with the Greek observers, this ship is pictured as already having reached the shore or harbor. This is not a ship at sea, but a ship, filled with a great company, which has already arrived safely at home.

Cancer, the third Chapter of Book III, contrasts sharply with Pisces, the third Chapter of Book II. In Pisces is the present conflict for His redeemed; the stars of Cancer speak of His redeemed safe from all conflict. Scripture also speaks of these contrasts. Each quote below describes our present reality.

Look up Isaiah 65:17-25. After the present reality described in the quoted verses below, write the contrasting future reality found in Isaiah.

1. "Man *who* is born of woman is of few days and full of trouble. He comes forth like a flower and fades away; he flees like a shadow and does not continue." Job 14:1-2 [NKJV]

2. "Why do You stand afar off, O LORD? *Why* do you hide in times of trouble?" Psalm 10:1 [NKJV]

3. "Therefore I hated life because the work that was done under the sun *was* distressing to me, for all *is* vanity and grasping for the wind. Then I hated all my labor in which I toiled under the sun, because I must leave it to the man who will come after me." Ecclesiastes 2:17-18 [NKJV]

4. "For all his days *are* sorrowful, and his work burdensome; even in the night his heart takes not rest. This also is vanity." Ecclesiastes 2:23 [NKJV]

5. "A man to whom God has given riches and wealth and honor, so that he lacks nothing for himself of all he desires; yet God does not give him power to eat of it, but a foreigner consumes it. This *is* vanity, and it *is* an evil affliction." Ecclesiastes 6:2 [NKJV]

6. "There is a vanity which occurs on earth, that there are just *men* to whom it happens according to the work of the wicked; again, there are wicked *men* to whom it happens according to the work of the righteous. I said that this also *is* vanity." Ecclesiastes 8:14 [NKJV]

We conclude Argo with more verses which speak to our hope.

"Are You not *the One* who dried up the sea,

The waters of the great deep;
That made the depths of the sea a road
For the redeemed to cross over?
So the ransomed of the LORD shall return,
And come to Zion with singing,
With everlasting joy on their heads.
They shall obtain joy and gladness;
Sorrow and sighing shall flee away."
Isaiah 51:10-11 [NKJV]

"The LORD has taken away your judgments,
He has cast out your enemy.
The King of Israel, the LORD, is in your midst;
You shall see disaster no more."
Zephaniah 3:15 [NKJV]

"… Jerusalem shall be inhabited *as* towns without walls, because of the multitude of men and livestock in it. 'For I,' says the LORD, 'will be a wall of fire all around her, and I will be the glory in her midst.' … 'Sing and rejoice, O daughter of Zion! For behold, I am coming and I will dwell in your midst,' says the LORD." Zechariah 2:4-5, 10 [NKJV]

"And there shall be no more curse, but the throne of God and of the Lamb shall be in it, and His servants shall serve Him. They shall see His face, and His name *shall be* on their foreheads." Revelation 22:3-4 [NKJV]

Lesson Thirteen – Chapter Four – The Coming One's Absolute Triumph

Day One – Leo – The Lion Rending

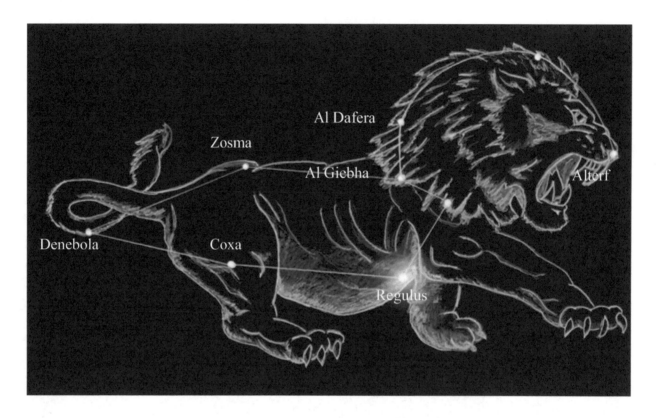

"Be silent, all flesh, before the LORD, for He is aroused
from His holy habitation!" Zechariah 2:13 [NKJV]

Can you believe it? This week we complete the circle of the revelation in the sky. It is a fitting end. The last events prophesied in Scripture and the heavenly scroll are the same; the Lord's judgment and final triumph over the great adversary and all his offspring.

Read Revelation 20:1-3. These verses describe the binding of Satan and his imprisoning in the abyss. This was pictured at the end of the second Book, in the constellation, Cetus. His destruction had not yet come.

How long is he bound?

Read Revelation 20:4-8. What does Satan do after his release from the abyss?

There is another description of a battle with the armies of Gog and Magog in Ezekiel 38 and 39. Read Ezekiel 38:2, 8-16.

What temptation have these men fallen under that has caused them to go up against the Lord's people?

> Turn back to Revelation 20 and read verses 9-10. Describe the battle.
>
>
> What is Satan's end?

The 1,000 year reign of Christ together with His co-heirs is peace and safety for His people. But there is still death for sinners (Isaiah 65:20) and evil exists outside. Today's constellation is an expression of the final destruction of death, Satan, and his offspring!

> "And God will wipe away every tear from their eyes; there shall be no more death, nor sorrow, nor crying. There shall be no more pain, for the former things have passed away." Revelation 21:4 [NKJV]

There is no confusion. All ancient Zodiacs picture a lion here. We easily recognize this lion as the Lion of Judah, "… 'Do not weep. Behold, the Lion of the tribe of Judah, the Root of David, has prevailed to open the scroll and to loose its seven seals.'" Revelation 5:5 [NKJV]

The ancient names are:
- Pi Mentekeon, Egyptian, "the pouring out"
- Aryo, Syrian, "rending lion."

> How does Isaiah 64:1 match the name Aryo?

- Al Asad, Arabic, "lion coming vehemently"
- Aryeh, Hebrew, "the lion." There are six Hebrew words for lion. This one has the Hebrew root *'ariy* which carries with it the idea of violence, plucking and tearing abroad. This word is used in the prophecy of Balaam regarding Israel.

> "Behold, the people shall rise up as a great lion, and lift up himself as a young lion [*'ariy*]: he shall not lie down until he eat of the prey, and drink the blood of the slain." Numbers 23:24 [KJV]

The ferocious lion in this constellation is the image of this prophecy.

The stars of Leo shine brightly and are easy to locate. His head and front is marked by a giant backward question mark.

We are fortunate to have several preserved star names:
- The alpha star in the heart of Leo is called Regulus, Latin meaning "little king." The king part of this name is correct, but this is no little king! Frances Rolleston has the root of this word a Hebrew word, *regel*, meaning "foot, treading."[1]

> What does, 1 Corinthians 15:24-26 say He must do until He has put all enemies under his feet?

This is interesting in out context. It is a present truth that He reigns even now, but we wonder if this is also speaking of Him reigning for 1,000 years on earth before finally defeating all His enemies?

- In the body is the star, Zosma, "shining forth." This star, together with the star below it were called by the Egyptians, Mes-su, "the heart of the anointed one [messiah]."
- Al Dafera or Adhafera, Arabic, "the enemy put down"

  "… And fire came down from God out of heaven and devoured them. The devil, who deceived them, was cast into the lake of fire and brimstone … And they will be tormented day and night forever and ever." Revelation 20:9-10 [NKJV]

- Al Giebha or Agiebha, Arabic, "the exaltation"

> How does the Lord say He will magnify Himself in Ezekiel 38:22-23?

- Al Terf, the first star of the sickle, Arabic, "the glance"

  "'And it will come to pass at the same time, when Gog comes against the land of Israel,' says the LORD God,'*that* My fury will show in My face.'" Ezekiel 38:18

- The beta star is Denebola, "the judge who cometh." We have seen the final judgment of the devil and his offspring in the verses already read. Returning to Revelation 20 there is still more to be judged.

> Read verses 11-15. Who else is judged here?

All the names and star names for this constellation are wonderfully supported in Scripture. There is no difficulty in understanding the declaration of this constellation.

> The LORD also will roar from Zion,
> And utter His voice from Jerusalem;

---

[1] Rolleston, Frances. "Mazzaroth by Frances Rolleston." *Philologos*. Web. 30 Aug. 2011. http://philologos.org/__eb-mazzaroth/202.htm

The heavens and earth will shake;
But the LORD will be a shelter for His people,
And the strength of the children of Israel.
So you shall know that I *am* the LORD your God,
Dwelling in Zion My holy mountain.
Then Jerusalem shall be holy,
And no aliens shall ever pass through her again.
Joel 3:16-17 [NKJV]

Day Two – Hydra – The Old Serpent Destroyed

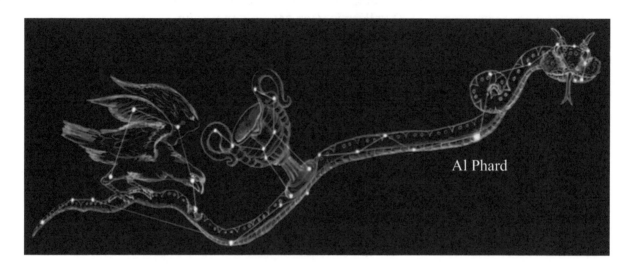

Al Phard

"In that day the LORD with His severe sword, great and strong,
Will punish Leviathan the fleeing [fugitive] serpent,
Leviathan that twisted [perverted] serpent;
And He will slay [destroy] the reptile that *is* in the sea."
Isaiah 27:1 [NKJV]

The above constellations are separate constellations all bound together by the stars they share with one another. This is the final end of the great enemy.

The snake, our subject today, is considered the largest constellation in the sky since Argo has been divided. It begins under Cancer, twists under Leo, continuing underneath Virgo, and ending under her feet. It is the representation of the "reptile that is in the sea" who is slain by the Lord's severe sword. This is not the devil punished, as in the two previous representations of him. The final chapter of the final Book is the final destruction of the great adversary.

> The devil, who deceived them, was cast into the lake of fire and brimstone where the beast and the false prophet *are*. And they will be tormented day and night forever and ever. Revelation 20:10 [NKJV]

Satan is not the keeper of the place of torment.

Read Isaiah 14:12-15. Where is Satan's place?

Read Matthew 25:41. For whom is everlasting fire prepared?

That man shares his punishment and torment is not the design of the Lord – but the result of man's willful rejection of Him.

> "Anyone who has rejected Moses' law dies without mercy on the testimony of two or three witnesses. Of how much worse punishment, do you suppose, will he be thought worthy who has trampled the Son of God underfoot, counted the blood of the covenant by which he was sanctified a common thing, and insulted the Spirit of grace? For we know Him who said, "Vengeance is Mine, I will repay," says the Lord. And again, "The LORD will judge His people." It is a fearful thing to fall into the hands of the living God." Hebrews 10:28-31 [NKJV]

The great sea snake is known today as Hydra. Hydra is a feminine noun and has a root for water in its name. "He will slay the reptile that is in the sea." The feminine name for this constellation is a current corruption. In the past, the masculine, Hydrus, an appropriate gender for a representation of Satan, was used. However, another snake constellation has been added by astronomers in the Southern Hemisphere. It was created and added in the sixteenth century, and, not being really creative, they called it Hydrus. This has forced the feminine version of the name, Hydra, to be applied to this constellation. When men stopped recognizing these ancient constellations as revelations of truth, they ignorantly corrupted them.

The Greeks had already begun the corruption by developing one of their various myths around it. This constellation has become, for the Greeks, Hydra of Lerna, a nine-headed water snake defeated by Hercules. Even in corruption, the truth can still be seen.

The great water snake is also found in the temple of Denderah.

The preserved star names are:
- Al Phard, the alpha star. It is Arabic meaning, "separated by breaking." This is the only star name still appearing on star atlases.
- Al Drian, "the abhorred" – identified by Rolleston but not on star maps.[1]
- Minchar al Sugia, "tearing to pieces of the deceiver" – also not on star maps.

The Scriptures do not directly answer the following question, but we think it is worth pondering.

Why do you think the Lord has reserved Satan's final destruction for the end of His 1,000 year earthly reign rather than earlier?

Yesterday, we looked at Ezekiel 38 as a parallel to the final battle recorded in Revelation 20.

---

[1] Rolleston, Frances. "Mazzaroth by Frances Rolleston." *Philologos*. Web. 30 Aug. 2011. http://philologos.org/__eb-mazzaroth/202.htm

Read Ezekiel 38:3-4. How does the Lord say He will lead out Gog and Magog?

We also know from Revelation 20:7-8, that Gog and Magog gather for battle led by the deceptions of Satan. Keeping in mind that Gog and Magog are described as led by a hook in the jaw, and Satan is the instigator of their crime.

Read the Lord's answer to Job out of the whirlwind in Job 41:1-2. Who else is being drawn out by a hook in his jaw in Ezekiel?

Leviathan is a common Scriptural reference to Satan, although the Lord probably was speaking of a very real creature with which Job was familiar. The release of Satan from the abyss at the end of the millennial kingdom was only to "pierce his jaw with a hook" and lead him to his own destruction. No man dare consider such a battle, but the Lion of Judah will overwhelmingly prevail.

Day Three – Crater and Corvus – The Curses on the Enemy

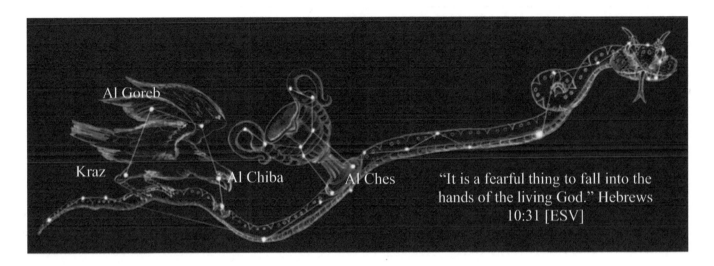

"It is a fearful thing to fall into the hands of the living God." Hebrews 10:31 [ESV]

The heavenly scrolls conclude with a pair, the cup and the raven on the body of the enemy.

The first of these has only one preserved star name, the alpha star in the base of the cup, Al Ches – Arabic – meaning, "the cup." This star is shared both by the body of the snake and the cup joining them together – just as the Lord's curse on this enemy is irrevocable.

This constellation is called Crater – from Greek meaning "mixing bowl."

> "But God *is* the Judge:
> He puts down one,
> And exalts another.
> For in the hand of the LORD *there is* a cup,
> And the wine is red;
> It is fully mixed, and He pours it out;
> Surely its dregs shall all the wicked of the earth
> Drain *and* drink down."
> Psalm 75:7-8 [NKJV]

The Greeks, though they became confused about the meaning of this bowl, did well to preserve in its name the idea of a mixing bowl rather than an ordinary cup.

The mixing bowl or cup of God's wrath is sprinkled throughout Scripture.

Beside the following passages note who will drink it.

Psalm 75:8 (quoted above)

Psalm 11:6

Revelation 14:9-11
Revelation 16:19

The final constellation is the Raven, called Corvus by the Romans. It also has been known as Al Goreb, Arabic, "the raven"

Preserved star names are:
- The alpha star in the eye, Al Chibar, "the joining"
- Al Goreb, "the raven"
- Minchar Al Goreb, "the raven tearing to pieces"
- Kraz, Arabic – likely a word for the sound a raven makes.

There is no disagreement in the names. This raven is to be understood in the act of consuming the body of the great snake. Such an end is a curse in Scripture. You will find this in Deuteronomy 28:26; 1 Samuel 17:46 and Proverbs 30:17.

Ezekiel 39:4 and Revelation 19:17-18 speak of the final battle. What happens to the defeated?

This raven is near Centaurus (the Despised) and the Cross. Persons who were crucified were not allowed burials but were left to be devoured by birds. This was part of the humiliation of crucifixion. But the raven is on the tail of Satan, not Centaurus, because Christ did not receive the curse reserved for Satan. In great contrast, Jesus was buried with the rich. Matthew 27:57-60

> "And they made His grave with the wicked –
> But with the rich at His death,
> Because He had done no violence,
> Nor *was any* deceit in His mouth."
> Isaiah 53:9 [NKJV]

To be crucified was to be assigned the curse of the wicked in death. But because Jesus was innocent He did not suffer the curse of the wicked, instead, He obtained honor in His burial.

It is fashionable today to hide or skip past this "fire and brimstone" message. We find it uncomfortable to discuss as well. But it is there in Scripture, unabashedly, as it is in the heavenly revelation also. We may pass over these uncomfortable passages in our Bibles, but we cannot turn the page on the starry revelation.

You may have noticed that these curses, while on the body of the devil, are most often in Scripture described afflicting wicked men. Look back again to the key verse for this entire heavenly scroll, Genesis 3:15.

Besides Satan and Eve, who will there be enmity (hostility) between?

Therefore, not only Satan, but all who follow him in the rejection of the Lord will inherit the curses God has prepared for Satan – they are the devil's seed. The curses of God have been earned by the Serpent – and the serpent's offspring also inherit them. That Scripture focuses on men as the recipients of the cup and the raven is a warning and ultimately an act of grace. Satan's course and end are determined and sure like the stars in the heavens. The same book that speaks curses for the enemies of the Lord also pleads:

> "Seek the LORD while He may be found,
> Call upon Him while He is near.
> Let the wicked forsake his way,
> And the unrighteous man his thoughts;
> Let him return to the LORD,
> And He will have mercy on him;
> And to our God,
> For He will abundantly pardon."
> Isaiah 55:6-7 [NKJV]

Unlike Satan, wicked men have the opportunity of calling on the Lord and forsaking their way and receiving mercy and pardon from God.

We have come full circle in the sky. We finish with a warning, but just behind it, rising to its place, is the constellation, Virgo. The Seed of the woman has taken the cup for you. The Lord Jesus Christ has willingly drunk the cup of wrath that the Lord has mixed for those who reject Him.

Look up Matthew 26:39 and John 18:11 – What does the Lord Jesus say he must do?

> "But He *was* wounded for our transgressions,
> *He was* bruised for our iniquities;
> The chastisement for our peace *was* upon Him,
> And by His stripes we are healed."
> Isaiah 53:5 [NKJV]

If you have delayed till now in reaching out for the forgiveness bought for you by our Lord Jesus Christ, let today be the day of salvation or you will suffer the consequences.

> "Of how much worse punishment, do you suppose, will he be thought worthy who has trampled the Son of God underfoot …" Hebrews 10:29 [NKJV]

For those who have reached out for that forgiveness:

> "Therefore, having been justified by faith, we have peace with God through our Lord Jesus Christ, through whom also we have access by faith into this grace in which we stand, and rejoice in hope of the glory of God." Romans 5:1-2 [NKJV]

Day Four – Book III – The Redeemer, His Glory – Review

You have now looked at all 48 ancient constellations. We hope it has been an exciting and eye-opening experience. It has been for us.

Book III – which has spoken of the Messiah's Kingdom has been especially enlightening. We are certain you recognized its chief pattern, its continuous use of pairs.

Below list as many pairs as you can remember from this Book.

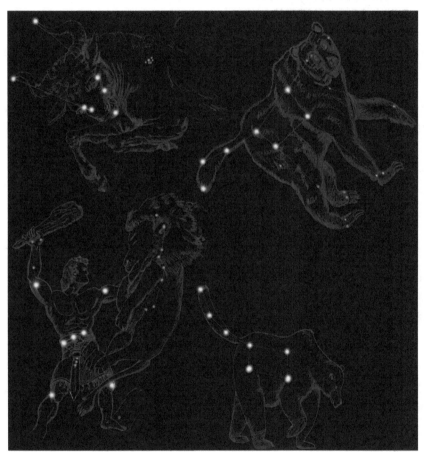

We also found the number of completion, seven, in several places.

List the constellations in which there are seven principal stars.

The Pleiades in Taurus' shoulder was called the seven sisters even though there are actually more than seven stars. There are seven larger stars in the cluster.

We left something out of this study that we feel is worth discussing. Remember when we were in Oarion and the Greater Flock? We looked at these constellations as they were mentioned in Job. The other star pattern mentioned there is the Pleiades. Let's look at the passage again.

"Can you bind the cluster of the Pleiades,
Or loose the belt of Orion?
Can you bring out Mazzaroth in its season?
Or can you guide the Great Bear with its cubs?"
Job 38:31-32 [NKJV]

All the constellations with seven principal stars are mentioned in this passage. When we studied Oarion we looked at loosing his belt, and when we looked at Ursa Major we looked at guiding the great bear, but we did not have time in Taurus to look at the question posed by God to Job, "Can you bind the cluster of the Pleiades." The word translated bind means bind together – bind anything to anything else. The name, Pleiades, means "congregation of the judge/ruler." Jesus' prayer for believers helps us understand this question:

> "Now I am no longer in the world, but these are in the world, and I come to You. Holy Father, keep through Your name those whom You have given Me, that they may be one as We *are*."
> John 17:11 [NKJV]

God asks, can you, Job, or any man, keep and bind My people together? Again it is a rhetorical question in the literal and spiritual sense – only He can keep us and make us one.

Let's summarize Book III.

In Chapter One, Taurus and its sub-constellations, spoke of the coming Judge. He comes to pour out wrath upon His enemies and rescue His redeemed.

In Chapter Two, Gemini and its sub-constellations, we saw the Kingdom of the Messiah. He will share His thrown with His co-heirs, He will dispel the wicked, and He will rule as Prince and Redeemer – the First and the Last.

In Chapter Three, Cancer and its sub-constellations, the possession of the Lord is held and kept safe from all conflict. The Good Shepherd will guide the Greater and the Lesser Flock to the Kingdom. A great multitude is seen safely arrived at home in the giant ship Argo.

Finally, in Chapter Four, Leo and its sub-constellation, we saw the Lion of Judah rending evil with His final triumph over the great deceiver. Sinful men are born during Christ's reign as king. These are deceived by Satan at the end of 1,000 years and gather to make war against God's people. Upon Satan and his seed, the cup of God's wrath is poured out and the curse of the raven devouring their flesh is accomplished.

What a book!

What was your favorite constellation from Book III and why?

Which constellation was the most enlightening or contained truths you did not know?

It has been an amazing journey through the heavenly scroll. We hope you have enjoyed it. We hope you have learned more about your Redeemer and His Word. And we especially hope it has drawn you closer to Him. Thanks for walking through it with us.

Appendix

Appendix A

The Structure of Psalm 19 from Bullinger's, <u>Witness of the Stars,</u> pgs 2-4

The Structure of Psalm 19 as a whole:

A| verses 1-4. The Heavens.

    B| verses 4-6. "In them" the sun.

A| verses 7-10. The Scriptures

    B| verses 11-14. "In them" Thy Servant.

Bullinger notes that the terms in the first half of Psalm 19, which speaks of the heavens, **A B** are literary (declare, utters, reveals, language, words). The terms in the second half, *A B*, are astronomical terms in their Hebrew roots though this section is about the law (converting – "to return" {like the sun}, enlightening – "to give light," warned – "to make light"). Hence, we have a whole Psalm interlacing the astronomical with the literary.

You see above that each half of the Psalm has two portions that correspond in thought, **A** to *A* and **B** to *B*. These quarters of the Psalm also match in the number of lines contained in each:

A| verses 1-4. Eight lines

    B| verses 4-6. Six lines

A| verses 7-10. Eight lines

    B| verses 11-14. Six lines[1]

---

[1] Bullinger, E.W. The Witness of the Stars. Cosimo, Inc. 2007. N.Y. originally published 1893. pp. 2-4.

Appendix B

In considering the account of the Bethlehem star, it is important to note that the appearance and subsequent disappearance of a new star is not a completely unique astronomical event. Such events can be found recorded in history; even as recently as 1604, a new star (actually a super nova) was recorded by Kepler in the constellation Ophiucus. In 125 BC, a star so bright it was even visible during the day was recorded by Hipparchus.[1] From the account in Matthew, it is likely that the appearance of a new star is what inspired the wise men to seek out Christ. First their use of the term "His star" and second, Herod ascertained what time the star appeared (Mt 2:7). There is also recorded tradition from early church fathers testifying to the appearance of a new star.

I am not an astronomer, but this is my understanding of how it is possible to follow a star to a specific place. A star at its culmination or highest vertical point in the arc it travels across the sky will mark or be directly above a specific latitude. (Latitude lines around our planet mark distance north or south of the equator.) Therefore, even though stars travel across the sky each night, the point at which they culminate would be considered the place they mark.

Latitude gives the wise men only one necessary point out of two needed to find the person announced by the star. They also need the longitude. The latitude circles the entire globe; so which direction upon it should they travel? It is believed by many commentators that the wise men were aware of the prophecy of Balaam recorded in Numbers 24:17.

> "... A Star shall come out of Jacob;
> A Scepter shall rise out of Israel,
> And batter the brow of Moab,
> And destroy all the sons of tumult."
> [NKJV]

They were looking for the King of the Jews; they saw His star. So latitude being determined by the star and longitude determined through prophecy, gave these magi coordinates specific enough to begin their search for the One the star announced. They wind up in Jerusalem asking for help in finding the new King because Jerusalem was close enough to Bethlehem in latitude and longitude to create some confusion. I think this account still shows how the life of Christ pricks all man's prejudices. I imagine that the wise men thought that if the Desired Son, spoken of in all the various constellations of heaven, had to be from the insignificant Jewish race, at least He would be born in its capitol city! Armed with more prophecy they travel on to Bethlehem.

The account says the star traveled before them and then stopped over the place where Christ was. The star can go before them because it makes an arc across the sky throughout the night. So as they traveled they followed it during the night looking for its culmination. They would consider reaching its culmination – or its highest point in the arc – to be stopping over a specific place. And, from the account in Matthew, culmination happened directly over the place where the Christ was.

---

[1] Rolleston, Frances. "Mazzaroth by Frances Rolleston." *Philologos*. Web. 30 Aug. 201, http://philologos.org/__eb-mazzaroth/207.htm#star

Appendix C

The final constellation of Book III, Chapter One – Auriga – pictures a shepherd who carries in his arms a she-goat and her kids. Goats, as a representation of His redeemed, is a bit troublesome for us. This is mostly due to the parable of the kingdom found in Matthew 25:31ff, the goats are those whom Jesus does not know and receive the judgment of everlasting fire. We do not believe finding goats in the arms of the Great Shepherd presents a great problem for the following reasons:

- Matthew 25 is the only place in Scripture where we have found goats compared to sheep and regarded in negative terms.
- The Israelites were shepherds to both sheep and goats.
- Both were kosher and acceptable offerings to the Lord. In fact, Ezekiel 43:22 says, "On the second day you shall offer a kid of the goats without blemish …" [NKJV] That a goat could be described as being "without blemish" infers that the bad reputation goats have received in the Matthew 25 parable is not a consistent Scriptural teaching.
- The parallel Old Testament passage to Matthew 25 speaks of separating sheep from sheep, "And as for you, O My flock, thus says the Lord GOD: 'Behold, I shall judge between sheep and sheep, between rams   [he-sheep]   and   goats   [he-goats].'"   Ezekiel   34:17   [NKJV]

We must be careful not to draw too strong a conclusion about objects used in the telling of parables. The chief aim of parables is to convey a key idea by relating stories with which the audience is familiar. A shepherd who keeps both goats and sheep would often pasture them together, and then separate them again at night for penning. So the Lord is making a commonly understood comparison.

> "All the nations will be gathered before Him, and He will separate them one from another, as a shepherd divides *his* sheep from the goats." Matthew 25:32 [NKJV]

This is a comparison to a common practice – He will separate the nations as a shepherd does sheep from goats.

- The parable does not reflect the Lord's opinion of goats. Parables use common objects meant to convey a bigger idea and are not meant to be used to draw conclusions about the good or evil of those objects. Consider the parable of the kingdom which compares it to leaven – Matthew 13:33. Leaven is otherwise used in Scripture as a symbol for sin. Should we conclude from this parable that leaven is now always to be understood as a symbol for something good? No, leaven's properties served the Lord's purpose in communicating what He wished about the nature of the Kingdom. We should understand leaven in the light of its purpose in this parable and not draw broader conclusions about the symbols used to communicate that purpose.

That the Lord exclusively, as far as we have found, calls His people sheep – and we find in our picture goats, still presents a bit of difficulty for us. We found something interesting in working through this mystery. There is a wide degree of natural differences between sheep and goats. Sheep are much more relational than goats. They can be a pet while a goat does not respond to shepherds this way. Sheep are more dependent on a shepherd, while goats tend to be independent. Sheep really can know their owner's voice and come when called – not so goats. That the Lord consistently calls us His sheep expresses His desire for relationship with us, not just that He guards and cares for us.

So why goats in Auriga? Maybe they are found in Auriga's arms because of an irresistible urge goats have for seeking the highest ground. You will always find goats on the highest spot available to them. Our picture shows them held by the shepherd high above the wrath being poured out. Goats would seek that place.

Appendix D

The 48 Constellations ordered by size

1. Argo[1]
2. Hydra
3. Virgo
4. Ursa Major
5. Cetus
6. Hercules
7. Eridanus
8. Pegasus
9. Draco
10. Centaurus
11. Aquarius
12. Ophiucus
13. Leo
14. Boötes
15. Pisces and Band[2]
16. Sagittarius
17. Cygnus
18. Taurus
19. Taurus
20. Auriga
21. Aquilla
22. Serpens
23. Perseus
24. Cassiopeia
25. Oarion
26. Cepheus
27. Libra
28. Gemini
29. Cancer
30. Scorpio
31. Aries
32. Capricorn
33. Coma
34. Canis Major
35. Lupus
36. Lepus
37. Lyra
38. Crater
39. Ursa Minor
40. Pisces Australis
41. Ara
42. Delphinus
43. Corvus
44. Canis Minor
45. Corona
46. Sagitta
47. Crux

The smallest constellation is the Cross, while the largest is the ship which has carried those belonging to Him safely home. This is a picture of Romans 5:15.

"But the free gift is not like the offense. For if by the one man's offense many died, much more the grace of God and the gift of God and the gift by the grace of one Man, Jesus Christ, abounded to many." [NKJV]

[1] Since Argo has been broken apart it no longer is listed as the largest constellation
[2] The Band, though it is a separate constellation is considered together with Pisces making 47 total constellations.

Star Appendix

10 Brightest Stars, from our view

Star Name	Name Meaning	Constellation	Best Viewing Time
Sirius	Prince of princes	Canis Major	January
Canopus	The possession of Him who comes	Argo	January below 37° N
Alpha Centauri (Toliman)	(the heretofore and hereafter)	Centaurus	May below 29° N
Arcturus	He comes with a band of travelers	Boötes	April
Vega	He shall be praised	Lyra	July
Capella	The she-goat	Auriga	December
Rigel	Foot that crushes	Oarion	January
Procyon	The Redeemer	Canis Minor	January
Achernar	End of the River	Eridanus	October below 33° N
Betelguese[1]	The coming of the Branch	Oarion	January
Hadar	Beauty or Comeliness	Centaurus	May below 29° N

---

[1] Betelguese is a variable star. It shines with variable degrees of brightness. This causes it to sometimes be less bright than the next brightest star in the sky, Hadar. And so in our table of 10 brightest stars, we've included 11.

About the Pictures in this Study

I drew all the pictures in this study. Some were based on famous drawings from "Urania's Mirror," 1825. Originally, since the copyright for all these pictures has run out, I had hoped to use these drawings in the study. But this proved unworkable for many reasons.

These constellations are drawings by a lay astronomer. I am not a scientist and did not use mathematical calculations to ensure the exact accuracy of the placement of the stars – especially when connecting constellations together. I have marked out the most prominent stars in each constellation as an approximation to highlight their placement. Their placement is close enough that the star pictures in this study are useful in helping anyone who wants, to identify them in the sky – and for this they are useful. Again, they are not scientifically, mathematically accurate; this was not my purpose.

I was more interested in the art of the pictures and how they may connect together to tell a story. As much as was possible, I endeavored to uncover what their original representation must have included, though there is no way to be certain these accurately reflect what the ancient prophets had in mind. I have also tried to depart some from the Greek/Roman style, but the influence of their style of dress – even their military dress – is still in them.

In pictures which represent the Lord, I have greatly varied the faces purposely. One must tread very carefully here. Please understand, these pictures are a representation of different aspects of His work, not the Lord, Himself – they should never be regarded as such. In many cases, the starry revelation uses various animals to represent an aspect of His work as well.

You can use these pictures to find these stars in the sky. On any given night, you can find them there and become familiar with, not only the meanings of their names, but their journeys through the heavens.

Made in United States
Troutdale, OR
09/17/2023